Pietro Di Donato

IMMIGRANT

✝ ✝ ✝
✝ ✝ ✝
✝ ✝ ✝ ✝ ✝ ✝ ✝
✝ ✝ ✝ ✝ ✝ ✝ ✝
✝ ✝ ✝ ✝ ✝ ✝ ✝
✝ ✝ ✝
✝ ✝ ✝

SAINT

The Life of
MOTHER CABRINI

McGRAW-HILL BOOK COMPANY, INC.
New York   Toronto   London

IMMIGRANT SAINT

First Edition

Library of Congress Catalog Card Number: 60-15756

16806

NIHIL OBSTAT:

   Edward Montano, S.T.D., Censor Librorum

IMPRIMATUR:

   Francis Cardinal Spellman, Archbishop of New York

New York: August 10, 1960

The nihil obstat and imprimatur are official declarations that a
book or pamphlet is free of doctrinal or moral error. No im-
plication is contained there in that those who have granted the
nihil obstat and imprimatur agree with the contents, opinions,
or statements expressed.

To

The Missionary Sisters of the Sacred Heart

Vatican City, August 19, 1960

Mr. Pietro Di Donato
Setauket, Long Island, N.Y.

Dear Mr. Di Donato:

I have read with deep interest your beautiful book *Immigrant Saint,* the life of Mother Cabrini, the great Saint of the Americas.

I wish to extend to you my congratulations for having been able to depict with precision and clarity of expression and at the same time with great historical fidelity, the stupendous figure of this Saint of our days.

From the pages of your book emerge with the clarity of a sculptured bas-relief the essential characteristics of the human and supernatural personality of this exceptional woman and in particular her courage and her audacity, rooted in her steadfast faith in the Providence of God; her enterprising spirit and her untiring activity springing from her burning desire to celebrate in her works the glories of the Lord; her profound humility which was a powerful and unceasing prayer for divine help. But the most moving aspect of her personality which you have illustrated so warmly in your beautiful book is her immense charity, the burning love of God and of her fellowmen which animated her whole life, which urged her on to seek the human miseries to which she could bring comfort and relief, which made her extend her activity far beyond the normal limits of human endurance; which kept her constantly united to our Lord whose suffering image she saw reflected in the brethren who received her help.

I wish your book all the success which it so richly deserves and I extend to you my best wishes and my blessing.

Sincerely yours,
Joseph Cardinal Pizzardo

1 ✠ ✠ ✠

AGOSTINO CABRINI was swinging his flail, threshing wheat in the courtyard. While he worked he listened to the voices of the midwife and his sister-in-law, Angela, within the cottage.

That morning his wife had been threshing wheat with him, when suddenly she said, "This child who seems to have been carrying me, wants to come into the world today."

Agostino and Stella had not expected to have another child, for Stella was fifty-two. The couple had known each other since childhood. They had been engaged for ten years, and only after they had respectfully buried their parents were they wedded. They suffered tragedy after tragedy. Nine of their children had died, at ages from three to eighteen. Only Rosa, Maddalena, hopelessly invalided by polio, and little Giovanni lived. This coming child was the late autumnal gift of their marriage.

Agostino paused and wiped the sweat from his forehead and tousled flaxen mustache. He wondered. The child was two months premature. Would it live? He chided himself for questioning. God knew best.

From the east high above the Lombard plain appeared a swift moving cloud of white. It was a flock of doves. Other farmers saw them, and ran to their fields with pitchforks and shotguns to protect their rice and wheat, but the doves did not come to plunder. They soared over the Sforza castle, past the

1

tall campanile of Sant'Angelo's church, down above the red-tiled roofs of the village and to the Cabrini cottage at 225 Borgo Santa Maria. The white feathery multitude whirred in a circle above the cottage and courtyard.

Agostino looked at them curiously. In his lifetime doves had never come to Sant'Angelo. Where had they come from? Why? He thought of his granary, but though he waved his flail at them, they tenaciously returned again and again. Rosa and Giovanni came from the house to help him. A dove became ensnared between the thongs of the flail.

"Father, please don't hurt it," begged Rosa.

The children caressed the dove as Agostino disentangled it from the flail. It flew to the bedroom window. As it perched upon the sill and cooed, the sunlight seemed to flash more brightly, and the cries of the newborn baby sang forth.

The midwife called from the window, "Agostino, benedictions. It's female and pretty."

He jubilantly signed the cross, then scooped up grain and threw it to the doves. The winged troops pecked the grain. With united impulse they reformed their flight and disappeared to the west.

In a few minutes, Agostino and the children were permitted to enter the room of birth. Rosa, a serious, usually restrained girl of fifteen, clapped her hands and cried, "Look, Father! What eyes, what beautiful eyes Saint Lucy has given the baby!"

The tiny fresh life at Stella Cabrini's bosom had the biggest of blue-green eyes and soft blonde curls.

Agostino whispered to his wife, "She is a precious flower, and may she forever precious be. I am grateful to God and you."

The sagacious midwife shook her head. "The little angel is like a lily, and just as frail. She is almost transparent, and has not the strength for this world. If she lives, I tell you now, it will be a miracle. Dear ones, I do not wish to alarm you, but you had best christen her without delay."

2

A few hours later, Stella Cabrini left her bed. In memory of two of the children she had lost, Francesco and Maria, she decided to name the baby Francesca Maria. It seemed this lily of a child had come by herself. Stella Cabrini could not explain to herself why, but she felt that God had a clear and signal purpose for giving her Francesca Maria. She bowed her head and vowed to do everything possible to keep the child alive. With her sister Angela, she bathed the baby in warm milk redolent with rose petals, gently massaged her with olive oil, and tenderly swathed her in soft linen.

The sun rolled far west, and cooling shades began to soothe the hot ancient walls of the village. With Agostino carrying his crippled daughter Maddalena, Stella bearing her baby in her arms, her sister Angela, and young Rosa and Giovanni following, the Cabrini family went into the church of Sant'-Angelo. As the first evening vespers of Our Lady of Carmel knelled from the campanile over town and plain, the pastor, Don Melchisedecco Abrami baptized the infant at the sacred font, and then wrote in the registry: "July 15, 1850, Francesca Maria Cabrini."

Agostino Cabrini was a pious man, who cleaved to the Commandments. The people of Sant'Angelo called him the "Christian Tower." He was not often to be seen in the village tavern, nor on the street corners with public idlers. The course of Agostino was the way of the apostle, direct and unobstructed. He had no need to go beyond the village limits to know the world fashioned by man. Man, the sole creature given the privilege to choose between good and evil, made his own woes, made tyrants that came and went like the winds. Agostino feared no mortal and knelt, with joy, to only one authority— God. Who else but God made life? Life was to be revered, and gratefully returned to God.

Such was the honest piety of Agostino, father of Francesca Cabrini. But the simplicity and faith of the Cabrini family was

3

not universal in their world. For years their homeland had been repeatedly harassed by war and civil war. That which we call Italy today was then a disorganized assortment of feudal territories, confused by the intrigues of royal families, oppressed in turn by French Bourbon influence and Austrian military domination. Generations of intellectuals and poets, noblemen and churchmen had dreamed of Italian independence and unification. But even among the patriots there was strife, dating back as long as half a century. In the 1800s, when Napoleon had asserted his sovereignty over Italians and soon thereafter had introduced the *Code Napoléon*, he paved the way for dissension between civil powers and the Church. Slowly, the clergy, beloved of the common people, were dispossessed of many of the lands, and subjected to other forms of tyranny. The result was a series of petty wars, bloody abortive uprisings of peasants and social idealists. These early years of revolution saw the birth of numerous patriotic secret societies in the Carbonari, the Federati, the Giovine Italia. The period was characterized by bitter dispute between Church and state.

It was in 1846, just four years before Francesca's birth, that the humanistic Pope Pius IX was elected. Simultaneously, the elements of the risorgimento, the "resurrection" of Italy arose. Giovanni Maria Mastai-Ferretti, Pius IX was of noble birth, yet at heart he was sympathetic to liberal ideas. By bitter experience he learned how they often incorporated the principles of anticlericalism. He recognized that the papal administration, if not so corrupt and despotic as its opponents claimed, was inefficient and intolerant, and its reform was one of his chief concerns. At the same time, he wanted the church kept intact and would not have it enslaved to either nationalism or liberalism. The price exacted for his determination was the endless bitter turmoil that surrounded the Vatican throughout his papacy.

It was among the rural folk that this humane and intellectual

4

leader had his staunchest allies—in the villages, like Sant'-Angelo, in the devout fathers and mothers, like Agostino and Stella Cabrini. The Christian Tower paid no heed to the voices urging rebellion against God and church, any more than to the political maneuvers of the many-factioned government. He kept his home as sacred as any temple of Christ, and it was as content as the richly yielding Lombard plain was prosperous. His devout family cherished the days of the unblighted years that followed Francesca's birth.

Stella Cabrini guarded little Francesca as though she were a rare flower ever about to perish. As she grew older, Francesca became aware that vigor had been denied her and that her uncertain health would never let her join the robust village children in their games. She did not complain.

One day as Rosa was braiding Francesca's long hair, she turned and looked up. "Miss Rosa, if you please . . . why do you call me 'Magpie' instead of Francescina? Is the magpie a good bird or a bad bird?"

"Because, little girl," answered Rosa, "like the magpie you have a long tail—which is your braid—like the magpie you are really good, and easy to tame, but also, like the magpie, you try to do everything too quickly and talk constantly. And if you expect to become an educated young lady, you must learn to listen."

"Then I shall be a magpie no longer. I will listen and learn, and become a schoolteacher, like you."

Rosa was the village schoolmistress, and at home taught Francesca the alphabet and numbers. When at last Francesca went to school, Rosa, whose standards for her sister were extremely demanding, insisted that she set an example in her studies. Often Francesca was too ill to attend. On these occasions, she remained obediently in her little room and dreamed. Her dreams were different from those of other children and more fervent. Her schoolmates dreamed of heroes and heroines of fabled lore, of Cinderella and fairy godmothers, of sorcerers

5

and werewolves, of elves and orgres and crusading armies with knights and knaves. Francesca knew these tales, but one by one, beside the great passion within her, they burst like bubbles. She had a wonderland of her own, and dreamed of Him who is most true.

On the long, icy nights of winter, the family would sit by the blazing fireside, eating hearth-roasted chestnuts, as Agostino read to them from the Annals of the Propagation of the Faith. On the horizon of Francesca's inner sky, the martyred Saints stood forth. *They are not the pastry puppets of children's myths; they are people magnified by their good acts; they are human and real. They walked the earth, were enamored of Him, braved the terrors of the unbelieving, and fearlessly died for His love.*

Father, smoking his long reed pipe with the red clay bowl, read of Saint Teresa: "He led her about and taught her, and He kept her as the apple of His eye. As an eagle He has spread his wings and hath taken her and carried her on His shoulder. The Lord alone was her leader." And the words were as hands, molding the inspiring images of Francesca's inner realm.

Father said: "There is only one true way, His way. We are here according to His will, and we are His children. He is the heart and the spirit of nature, the heart and spirit of arts and labors. He is the Son of God, and King of kings. Love is His bread and wine, love is His law which maintains in balance the universe." Francesca absorbed his words with a heart already open to their message.

One summer morning Rosa took Francesca to spend a day with their mother's brother, Uncle Don Luigi.

They found the old priest cutting roses in the garden behind the rectory. He greeted them and chuckled. "My illustrious nieces, schoolmistress Rosa Cabrini and Miss Francesca, student of wide-eyed prescience! Signorina Francesca, have you come to take care of your helpless old uncle?"

Don Luigi is the famous thief of himself; Don Luigi robs

6

Don Luigi for the distressed; he gives the very shoes on his feet, the clothes he should wear, the meals he should eat, to the poor. He never thinks of Don Luigi. Rosa asked how he was, but he answered, "While playing a Scarlati cantata on the clavichord I composed a fine poem; would you like to hear it?"

Was he moderating his generosity?

"Rosa, what oceans of honey my bees are providing!"

Was he still handing out to the needy more than he had?

"Tell good Agostino I have mastered my chess, and will surprise him in our next game!"

"Uncle, are you taking care of yourself, as you promised me?"

"Rosa, my dear Rosa, the Spirit of charity is the asset that covers all liabilities!"

Rosa instructed her little sister upon deportment, and drove off with the horse and buggy.

Francescina was particularly fond of Uncle Don Luigi. He was easygoing and had her mother's clear brown eyes. Uncle Don Luigi treated her as if she were a young lady and a special guest. She liked to have him tell her about the faraway lands where missionaries went to bring souls to the Lord. He described the heathen Chinese and their strange habits as though he had been there himself. She asked him if she could be a missionary. Was it hard to learn the Chinese language? How did missionaries get to China? Why didn't the Chinese know about the Lord? Why were there poor people and sick people, and why were there people who did bad things?

Uncle Don Luigi raised his eyes. "Young lady, serious problems like this, important thoughts, are too much for man; you must tell your wondrous ideas personally, privately, to Our Lord, Jesus Christ."

She reflected, and answered confidently, "Uncle Don Luigi, thank you, I shall."

Don Luigi's garden extended to the nearby Venera River which moved swiftly between low walled embankments. When-

7

ever uncle Don Luigi left her by herself in the garden he cautioned her not to go near the river's edge.

Alone, she wandered about the garden, inspecting the flowers. *The roses are grand ladies pink and red, the geraniums are intelligent young women.* She gathered some and brought them to the riverside. Along the embankment were daisies and violets. *The daisies are sunny girls, and the violets are smiling maidens.* She fetched paper and scissors from the rectory and fashioned paper boats. *She is Mother Superior Francesca, and the pretty flowers are her nuns.* She arranged the flowers in the paper boats.

"Sister Daisy and Sister Geranium and Sister Rose and Sister Violet, I am sending you across the ocean to far away China to save souls for Our Lord. Do not be afraid. Be brave and do not cry. I, your mother, will pray for you, and you will be safe. God bless you, Sisters of the Flowers."

She leaned over the embankment, launched her boats, and bade them farewell as they sailed downstream on the rapid current. She remembered losing her balance and falling into the river. Then she recalled nothing until she opened her eyes. *She is lying on the river bank quite a distance from where she fell in. A group of people are standing about her. Her frightened uncle carries her to the rectory. A woman removes her clothes, drys them in the sun, and dresses her. Uncle Don Luigi shakes his head.* "We must not let Rosa hear of my negligence; she would scold us properly. No one saw you fall in, and no one pulled you out of the river—unless it was done by your guardian angel. Child, what were you doing that made you tumble into the river?"

She told him of the sister flowers she was sending to China.

"Why flowers, Francesca?"

"Because they are pure and pretty, and raise their little faces to Our Lord."

"Ah, well and good," he sighs, "but be it as you say, while

8

your missionaries were on their way to transform heathens into Christians, you almost took a trip to the next world!"

After the frightful reality of near-drowning, she questioned herself: "How can I be a missionary when I fear to leave my home and cross the deep sea?"

The morning of July 1, 1857, was an important one for Francesca. There was great excitement, and a flurry of elaborate preparations.

Rosa scrubbed Francesca's face, and with a stiff brush dipped in olive oil, brushed her thick blond hair so forcefully that it brought tears from the child.

"Stand still," commanded Rosa, "these curls seem frivolous. Stop wincing; you are not going to a children's party. Today you are to receive the Sacrament of Confirmation. We will not have you approach the sacrament with tossing curls. Do you realize the sanctity of this occasion?"

"Yes, I do, Rosa." She wanted to tell Rosa of her worshipping love of Him, but did not dare.

When little Francesca was ready, Stella Cabrini smiled with pride. Despite Rosa's efforts to make her young sister look somber, blue-eyed, golden-haired Francesca, in her white embroidered dress and veil, was most cheerfully pretty. Stella Cabrini kissed her.

"Daughter, thou art the picture of a tiny bride."

The Christian Tower, wearing his old black wedding frock coat and Sunday beaver hat, his wife and Rosa and Giovanni, nicely and spotlessly dressed, led Francesca to the village. Along the road they greeted neighboring farmers who also were taking their children to receive the sacrament.

With her family, Francesca entered Sant'Angelo. About and above her, in marble, statuary, wood, glass, and portraiture, was man's song to his first and lasting love, his creator. She had been instructed, and understood the mysteries of her faith.

This is the temple of the King of kings, where all are equal in dedication of prayer and praise to Him. The choir with the high altar represents His head, the transept His arms, the central nave His body. The high altar points eastward toward the Holy Land, where He was born, where He studied, where He grew up as a carpenter, where He suffered and died for His children who are mankind.

Following Mass, she knelt with the other children at the altar rail. What were they thinking and feeling? With her she had brought a secret—the passion of her devotion to Him. Literally, she had fallen in love with the Son of God. Bishop Benaglia, the pastor Don Melchisedecco Abrami, her parents, and Rosa were unaware of that secret. Only He could surely know. Did His Father and Mary know? She gazed at the statue of the Sacred Heart. He was looking down upon her with outstretched arms.

Bishop Benaglia anointed her forehead with the sacred chrism, and patted her cheek. The Sacred Heart smiled with the beauty of perfection. As she embraced His smile, the sun flared through the windows. A circle of light beyond containment dazzled her, then another and another, seeming the beams of all suns combined. Her child-heart was enveloped in joy not of the earth. She felt that He had chosen her, that she was to be among His brides, His beloved.

Because I hide these things from the wise and prudent and reveal them to the little ones. Francesca, bud forth as the rose planted by the brooks of waters: give ye a sweet odor as frankincense. Send forth flowers as the lily, and yield a smell, and bring forth leaves in grace.

In later years she was to say, "The moment of the anointing of the sacred chrism, I felt that which can never be described. From that moment I was no longer of the earth. My heart began to grow through space ever with purest joy. I cannot tell why, but I knew the Holy Ghost had come to me."

10

Walking home with her family, she did not hear them as they spoke to her, for His radiance intoxicated her. She looked neither to the right or left. He had visited her spirit, and to stay. She would become His bride. She would be as nothing and obey His will to bring home to Him the souls of His children. Only thus would she grow to love Him more and more.

Before retiring, Stella Cabrini looked in upon her children, caressing them with her eyes. Rosa, Maddalena and Giovanni were asleep in their rooms. She opened the door of Francesca's room. Francesca, in her nightgown, knelt at her bedside, communing with an unseen presence. Her expression was enraptured. Stella Cabrini closed the door.

In Francesca's Lombardy, as in every region of the Italian land, the house of God was the enduring monument that survived all the political and dictatorial follies of man and state. It was the comforting and uniting center of every village. The original Lombards were a high Germanic people, a pagan race of fierce tribal warriors who invaded Italy in 568. They killed large numbers of the Roman nobility in northern Italy and settled there to stay. The big, fair Lombards quickly came to love their rich plains. Their industriousness and the fertility of the land made them prosperous. They were devoted to cleanliness, order, and reason. In the course of time, they assimilated much of the Roman civilization they had supplanted, and ardently adopted as their own the Catholicism and language of the conquered Romans. Assemblies in front of the parish church gave them the beginnings of local self-government, and their devotion to the law of Christ reinforced the naturally solid character of their people.

Not all the children of Francesca's village had her dedication to the faith they practiced, but in common they knew in their hearts that the church was theirs. At every important moment in their lives they turned to the Church, as to their parent, for guidance, blessing, and consolation. Conversely, an event at church was a matter of moment to every family of the village.

When a missionary returned from the Orient came to Sant'Angelo to speak, the peasants flocked to hear him as if he were the loftiest of dignitaries. His stories of a missionary's adventures for God were a vivid, moving experience for the parishioners. When, at the Cabrini home, the family discussed the heroic laborers in the missions, there were tears for those who had lost their lives with violence in the fastness of China.

Suddenly Francesca announced calmly, "I shall be a missionary."

"For an ignorant little girl you presume large dreams," Rosa said. "A missionary order would certainly never accept a girl who is ill most of the time. They would need strong girls. Do you know that a missionary must master many subjects and trades to meet every situation among the sick and needy and dying?"

"Rosa, do not discourage her," Stella Cabrini advised. "Spirit is stronger than bodily conditions, and Francesca shall become whatever her Lord wills."

Throughout the seasons her mother told her about Him, His natural boyhood, His apprenticeship to human toil, His profound and searching wisdom, His acceptance of His mission, the performance of His ministry, and its completion with the sacrifice of His young life on earth for the willful sins of mankind. Stella Cabrini did not realize that this story, which every Christian mother tells to her children, was more than a religious story to Francesca, that Francesca felt it and saw it as vividly as if she were there when it happened.

Francesca's childhood was not all lived in dreaming. She took part too in the domestic rituals of rural life. There was the pleasant harvesting of the fruit from the vineyard, and the merry barefoot treading of the grapes; the preserving of fruit and vegetables in earthen crocks, to feed the family through the field-slumbering winter; the singing churn that stirred thick milk to butter and cheese. Foremost was the weekly baking of great round breads in the wood-fired brick oven. Meats had to be salted and smoked, and the satisfying hot and sweet sausages made. Chestnuts were shelled, dried and ground into flour for the polenta pudding. There were the lambs' fleecy coats to be shorn, washed, spun, and woven into lasting woolens.

Hard as the Lombard farmers worked, they had time, too, for festive occasions. There was the county fair, when breeders of livestock and their domestic beasts and fowl ruled the day. Farmers' produce was displayed at the fair, and the women took part in culinary competitions. There was the annual spring carnival of rustic Roman tradition, when the people sported with comic costumes and floats, monstrous deities and pagan masks of old. There were the clapping hands, the stamping feet and the whirling of the saltarella and the tarantella, to the music of the resplendently attired village band.

During the holidays and feast days Francesca, with mother and father, sister and brother, visited the lively marketplace. The torches flared; the homely buildings were gaily bedecked, carts sold sweetmeats and novelties. There were carefree Lombard melodies from many instruments. Willing folly swelled, and the cobbled stones resounded under the heavy boots and swift feet of the dancers. The make-believe of the puppeteers beguiled the children. The strong man was beheld with awe, and the bear who walked and danced, and the monkeys tripping about were fascinating spectacles. Tumbling acrobats held the eyes, and fortune-tellers held the heart. Magicians confounded, and hawkers startled the ear. With such amusements reigning, adults and children were of one age.

At these celebrations, Francesca's heart beat faster, her face warmed and her eyes lighted. Perhaps if she were not sickly she would shout and dance and sing with the others, for surely He rejoiced when His earth children were happy.

But when she visited the village square the mornings after the feasts, the sunlight revealed only debris, torn festoons, painted paper.

In 1859 another kind of public excitement came to Sant'-Angelo—a strange, terrible excitement. There were uniforms and speeches, parades and slogans: "Lombards, free yourselves of Austrian tyranny!" "Break the stranglehold of the clergy!" "Long live the red shirts of Garibaldi!" "Victor Emmanuel and the House of Savoy for Italy united!" There was war.

The war had not come overnight.

The revolutionary spirit that had pervaded Italy since the Napoleonic domination of the early years of the century had prevented the country from enjoying true peace. The liberal party wanted a unified, independent Italy, united behind the great Garibaldi and King Victor Emmanuel, of the House of Savoy—then the only native royalty in Italy. An important figure in the liberal party was Agostino Depretis, a cousin of Agostino Cabrini. The immediate cause of the war of 1859 was a treaty which Count Camillo Cavour, the patriot who was called the "Machiavelli of Liberalism," had signed in January of that year with the Second Empire of Napoleon III. The treaty, which concluded an alliance between France and the Piedmont Region of Italy, aroused the ire of Austria, and in April, 1859, Austria retaliated with an invasion of Lombardy.

In the early spring the citizens of Sant'Angelo knew the Austrians were preparing to march upon Lombardy. Armed and bearded red-shirted horsemen galloped over the ancient roads and waved the red, white and green banners of Savoy.

The drum, the shrilling fife, and the gay hunting horn, sounded urgently.

But the house of Agostino Cabrini, the Christian Tower, was calm, although without men were inciting men. Men were not turning to God, were not rising to God.

The Austrian invaders rumbled and blared into Sant'Angelo. Fathers and sons and husbands of Sant'Angelo fled south. What were Austrian fathers and sons and husbands doing in Sant'Angelo?

Austrian soldiers occupied Agostino's house, barn, and stables. Their captain was perplexed that the Cabrini family was unfrightened and hospitable. He observed with curiosity the genuinely pious practice of this family. One evening he asked Agostino, "My good signore Cabrini, I understand that you are cousin to the radical nationalist Depretis—where do you stand?—you can safely tell me. What do you think of this conflict? Whom do you consider as friends: Victor Emmanuel with his scheming ally Napoleon III, and the revolutionist Garibaldi, or the civilized Austrians who are your protectors? Who is right, and who wrong?"

Francesca listened intently as her father answered, "Captain, you and they, governments other than that of Christ, are tragically wrong. He who created me is my King eternal. And all is darkness that is not Christ. Captain, I am sorry for those who live by the sword, and I pray for their souls."

The white-uniformed Austrians marched south. In a few months it was summer, and again they passed through Sant'-Angelo. Now they were beaten and in flight. How pitiful, how grotesque were they who had come as conquerors, and left in chaotic defeat, bleeding and groaning. The fallen of both armies were buried to rot in the fat Lombard plain.

Garibaldi came to Sant'Angelo, and so did Agostino Depretis. While Depretis made victory speeches, his cousin Agos-

15

tino Cabrini silently gave food, money, and consolation to the families of the war victims.

Agostino said to his children, "Each generation is accursed by those who would play the lottery of idols. As they cannot create, they destroy. Their governments are cruel traps, a waste of body and soul, to be interred and forgotten as was Babylon. The strivings of the generations without the love of Christ are vain, for His is the everlasting nation."

Francesca could not seem to get enough of learning, pursuing grammar, arithmetic, history and geography. By lamplight she traced her atlas, thinking of Francesca Cabrini, the missionary, riding trains, sailing oceans, tramping through jungles and climbing mountains. She had taken to heart Rosa's advice that a missionary must be able to cope with all kinds of problems, and she applied herself to chores by her mother's side, learning to wash and scrub and iron and sew, to cook and bake, to shop. When she labored over her schoolwork, Rosa felt the extraordinary force emanating from the little girl. Rosa did not praise her, but felt a silent pride in her.

Under Rosa's guidance she completed the primary grades at the age of thirteen. For higher education she was sent to the Daughters of the Sacred Heart school in adjacent Arluno. The nuns who instructed her seemed to her black-robed temples. They were His stalwart brides. Their patience and consideration for her were manifestations of their love of Him. The five years in the Arluno school broadened and deepened her hungry mind. She avidly mastered Latin, Italian, French, history, mathematics, geography, and natural science. Her favorite subjects were classic literature, geography, and particularly history. She learned of ancient civilizations, races, and social systems, of myth-shrouded Egypt, Old Testament Hebrew titans, Chaldean wisdom, Grecian grace, and of the builders of imperial Rome. Most dear to her was the Rome of and since Constantine.

The culture of her own Lombardy fascinated her. Immortal artists created their exquisite works there: Tintoretto, Mantegna, Bellini, Raphael. On the wall of the refectory in the church of Santa Maria delle Grazie is Leonardo da Vinci's "Last Supper." At Monza is a cathedral containing the Iron Crown with which the German emperors, Frederick Barbarossa and Henry VII were crowned kings of Italy; the strip of iron inside the crown is said to have been made from a nail of the True Cross. She read of Naples, "merry in sadness, sad in merriment"; Pavia, city of the hundred towers; ancient Brescia and Bergamo; Cremona, colonized in 218 B.C., the home of Stradivari and Ponchielli; Mantua, that gave birth to Virgil; Pistoia and its Hospital del Ceppo, founded in 1277, with Giovanni Della Robbia's terra-cotta reliefs of the seven works of mercy—those very works she intended to perform for her Lord. It was in her Lombardy that in 728 the Bishops of Rome instituted the great human *Domus Culta,* the cultivation of the home, offering the family unity and the common social bond that did so much to dignify life.

Quietly and steadily her intuition developed. Knowledge did not come by magic. She kneaded and worked her fine clear mind. Swiftly her spirit absorbed, selected, and added to its practical store.

Though ill during the weeks of final examinations, she did not spare her studies. She passed with highest honors and obtained her schoolteacher's license. She was now a young woman of eighteen who looked like a pretty fourteen-year-old girl. Her luminous blue-green eyes were her sole feature of strength. Yes, she had set her course to become a religious. Her decision was not dictated by any timidity of the outer world or need of refuge, or by any feeling of feminine inadequacy, for she was delightfully formed and lovely, and many a good Lombard youth would have wished her queen of his home and future. She was the embodiment of conscious principle, and her soul which was more real to her than her flesh

17

and the world about her, had chosen for her the ideal husband. She presented herself to the mother superior and expressed her wish to become a Daughter of the Sacred Heart.

Mother Grassi contemplated her with motherly kindness. The religious must have body and limbs to equal the steel of her spirit. The nun has to put her hands to labors that would try a healthy man. Mother Grassi gently shook her head and said, "Bless you, enlightened child, but the way of His brides is most arduous, and our community may bring in only the physically strong. It is with regret that I refuse you." She kissed Francesca's brow. "Abide and do not be discouraged. He Whom you cherish so has His purpose for you."

It is not now, then, thought Francesca. And she bowed her head to His plan.

2 ✠ ✠ ✠

SHE WAS HOME again. The Daughters of the Sacred Heart would not accept her. Very well, she would translate her love of Him into imitation of His acts to the utmost of her ability within her own home. Until God should call her parents, she decided, she would devote herself to their comfort and happiness.

Upon Agostino signs of the end were already written. His tousled hair and mustache were whitened, his keen hearing and vision were failing, his large muscular frame had become gaunt and stooping, and now and then he had a fainting spell.

It was the fall of 1868. It was also the last harvest for Agostino. He would never again make the scythe dance through the heavy-headed wheat, gather the bursting red grape, the tart green olive, the sun-smelling tomatoes, lift from the garden the succulent gourds, pick the corn, milk the gentle cows, or stroke the sleek coats of his horses and mules. He would never again feel the late autumn sun gild the plain, that tabled rich Lombard bosom of a vanished sea. He would never again see his neighbors in the far-stretching fields and hear the instruments play as they reaped and sang harvest thanksgiving song. It was the last time he would see the harvest moon silver his land. Yet Agostino plied his failing strength against familiar chores until a morning of the following February. As he finished dressing to go to Mass a trembling seized him and he was suddenly rendered powerless. He stumbled to a chair and sat down. An iciness came over him. ". . . Stella, please," he mumbled, "hot coffee . . ." Hurriedly Stella poured the steaming coffee, and placed the cup before him. He was unable to grasp it. Agostino was paralyzed.

It was now Francesca who was the Christian Tower of the Cabrini family, as she sustained the spirit of her slowly dying father. In the kitchen of the simple gray-stucco cottage she kept the once-mighty Agostino warm and comfortable. She and Rosa tenderly waited upon her ailing mother and invalided sister Maddalena. Each morning she called for and accompanied the pastor, Don Bassano Dede, who brought the Holy Communion to Agostino. And she read at night to the family from the missal. With spring, she, Rosa, Giovanni, and hired help worked their father's fields, and the yearly miracle of seed and awakened earth burgeoned.

For months, the Cabrini home was a quiet Christian isle, Agostino's life was a tide ebbing without return. Death hovered possessively over him. On February 22, 1869, as it fluttered down upon him, he whispered to Stella, "I must leave thee and our dear children. I go now. I accept willingly the death my maker sends me. Stella, soon, you and I will be rejoined."

Francesca witnessed the end of her father's life. Agostino greeted death with the same calm that had marked his life, as patiently as he had farmed, had taken his honest pleasures, and had worshipped. His death was the elevation of his virtuous life, and the grateful return of the gift to the Giver.

Before that year was over Francesca was to bear three more sorrows. Elderly uncle Don Luigi, retired now from his parish, had come to live with his sister and her children. He and Stella Cabrini would sit on the long summer days among the sun-kissed roses beside the cottage, recounting the goodness of the past. Together they would softly say their litanies. Smilingly, resignedly, they awaited the quieting, rewarding

20

angel of the Creator. When white winter stole the roses and left bare the stems, they were called. As Francesca held her dying mother in her arms, her mother whispered, "My child of light . . . from above my prayers shall follow thy feet. . . ." Within months Maddalena, who had been crippled since childhood, followed her parents to the grave.

Francesca did not mourn the passing of her loved ones. They were with her Spouse, and knew more than was given them to perceive on earth. They were safe from the trammels and passing kingdoms of men. While they lived, they had ever had His mansions before their eyes; there now they had arrived.

Melancholy could not find Francesca Cabrini, for there was much to be done for His children near and far. Tragedy, which terrorizes and crushes the spiritually blind, ennobled her. She worked the farm with Rosa and Giovanni. After the day's toil, instead of resting she sought those in need and went to their aid.

On the outskirts of the village a wanderer lived in a poor hovel, destitute, and suffering with cancer. She learned of his plight and immediately went to him. The man, a bearded mute, was a mass of open sores. She compressed her lips and set to cleaning and feeding him.

She cared for her patient for a year. Each day his eyes sought her smile and spoke gratitude. In his dying hour his hand rested in hers.

What did the Sant'Angelo people think of Francesca Cabrini? They knew she was the daughter of the Christian Tower and of good Stella Cabrini and saw well the inherited expression of her character. She was a surpassingly fair flower of Lombardy. For one of their sons she could be a yoke of love and peace. But it was known in Sant'Angelo that although not accepted by the community of the religious, she had in spirit promised herself to Christ.

For the people of Sant'Angelo the spring of 1872 was a grim season. Under an ominous sun, while farmers sowed the plain, an uninvited guest came noiselessly, attired in the black mantle of smallpox. Bravely heedless of contagion, Francesca went to the stricken day and night, with Rosa following and constantly fearing for her.

"Rosa," she admonished, "how can you fear for me when 'tis He who compels my actions? Do you not trust Him?"

She stifled her repugnance to the sight and stench of the sick, and with her small delicate fingers drained their festering boils. Now that she healed and consoled, her growing love of Him was richer than treasures. Now as He worked mercifully for the sick through her frail being, her passion for Him intensified.

When inevitably Francesca was stricken with smallpox, it was the devoted Rosa who tended her, alternating skillful nursing with fervent prayer. And throughout her illness Rosa never left her bedside. Before Francesca lapsed into the delirium of the crisis, she gazed at the shrine of the Sacred Heart upon the dresser.

"Rosa, Rosa, He is smiling at me. He does not want me now. He spreads His wounded hands over distant lands and motions that there I have much work to accomplish for His children in His name, in His love, before He will call me. . . ."

The pastor of her early childhood had been the priest who baptized her, Don Abrami, but since her fourteenth year she was under the spiritual guidance of Don Bassano. After the passing of Francesca's parents, the old-fashioned Don Bassano was paternally close to her, Rosa, and Giovanni. During her convalescence from the smallpox Don Bassano visited her every day. She recovered slowly, but without a trace of the marring pox upon her lovely face. One day, after she was able to get up and about, Don Bassano came to her and asked her if she would substitute for the schoolteacher of Vidardo, who

22

was ill. Vidardo was but a mile from Sant'Angelo. Yes, she would do it, for she was obedient to her pastor. Moreover, she knew that the aspiring missionary should have practical teaching experience.

In Vidardo her reserved manner was misunderstood and she was received rather coldly. The first morning in the classroom she stood timorously before the curious and critical children. They measured her. She was slight, girlish, pretty, and uncertain.

"I am your substitute teacher, Miss Francesca Cabrini. Good morning and God bless you, dear children. We will begin our day with prayer."

The children were quick to inform her that Mayor Zanardi was of the liberal party, that he was an enemy of the pastor, Don Serrati, and definitely forbade religious instruction in the public school. She lowered her head and quietly prayed for her class.

Her first month was difficult. The children fought and played and turned the classroom into a daily carnival. She did not use angry words or force with them, and they were perplexed. After they left she cleaned up the debris left by their pranks, restored the room, taught a small class in religion in Don Serrati's church, and then walked the long country road home to Sant'Angelo. Under the trees and through the fields, she communed with Him about her unruly school children and the bombastic anticlerical Mayor. What was the answer? What else but love for Him and consequently for His children, no matter how they behaved. Love was not provoked to wrath. Love would conquer eternally.

The children eventually exhausted their mischief upon her and were ashamed of themselves. They learned that her love for them was genuine and unconditional, and they opened their little hearts to her. They embraced her manner of discipline, and reached happily to her for the outlawed religious instruction, even following her to the parish church classes

23

after school hours. The liberal Mayor Zanardi had a young daughter, and the child was among Francesca's pupils. Through the enthusiasm of his little girl, the Mayor reconsidered his view of religion. He befriended Francesca, and after a time he allowed her to return him to the faith.

Her supposedly temporary teaching job lengthened, and daily for two years she was to be seen throughout the seasons, whatever the weather, walking to and from Vidardo. Because she was active in the parish of Don Serrati, she humbly submitted to his spiritual and paternal authority. Often she would tell Don Serrati of her hope of becoming a bride of heaven in the eyes of the church. He did not encourage the possibility, for he was seriously concerned about her health. He would pointedly mention the fact that during her spells of lung attacks she coughed drops of blood, and he would shake his head.

She offered herself to the Conossian Sisters and again to the Daughters of the Sacred Heart, but both rejected her. Francesca remained unaware that they were acting on Don Serrati's advice. The good man no doubt sincerely felt that the duties of the religious would prove too much for her frail being.

During the time that Francesca was teaching in his parish, her friend Don Serrati was elevated to the dignity of monsignor. To take up his new duties, he was sent to the town of Codogno, which was not very far from Vidardo. The change in his station was to bring about a profound change in Francesca's life as well.

Not long after Don Serrati took up his new duties in Codogno, he found himself beset with a problem that seemed insoluble. The parish was the site of a small orphanage for girls called the House of Providence.

Codogno was one of the many towns throughout Italy where the new united antipapal government had deprived the church
24

of land, means, and influence, and where the parish and religious were at an unfair disadvantage and uneasily on the defensive. The parishes under the circumstances, could not afford to build, buy, or rent the charitable institutions they needed. Some years before, the parish of Codogno had made an arrangement with a woman named Antonia Tondini. She bought a building to shelter orphans, and the parish paid her a stipulated sum per month for the proper keep of each orphan.

Since this woman owned the house and property, she regarded herself as rightful owner and sole authority of the orphanage, although the children it housed were supported by parish funds. The Tondini woman was unmanageable. It was common knowledge in the parish that she kept the orphans in disgraceful condition. Moreover, Tondini's friend and partner, Teresa Calza, lived in the house with Tondini, and she too was inflicted on the children as an authority. The cook, Giuseppa Alberici, was a kind but meek woman, who herself could do no more than tolerate the temperamental ways of her employers.

Thinking to effect a transformation in these women, Monsignor Serrati lighted upon the idea of offering them religious character, hoping against hope that if they viewed their responsibilities through nuns' eyes, they might improve. He succeeded in persuading them to serve a brief novitiate with the Sisters of Nazareth. Serrati then conferred upon them the religious profession, and thus they donned the Habit of lay sisters, or religious associates. But the monsignor's well-meant inspiration turned out to be an embarrassing failure, for, wearing the authority of the habit, they exercised their abuse of the orphans with all the more security.

Serrati thought of young Francesca Cabrini; she had accomplished small wonders with the school children, the Mayor, and his parish in Vidardo. He sent for her. She responded obediently to his wish. When she came to Codogno he had not the courage to tell her about the House of Providence and Antonia Tondini in detail. He told her he had an interesting project for her, that of helping to reorganize the orphanage; it would not keep her there long, probably a few weeks; then again, the fine dry air of pleasant Codogno might be beneficial for her weak lungs. If her health should improve, who knew but that he could help make a real nun of her. Francesca agreed with alacrity, and returned to Sant'Angelo only long enough to collect a few personal belongings.

She did not know that she would see her sister and brother only a few more times, and that they would go far away and out of her life, for Giovanni would soon emigrate to Argentina, and Rosa would follow him and devote the rest of her days to his care. The gray-stucco cottage with its red-tile roof, the ancient brick-paved kitchen and fireside, mother-and-father's room and huge bedstead, the family crucifix centuries old, the bower of her tiny room where as a child she had so often contemplated His heavenly spirit, the granary, stable garden, and trained fields, the good farm neighbors, the chapel and chimes of Sant'Angelo, all would be left behind as halcyon memories, and she would actually never see Sant'Angelo again.

On August 12, 1874, she returned to Codogno ready to report to work in the House of Providence. Just what she was to do there was not yet clear to her.

The address of the orphanage took her into the crowded industrial and tenement quarter. To her distress, she discovered that the House of Providence was a depressing three-story structure that had been a factory. It was adjoined by a tall tenement and a tannery; across the way was a dyeing mill and a workingmen's tavern. She hesitated before the entrance. Above the rumble of heavy wagons over the street stones, she heard a voice shouting from within, "Salesia! Curses on the hour your bricklaying father left the earth for me to bear your stubbornness! And you, Veronica, you will mind me or go back to the gutter where they found you!"

26

She waited for the confusion of screams to subside, and pulled the bell cord.

"Salesia! Answer the door!"

A barefoot and ragged girl of thirteen with a smoldering expression on her cherubic face opened the door.

"Good morning. God bless you. I am Francesca Cabrini."

The girl disappeared into the kitchen, to inform her keeper of Francesca's identity. Sister Tondini and Sister Calza made her wait a long while before finally coming out into the all-purpose room.

Francesca curtsied and respectfully introduced herself.

Antonia Tondini, a tall, swarthy, frenetic woman in her late forties, returned her greeting with a hostile grunt. Monsignor Serrati's and the Bishop Gelmeni's plan to have Francesca do some good for the House of Providence did not appeal to Sister Tondini.

Francesca's entry into the House of Providence, in any capacity, meant trouble to Sister Tondini. It meant interference with her careless methods. Worst of all, it threatened her privacy. Everyone had long suspected, but no one yet had been able to prove, that Tondini had been mishandling the parish's orphan funds.

Antonia Tondini decided to rid herself of the frail young newcomer immediately.

"Serrati told me he was sending you here," she exclaimed. "But schoolteacher, saint, fool, spy, dupe or whatever you are, I did not need nor ask for you! Serrati has a lot of nerve to thrust you under my roof—but if you stay and trouble comes, you'll see how quickly the civil authorities will back me up! I, Antonia Tondini, and not Serrati am the sole proprietor of this house, one hundred per cent! My thirty-thousand-lire purchase money speaks to me. Do you bring talking lire?"

The outburst left Francesca shocked and breathlesss. Were these unkempt women really His brides?

"If you insist on staying, you hang yourself on Serrati's

27

hook! Do your own pleasure." Having delivered this welcome, the formidable Sisters of Providence turned from Francesca and marched back into the kitchen.

Tears of astonishment came, and she could not restrain them. The Annals of the Propagation of the Faith, the stories about saints and martyrs had depicted glorious heroism in the face of savage tortures and purifying flames. The whole spectrum of eternity awaited the bride subjected to such tests. The stories spoke of cruel heathens alien to His light. But the children of darkness were not supposed to be here, in civilized Italy. Furthermore, how could the foes of the Spouse pretend to be His followers?

Her instinct was to pick up her valise and hasten from the House of Providence. But would Mary be disconcerted by Sister Antonia Tondini, and run from the neglected orphans? Was she to fail Him so soon?

The orphans eager to see the newcomer, had been hanging about and had witnessed Tondini's onslaught. Three of the older girls came to Francesca's side as soon as their "protectors" were out of sight. Salesia, the sturdiest of the orphans said, "Miss Cabrini, you are crying. We understand. Those awful women beat us with tongue and hand and thus we know too well what tears are. Monsignor Serrati told us so many nice things about you. You are much prettier than we thought. Oh, I am called Salesia, and these are Veronica and Columba —although I am bigger, they are older." Veronica put her hands to her mouth and whispered, "Sister Alberici is on our side but dares not show her sympathy."

"Have you a father and mother?" asked Columba.

"They are at rest above with all of your dear parents."

"I am sorry," said Columba, "that you are orphaned, like us."

Salesia said, "Miss Cabrini, I am orphaned six months and have been here less time than the others, but I know this place. Tondini means what she says. Even Bishop Gelmeni

28

and Monsignor Serrati are afraid to come here because of her. Has Tondini frightened you, too, away from us?"

"Children," Francesca said, "this shall be my home with you."

The orphans came bashfully around her. Their wan under-nourished faces were all eager friendly eyes.

They were new rays of His love that instantly lighted her heart, and she smiled. "I, Francesca, tell you, you are not abandoned of parents. God's Son is now your Father, and you shall be as daughters of mine in spirit." Salesia impulsively threw her strong arms about her.

The House of Providence was utterly dismal and hardly removed from a bedlam. That night Francesca lay awake on an improvised bed of boards in a bin-like room with the girls asleep about her. Her love must now leave the idyllic nest and take wing against storm. He had not come to follow; His Mission was the Way to be followed. His life was given to works, and prayer was his resting. Could she recoil, and follow with lagging steps? She must put her hands to the House of Providence while her heart communed with His, and He would guide her hands.

The orphans of the House of Providence lacked everything but want. Where to start first? She arose at dawn and gazed upon the slumbering girls. The House of Providence had blighted them with hunger, spiritual thirst, and physical neglect. Without delay Francesca wrote to Rosa, asking Rosa to use her modest inheritance and her Vidardo schoolteacher's savings to purchase soap, linen, sewing kits, fabrics, and medicines and to send them all to Monsignor Serrati, so that it would seem the House of Providence had received the urgently needed supplies from him.

At every turn the aspect within the orphanage was bleak; Sisters Tondini and Calza were walls of suspicion, obstruction, and hatred. Her sense of cleanliness and order was revolted. Malodors contended and converged. In front of the orphanage the gutter was an open sewer for the tenements. The acrid smells and filth-carrying flies of the tannery invaded the meager play yard behind the house.

The sisters, positive at first that Francesca would lose her spirit and leave, disregarded her as if she were not there. When she addressed them they smirked or shrugged and left her unanswered. Her heart bled daily as Tondini and Calza dealt blows at random upon the girls, and particularly when the children sobbed and wished themselves dead and freed from the House of Providence.

Months went by. When winter came and Francesca had still not fled, Tondini resolved to shatter her will. At night as Francesca and the girls shivered in their beds, they were treated to a recital of insults from below. Heated from wine, rancor, and the kitchen stove, Tondini and Calza would raise their voices in a virtuoso display of malice. "A peasant's daughter putting on scholarly airs! Nicely she stole the teacher's job in Vidardo! She talks about sanitation—and she herself coughs blood! The undertaker is looking for her. That humility is false, for humans cannot be angels! Cabrini is a serpent wearing dove's feathers! What made her leave her own home town, heh? Why doesn't she get married and practice saintliness on a husband instead of strangers, heh? Actress of piety, she is not wanted even as a nun! Intruder on my property! Careerist! Her motive is to take over the orphange for her pocket, but she can't win under my roof!"

Then, having vent their nightly venom against her, they would turn upon each other, quarreling violently about the orphanage fund Tondini was looting and slipping to her nephew.

It was impossible for Francesca to shield her heart from their cruelty, but the tears she could not repress flowed silently. She was ashamed of her tears and nightly after having wept she reasserted her promise to Him that she would conquer her

30

tears, for tears were escaping energies that should go into her mission.

She remembered her father's patient agricultural labors, and his faith in Him Who unites the goodness of earth with the purity of sun and rain. She took up her own labors in earnest, and in her hands small miracles budded forth. She begged Him to forgive her for the limited time she allowed to meditation as she outlined the many necessary chores of her plan for His children. She could not offer His children vistas of the soul while their flesh was covered with infections and dirty clothes.

She, the young, would lead the younger to the light, and a little sisterhood of Christ would come to life in Tondini's hell. What would He first do? His mercy would swiftly remove from His children the torments of their bodies, wash their feet, anoint their heads with fragrant ointments, and then lead them sparkling clean into the temple. Thus she did what He would have done: fine combs tracked out the lice from the girl's tresses, and baths, salves, and powders cured their skin diseases. Washing and sewing reformed unsightly petticoats and dresses, and she taught them to make bonnets, and to cobble their worn shoes after a fashion. From her they learned, "We will not depend upon others, we must and will do it ourselves!"

She hurled herself against the evil of filth with soap and mop and disinfectants, and her dynamic activity exhilarated the girls to a kindred enthusiasm.

The hygienic conquest of the House of Providence made Tondini fume with chagrin. Any improvement of the orphans' lot was a reflection upon her. As long as she had enjoyed full authority, she could claim that nothing could be done that was not being done, that the situation was hopeless. Now Francesca proved her wrong.

"Cabrini! Your soap and water gouge the paint from my walls and ruin my floors! How dare you toy with my house! I am the owner and your superior! Troublemaker, how many

31

times a day must I tell you to get out of my house? Your schemes against me will fail! One of these lovely days I'll talk to you with my hands! I'll take you by the throat and throw you out of my house!"

Francesca would bow her head. In those ugly moments the orphans would turn their heads and weep for her. Her reward came at night in the bedroom with the girls. She told them, "Remember always, in your work and study and play and dreams, that you are His beloved children. You are the flowers He gave to me."

Big Salesia could not help letting loose the store of her wrath against Tondini and Calza. "I am keeping score of the beatings. Before I leave this place, I will pay them back beating for beating, and with interest!"

Francesca set the example of pacification. "Salesia, Salesia, not their way, but His Way. We must return darkness with light, epithets with forgiveness and prayer. His gifts were not meant to be cast away by strife. Love is time, love is space, love is forever, and He is love."

For Francesca, who could never find enough time to devote to undistracted adoration, constructive action became itself a form of prayer. She conveyed to the girls in her care her conviction that work, undertaken in love of Him, was a kind of worship. She revealed to them how priceless was time, and told them that each moment must be the song of cleanliness and well-being, and learning. Under her care, they absorbed knowledge of geography and mathematics, spelling and writing and history. She did not seek her bed until she heard them in prayer and saw each peacefully asleep. Then as she reached her heart to His, possible dangers to her girls crossed her mind: some of them would be arriving at the troubling age; she would have to be the personal mother. Her bosom must protect them from the welter of hurts, and she must endow them with self-protecting strength. She must not fail His children!

32

My Lord, my Passion, be ever at my side, look down ever upon me, and with Thee all things I can do. Good night, my Love.

Disregarding her precarious health, she bore her girls safely through the long winter, guarding them from illness and discomfort. As she performed each duty, the ceaseless vision within her was already turned upon the next. She must see that there were more clothes, more schoolbooks. She must press Monsignor Serrati to improve the girls' diet. Salesia wore out her shoes sooner than the others; this one with her rheumatic fever and that one with her poor liver needed special attention and must rest more often. Someday there must be a melodium for musical Passerini. With dried corn leaves and ticking she could make new mattresses. Giovanette was petulant and probably needed stomach treatment. Then there was the matter of Gesuina's teeth. And bless Salesia, who so kindly helped to discipline the girls!

No matter how she looked at it, the House of Providence was badly and inexcusably located. The orphanage should be a sound, safe, roomy building in the country, abounding with His wonders of nature, gardens, birds, sun, grass, and trees. How could she possibly raise her living flowers without invoking the raging and continual madness of Tondini? When, where, and how would she really become the missionary to far Christless lands?

At night in the bedroom, with her flowers gathered about the candle's glow, she tenderly increased religious instruction, and her gentle words lifted their hearts above bondage to Tondini, above the efforts and setbacks and tears of the day.

One day seven of the girls, Passerini, Veronica, Salesia, Agostina, Franceschina, Gaetanina, and Columba came to her solemnly. One of them, speaking for the group, whispered with inspired sincerity, "Oh, Francesca, we too want to become missionaries with you. We want to be His brides by your side.

33

We want to live and die for His love as your daughters. . . . Promise us, Francesca, promise us." Her first seven joys. Seven gladnesses to His Sacred Heart.

One, two, three years passed as Antonia Tondini put obstacle after obstacle before Francesca and scorned and blasphemed her. She was now twenty-seven, and would no longer be denied the robe of His bride. She presented her seven flowers and herself to Monsignor Serrati, and together they begged to consecrate themselves to God by means of the holy vows.

Monsignor Serrati contemplated her fondly. Francesca Cabrini, the small, golden-haired, beautiful young woman whom he had placed into Tondini's inferno. Time and again Antonia Tondini had stormed to him and reviled her. But when he questioned Francesca about Tondini, she showed herself incapable of resentment or bitterness. He, knowing the truth, was amazed by Francesca. She covered the misguided actions of Tondini with the cloak of charity, all the while bringing the strength and comfort of Christ to the orphans. A paternal smile spread over his face.

"Francesca Cabrini, forgive me! Long before this moment I should have known that the Bridegroom of Heaven had already betrothed thee." He graciously consented to accept for Him also her seven flowers. As he blessed her he lifted her lowered chin. "Soon, on the day of your nuptial, you will be 'Mother Cabrini,' superior of the House of Providence!"

On September 14, Francesca and her seven orphan girls offered up to Him their vows of poverty, chastity, and obedience.

At long last she was a religious. How dear to hear for the first time the little orphans lisp and whisper and say and cry, "Mother Cabrini. . . ." With her vows she had taken as her middle name the name of the great missionary Saint Francis Xavier, so that henceforth she would be Francesca Xavier Cabrini. Now all that remained was to become a missionary.

34

She and her daughters were then as eight temples in the orphanage, and the House of Providence roofed two worlds, her light and Tondini's bitter shadows. That the House of Providence could exist as an unshaped convent containing a small group of nuns under the protection and supervision of Bishop Gelmini was evidently one of the improvisations of those trying times in which the Church found herself. Under the wild, raw blows of new-sprung liberalism the way of the devout was extremely difficult.

Five months after Francesca was admitted to the religious profession, Pius IX died, and on February 20, 1878, Cardinal Vincenzo Gioacchino Pecci, was elected pope and became Leo XIII. This was to be the great pope of Francesca's life and mission. There is no doubt that his mind and spirit deeply influenced her own.

Leo XIII was born at Carpineto on March 2, 1810. His family was Sienese in origin, and his father, Col. Lodovico Pecci, had served under Napoleon. His mother, Anna Prosperi, was a descendant of Rienzi, and was a member of the Third Order of St. Francis.

He had been educated by the Jesuits at Viterbo and in Rome. On December 31, 1837, he was ordained priest, and in 1847 he was made Bishop of Perugia. Throughout his thirty-two year episcopate he had a reputation as a social and municipal reformer. He built and restored many churches, striving to elevate the intellectual as well as the spiritual tone of his clergy, and showing in his pastoral letters an unusual regard for learning and social reform. He was resolute in his protests against the deprivation of the pope's temporal power in 1870, the confiscation of the property of religious orders, and the law of civil marriage established by the Italian government.

As successor to Pius IX, Leo XIII was confronted on all sides with hostile governments imbued with secular philosophies. Modern capitalism, the machine, and revolutionary theories seem to have been born at the same time. Theological speculation and ethical reflection did not know what to make of the old traditional hopes for the future. The new generation revolted against the mystical and abandoned the old system of solid morals. With the intoxication of the intellect came a progressive deterioration of the spiritual values, a turning away of men's souls, and a transformation of man's passionate relationship to his Creator. The result was the heartbreaking loss of the felicity of the human and holy family that left man a factory cog, a lost and arid isle.

Leo XIII had strong convictions as to what the role of the Church must be in the giving of a healthy positive answer to the moral problems raised by the modern age. He believed that theology had to be reconciled with science as faith had once to be accommodated with reason. His model was St. Thomas Aquinas. He was not afraid of learning. The man who became pope at the age of sixty-eight, when Francesca Cabrini was twenty-eight and a nun only a few months, was a man of literary taste and culture, familiar with the classics, and anxious that the clergy should unite the humanities with their theological studies. Leo XIII believed firmly in the value of education at all levels. He encouraged the study of astronomy and natural science and advocated critical and scholarly Biblical studies. As soon as he became pontiff his hope was to forge a real reconciliation between the Church and the people of his day.

Like all Catholics, Francesca was moved by the passing of the staunch pope, Pius IX, who had opposed so bravely the freethinkers of his day. And like all Catholics, she greeted the accession of his successor with hope and prayer. But she could little anticipate the role he would someday play in her life. Indeed, she must not have given much thought to the matter at the time, if for no other reason than that she could not have had the time.

During the months after Francesca took the veil, the number of orphans brought to the House of Providence kept increasing. Francesca's burdens grew no lighter. She was teaching His children His Way, preparing them for Confirmation and Holy Communion, building their bodies and minds, manners, abilities, and giving personally to each the warmth of her boundless love. Her position as the official and spiritual superior in a house owned and managed by an uncontrollable woman was almost impossible. All the exquisite tact, prudence, and kindness she exerted with Antonia Tondini was of no avail. Her heart bled for the girls who were daily made to cringe and suffer at Tondini's hands. The older woman's brutality to the orphaned girls sowed in her heart the deepest compassion for the bereft and abandoned young. Whenever she approached Tondini for an accounting of the orphanage funds, Tondini flew into hysterical tantrums and threatened to kill her.

One night as she and her seven daughters were softly singing hymns, Tondini and Calza, heady with wine, pounded upon the door and broke into the room.

"Now you'll taste the justice of my hands, since you pay no heed to my tongue!" shouted Tondini, smashing at her face. Sister Salesia pulled Tondini from her and raised her fist to Tondini. Though bleeding from nose and mouth, Francesca stayed Sister Salesia's righteous hand, and smiled. "We will return violence with peace, Salesia my daughter, and hate with love."

For three years after she had taken her vows, Francesca remained at Tondini's House of Providence. Tondini's incorrigible stealing of the orphanage funds deprived His children of their just bread. He had not hesitated to lash out at the profiteers in the Temple. Francesca now had to grow to the true strength of a mother and look out for His children. Enough was enough. At last she informed Bishop Gelmini of Tondini's thievery, and demanded righting action.

Bishop Gelmini and Monsignor Serrati sent for her. In the rectory she sat with the two humble men of God. She could not possibly know that the smiles on their faces were heralds of her dream. The Bishop nodded to Monsignor Serrati, and with a ring of pleasure Monsignor Serrati intoned, "Francesca, my child, six long years ago, knowing well that you would not refuse me, I asked you to help me for a few weeks with the despairing problem of the orphanage. "Sisters" Tondini and Calza—God forgive me—sisters of the Adversary, dominated the House of Providence to the distress of parish and all. Verily, I expected you to run from them and not immolate yourself upon their horns, and then I feared that your determination to stay there would be the death of you."

Monsignor Serrati enumerated her trials and lauded her accomplishments. When he concluded, she whispered, "Monsignor, I am nothing. I am merely His witness."

Bishop Gelmini said cheerfully, "We are dissolving the House of Providence, and excommunicating the unholy sisters. Your orphans will be removed to other homes elsewhere. But what is to become of you and the seven daughters you inspired?" For a suspenseful space he grinned. Then he continued, "Dear child, I know that you have always dreamed of becoming a missionary. Well then, the time has matured for you. There is no institute of missionary sisters in these parts. So, Mother Cabrini, found one yourself!"

She raised her eyes, and arose. Child of obedience, His obedient bride, she answered with humility, with softness, with simplicity, "I shall search for a house."

That was the first night in the House of Providence that she went to bed with an unclouded peace. Before she surrendered to slumber, she returned the confidence He had placed in her with the deepening, widening, heightening passion, the love that senses and soars with ever-expanding time and space.

It is the twilight of the new day. She knows not or questions whether her vision is dream or waking. He is pointing to the Franciscan church in Codogno, then to Saint Peter's and the dovecots within the cornices, then He directs His hand

38

toward the west-reaching ocean. Following morning prayer, she hastened to the Franciscan church which was in the quiet wooded section of town. There seemed to be nothing but trees behind the church. She persistently searched the vicinity, and in the woods discovered an ancient abandoned monastery. It was an appealing two-story building with a low-pitched tile roof and airy, arched continuous porticos opening out upon a large enclosed courtyard.

This would be the cradle for the mission of the Sacred Heart! The house where He would attend His new brides!

3 ✤ ✤ ✤

SHE IS thirty. She has overly paid obligations to subjection, timidity, and patient waiting. These terms are below mothers. He has signaled her to found the order of His heart. From now on she will put hand to people and events.

She went to Monsignor Serrati and solicited his approval of the house she had found for her order. After seeing the commodious old monastery, he marveled at the correctness of her choice. At once he sent an architect friend to find the owner and negotiate purchase. The property had been a Franciscan monastery until it was suppressed by Napoleon, and had been all but forgotten by the inhabitants of Codogno. It could be acquired for a negligible price, but the owner was a liberal and fiercely against the Church. Monsignor Serrati wrote out the purchase draft and instructed his architect friend, "With innocent artifice for which God will forgive you, tell the Church-hating owner that you are buying the monastery for the storage of cement. In good time—when it is too late for him to do anything about it—he will be apprised that the cement is of the spiritual kind, cement to adhere together bricks of the soul, cement to build the edifice of Francesca Cabrini's Missionary Sisters of the Sacred Heart."

Francesca could not and would not part with His orphans. She decided to take them with her and make of the monastery a missionary convent and orphanage combined. There was no

40

reason for His little ones to remain longer in the House of Providence.

The termination and fall of the House of Providence brought silence and amazement to Tondini and Calza. Guiseppa Alberici, the meek and inoffensive cook, wept as Francesca and the girls made preparations to leave. Francesca said to her gently, "Would you be one with us under His roof?" Guiseppa Alberici wiped her tears. "Mother Cabrini, yes! It is God's will for you to ask me. . . ."

Swiftly Francesca supervised the meager packing, and on the afternoon of November 12, 1880, after Bishop Gelmini, Monsignor Serrati, and a sacristan loaded three donkey carts with beds, mattresses, blankets, and sacks of paraphernalia and rode off, she, her seven collaborating brides, and the happily excited orphan girls, toting their belongings, proceeded from under Antonia Tondini's roof. Their fondest dream had come true, they were going to their own true home. Neighbors' eyes dampened with joy for the orphans and nuns, and they hailed them farewell and good future. The nuns and orphans paraded through the streets past tenements and factories, out to the country area and to their own bare but impressive home.

For moments the girls looked with awe at the inviting building and trees, hardly believing their eyes. Then with cries of joy they ran through the tall grass and wild flowers, twirling, skipping, and leaping.

Francesca, Bishop Gelmini, and Monsignor Serrati stood in the Fall sunlight watching them, and in reverie she spoke, "Today His children know laughter, and their ringing voices are the bells announcing this, the new House of His Heart."

Her daughters and the girls flurried about unpacking and carrying and setting up the household goods under her direction. What matter that His house had opened without means, only a bit of hastily prepared cold food for each, chairs and utensils lacking, and not even a table? They were home! During their impetuous move from the House of Providence, no

41

one had thought to bring along candles and lamps. She led her Daughters and girls through the corridors to the make-shift bedrooms in the dark as securely as if the house were lighted. She laughed at their wondering. At last their Mother Cabrini was laughing!

The early days of the Codogno house were to be among the most precious of Francesca's life. In the house of the Bridegroom blessed was the pallet bed of that first night, blessed was the house to be lived in in His name, blessed was the dower of His seed.

In this house she would gather more virgins for Him and initiate them as sharers of her marriage, and for them, He, His Father, and the Holy Spirit waited.

The daughter in the adjoining bed awakened, and was startled. About Francesca Cabrini's short golden hair and face there was light. Her expression was of transfiguration, her eyes reflected a flaming vision. The daughter cried with alarm, "Mother! Mother!" The light dissolved. The room was dark.

"What is it, my Daughter?"

"The light! Mother, did you see it?"

". . . Yes, Daughter . . . 'Twas nothing. Pray yourself back to calm and slumber."

And thus it was that from then on Francesca Cabrini would sleep in a little room by herself.

There was much to be done before she could hope to see her infant order prosper. In her mind she catalogued immediate duties: appeal in person from door to door to the people of Codogno for donations of furnishings and money. Arrange for credit with the flour, grocery, and charcoal merchants, with farmers for milk, eggs, vegetables and meats, and with the fish vendor for Friday's food. Furnish the chapel. Start a private school within the house, for income to help support more orphans.

Busy as she was, even while she worked at the domestic chores she was formulating regulations for her order. Her

42

standard would not be a theological maze of gestures and useless mortifications. It would point clearly to the imitation of Christ. She was the bride who would go to the Spouse for directions. His words had been spoken on earth by Him and were not to be altered. The institute would have the spirit of the Holy Family. All would be equal in love without preference, acclaim, or favor. Simplicity would show the proper path. The Lord said to Ananias, "Arise and go into the street which is called Straight, and inquire in the house of Judas for one named Saul, of Tarsus." Simplicity would be her street called Straight. The Missionary Sisters of the Sacred Heart would wear plain practical Habits without frills to hamper their labors. Faith demanded detachment from people and things, for the inclinations of such personal attachment limited that universal love exemplified by the Spouse. Each new house would be independent of other houses and would support itself, by begging, subscription, soliciting donations, taking in paying pupils, whatever means the locality suggested. The mother superior of each house would be chosen by her without sentiment and strictly for the most capable administrative abilities. She remembered all too well her protracted efforts to join the religious and was determined not to refuse the worthy even if they were not physically strong. The candidates admitted as postulants to the institute would be given more than sufficient time to decide upon the religious profession before they gave their vows. They were to be won only by their voluntary love of Christ and not by any other means. None were to be coaxed or forced under the standard "Imitation of Christ," but each should take up with her entire body, mind, and soul her vows of poverty, chastity, and obedience to the Spouse. Anonymity would be their modest and fortifying decorum. Goodness must pour from her daughters without calculation or demonstration. Goodness must be a pure giving, and sacrifices for the Spouse would not be defined as such but as privileged treasures. She knew that the purity of love and its

43

works were beyond human recording. She knew that love not loved and lived was but a dead word. Her daughters would seek identity in the Sacred Heart, and by passionately longing for Christ, become their true selves. She must make her daughters strong and fearless by having them realize that in God's own time and God's own way all justice must eventually be restored to the serenity that permeated paradise, and that the climax of their Christian love, life and toils would be the vision of, and the union with Christ.

To her house came more and more orphans and aspiring brides. Within a year after Francesca had bought it, the house had to be enlarged. Eagerly she drew plans for the annex, but the estimates she obtained from contractors called for twice the amount the diocese was able to give her. She bargained frankly with workmen and supply dealers, and her manner melted them to compliance. The young nuns, orphans, students, and their relatives helped in the digging and shoveling. As they mixed the mortar and carried bricks to the masons, she and her daughters carefully noted how the masons plied their craft. In the late afternoons, after the masons had left for the day, they consulted with Sister Salesia who had worked on walls with her bricklaying father, and under Sister Salesia's foremanship they mixed mortar, carried heavy hods to the scaffolds, and became masons. Fumbling but dogged, with trowels they picked and dipped and spread mortar upon the walls, buttered the ends of the bricks, and pressed them down into the furrowed mortar bed. Imitating masons, they cut bricks with hammer and chisel, calling the line for the next course, and slowly raised the walls with exhortations, prayers, mistakes, and laughter until darkness, which found them mortar-splattered from head to foot, their hands bruised and their limbs aching. Francesca gained the respect and generosity of the workmen.

With the carpenters and other craftsmen, she and the chil-

44

dren worked, and in little time the mother house of the Missionary Sisters of the Sacred Heart was doubled in size.

Gradually, Francesca's school and orphanage in the Codogno house became known in surrounding dioceses for its scholastic quality, efficiency, and spiritual deportment.

Don Gallone, provost of Grumello, a town not far from Codogno, having observed and admired her work in Codogno, asked her to open a school in his diocese, for in Grumello there were many families who despite the liberal government wanted their daughters educated under religious guidance.

The opening of the first branch of the Missionary Sisters of the Sacred Heart gave Francesca almost as much happiness as the founding of the mother house in Codogno. How reassuring is the first fruit from the tree! In November 1882, accompanied by four of her daughters, she climbed onto the seat of the shabby country wagon piled with household articles, picked up the reins, and urged the mare towards Grumello. This was the first time daughters had to leave, to pursue the mission she dreamed of spreading to distant lands. How poignant it was to have to part with a single one of them!

Her little Institute represented the purest forces of religious character. Her type of charity and scholarly competence was needed and recognized, and soon calls came to her from other districts to open houses—Milan, Casalpusterlengo, and Borghetto Lodigiano.

By 1887, seven houses had grown through her hands. She was thirty-seven and more impatient than ever to do the real missionary work she had dreamed of all her life. She told Monsignor Serrati that she definitely wanted to establish her institute in Rome and obtain approval for missions to far lands.

Monsignor Serrati drew back from the magnitude of her impulse.

"Francesca, my child, would you go to Rome—just like

45

that? Seeing the pope is an honor, and chatting with him nicely for a few minutes in the proper formal manner is all very well—an event to cherish the rest of one's life—and for that you have my total blessing. But captivating him to your dream of world mission! Just now when the life of the Church is at stake against freethinkers and whatnot, you want to convince him to send your baby institute around the compass—! Do you expect the vicar of God on earth to collaborate with ...with you, my child? Francesca, Francesca, heed my paternal regard; these superhuman crosses and ventures we shall appropriately leave to saints!"

If Francesca was discouraged by the good churchman she could not long remain discouraged, for one night she had a dream. Christ appeared to her as a child and said, "Francesca, go to that ground where they crucified Peter. Go to the rock where flames the light eternal. Francesca, Rome is thy portal."

Again, she approached Monsignor Serrati about her desire to go to Rome. Again he tried to discourage her. "The woman religious," he said, "can be nothing but the quiet handmaiden to the towering prerogative of the Church fathers. Even after extended years an order of sisters is little empowered. You have already accomplished a great deal for a religious; you have a mother house and six branches. I say to you, halt with the Milan house, and be content with what you have achieved. You must preserve your slender health. Let robust priests and Jesuits carry the frightful burdens of missions. Francesca, remain tranquil in this our very own Lombardy."

She smiled respectfully, but firmly answered, "Dear and good Monsignor Serrati, I will not be deterred from the Way."

"Would you go to Rome unannounced? Without being sent for? You will return and be the sad spectacle of the province. I know."

"The hour has arrived. I must go to Rome."

Monsignor Serrati was sorry for her and shook his head. "Child, child, we are in the age of civil and clerical strife,

46

atheism, machine idolatry. The affairs of the Church are complex, and high above small religious like us, the titans wrestle, deaf and blind to us. Your order is an infant. Do you think this infant can scale the ponderous steps up to the holy seat? Big things can be moved only by illustrious credentials and large capital. Francesca, just where are your credentials and capital?"

She held before Monsignor Serrati her spiritual wedding ring. "This circle binding me to His heart is my credential. He and Mary speak for me."

Monsignor Serrati nodded. "So be it. The dove overcomes the monsignor. But will Pope Leo be moved by the dove? God bless you."

With misgivings Monsignor Serrati wrote letters to friends who had contacts with Rome. He made the effort to please her although he knew that as a provincial prelate his words carried little weight. In any event he would be unhappy over her headlong invasion of Saint Peter's. Surely her goal was hopeless and she would return with crushed spirit. And if the fantastic came to pass and she won the leonine Father to her dreams, her departure from Codogno would be a loss for him and his diocese. So be it.

It was September 24, 1887. By her side on the train was Sister Serafina. Between them was a tattered straw valise. They looked like girl nuns, and their worn shoes and simple habits of economical cloth showed their poverty. But they were on their way to Rome.

The train ran along the coast and for the first time Francesca beheld His sea, the level liquid expanse of her childhood dream. This was now the ocean she wanted to fly over with His light. Oh, for a great ship called "Christ Bearer" with which she would encircle the world! How vast to the horizon was His sky and sea, how blue His sky, how green His sea!

The train arrived in Rome. Ah, Rome, His city eternal on

47

earth. Rome was His Word's edifice, whose foundations were martyrs' blood. Rome, first city to fly the burning banner of His word above and beyond all passing governments of man. Rome, Christ hearth, radiating throughout the world the flames of indestructible love.

She had the address of a Franciscan convent where she and Sister Serafina were to stay. But before she would go there to rest after the journey, Francesca sought and found the little old church of the Gesu, and before the altar of St. Francis Xavier, she prayed for her mission.

On the way to the convent she saw part of the busy city. Fine horses pulled expensive carriages, and rich men and women revealed their wealth by their arrogant mien and costly attire. In the streets were innumerable cassocked priests, and nuns of many nations in various and often elaborate habits. Her resolve trembled. She was a rustic religious who had founded an as-yet regional and unrecognized missionary community. The ladder to the holy seat was crowded with other zealous religious. Who would help her climb to Saint Peter's? She asked absolutely nothing for herself; she begged only to work and die to direct the distressed to His love. Why was it that entering the great city could make a great dream seem small and unimportant? Before dusk she found shelter and sympathy for herself and Sister Serafina with understanding Mother Maria della Passione in the Franciscan convent.

Francesca well knew of the strife between Church and state that Monsignor Serrati had spoken of. It was the dominant fact of the times. She knew the ungodly influence of the secular philosophies such as positivism and Marxism. She knew how tragically the indiscriminate impact of intellectualism upon the family and personal discipline had created problems far worse than those it sought to cure. She knew, too, that her Catholic Church, though oppressed by the new forces, was not dormant. Leo XIII was in every sense the right pontiff for the age. Francesca knew that the mighty forces of his whole

48

intellect and energy were dedicated to the promotion of the Christian reunion. He had never ceased to consider the many-coated Italian government a ursurper, and gradually he was winning respect for papal independence.

With the serious struggle going on between the Vatican and the government in Rome, who would care to listen to Francesca Cabrini from Lombardy? Who would foster her missionary dream? But other unknowns, she reminded herself, had come to Rome before her, and had not been forgotten. She thrust aside her doubts.

She discovered that the authority to appeal to for her purposes was Cardinal-Vicar Parocchi. Immediately she pressed for an appointment and after three days the important prelate consented to see her. With Sister Serafina clinging to her side she was led into the chamber of the cardinal-vicar. She sat by the desk opposite His Eminence.

Cardinal Parocchi studied her for a few moments and then asked, "My child, who are you?"

"A missionary, Francesca Xavier Cabrini."

"Oh . . . ?"

Again, she doubted herself. Her labors of love for His children were understood in Codogno, but what could they possibly mean to the giants of Rome? But then again, her Spouse stormed her heart, and she would storm Saint Peter's!

"Well then, young Sister," continued the cardinal profoundly, "you are a missionary? Pray tell me, missionary of what?"

"Of the Missionary Sisters of the Sacred Heart."

Could she tell the mighty cardinal she impetuously came to Rome unknown and with hardly train fare? That with each breath she wanted to obtain the pope's aid and blessing to fly without delay to His children in far off darknesses? Could a man, even though cardinal, realize a nun's volcanic passion for her heavenly Spouse?

"Missionary Sisters of the Sacred Heart? I regret that I have not heard of this new order. Where has it been instituted?"

"In Codogno, seven years ago."

"Ah, good. I myself was from the Lombard plain. Who is your foundress?"

"His Mother who bore immaculately His Sacred Heart, she, the Madonna of Grace."

He contemplated this little woman.

"Our Madonna of Grace? Really?"

"Yes, Your Eminence."

He could not help but smile.

"For exactly what reason have you come to me?"

"We want to build our house upon His rock."

". . . I see. But child, child, do you know that Rome is surfeited with religious houses? And that we are fighting with the government to retain those we already have?"

"We do not come to convert Rome. We only desire that the holy seat be our catapult for foreign missions."

"I am well answered again, my child. Now please, can you specify in particular the animating spirit of your order?"

"We can answer that only after our wings are unfolded and truly tested for the missions of Christ."

Her swift honesty pleased him, and he smiled. How open the countenance, how clear the conscience of this little religious. Yet, if he were to comply with the wishes of all infant orders and knockers upon Saint Peter's doors, every building in Rome would house institutes. He did her the courtesy of scanning her papers, brief as they were, regarding the Missionary Sisters of the Sacred Heart. Yes, inspired intentions and willingness to sacrifice for the Lord was admirable, but that was far less than sufficient to move one cog in the ponderous centuries-old clockwork of weights and balances and counterweights of the Vatican. Where were her papers of important recommendations? Where the financial resources? Regardless where the money came from, could she raise a half-million lire to open and sustain a mother house at Saint Peter's

50

feet? And as for foreign missions: yes, yes, the Orient was Christless and the New World of the Americas bled for the want of Christianity, but it was unthinkable that Mother Cabrini's little order could effectively missionize those uncertain and chaotic areas of the earth when much older, more elaborate groups were having a hard time trying to do it. The cardinal-vicar concluded, "Francesca Cabrini, youthful mother, you are well appreciated in Codogno. Leave to the hands of the strong the foreign missions."

"Your Eminence, the Madonna did not draw back her divine delicate hands from hardship and danger."

"A true and laudable thought," said the cardinal, "but your institute is too small, its background brief, and it has no money. For now I suggest that you take your dream back with you to Codogno."

"Your Eminence, do you request, or suggest?"

His controlled features did not reveal his rapidly mounting admiration. This woman of God was quite different from any nun he had known. "Suggest," he answered finally, with a shrug.

She arose. "Forgive me, Your Eminence. I will stay in Rome, for I know Our Lord will change your heart. I thank you. God bless you."

Not until she was out in the street did she allow big tears of disappointment to flow.

"Ah, Mother, do not cry," said Sister Serafina. "Surely our Lord will change the cardinal's heart." And with their heads together they consoled each other and wept their way to the Church of the Gesu to speak with Him, to renew courage from His love.

Then began the fatiguing search for approval and aid to establish the Missionary Sisters of the Sacred Heart in Rome. She went without meals from early morning to night, knocked upon every possible ecclesiastical door, waited interminable hours in antechambers, wrote letters, walked, walked, walked feverishly with broken shoes through rain and cold and snow, climbed the stairs of palaces, followed leads, but received nothing but cautious advice and discouragement.

The first of the many times that they walked past the grounds of the Vatican, Daughter Serafina timidly asked her why they did not go in.

"Daughter, after our Spouse intercedes for us and we are permitted a cote in the Vatican, then we will peacefully drink into our souls the exalting wonders of Saint Peter's."

She obtained a few more interviews with Cardinal-Vicar Parocchi, during which he marveled at the scope of her mind and the forceful glow of her character. He could not resist her. Finally, he told her, he would have a final decision for her on October 22. In his chamber on the afternoon of that day he clasped his hands and with a severe cardinalite expression asked her, "Now, Francesca Cabrini, will you be obedient?"

She replied directly, simply, "Obedient I am. Obedient I shall aways be. Obedient unto my death."

He smiled. "Good. Well then, instead of the house you desire here for your Missionary Sisters, I request you . . . to open two houses!"

"Bless you, Your Eminence," she said softly. "Our Lord has deigned to change your heart as I so prayed."

"Yes, dear child, but not the scarcity of my purse. The anti-clerical government has made us poor. I want you to establish a free school here in Porta Pia, and a nursery in the suburb of Aspra. In truth, I am giving you two small crosses. I can equip the schools, but your sisters will have to support themselves and pay rent."

She hastened to the Church of the Gesu, told her gratitude to her Spouse for delightful hours, and that night wrote the jubilant news to her daughters and Monsignor Serrati in Co-dogno.

52

". . . and we are ascending the tree of our desire to see and hear our Bridegroom closer—but remember, from the shining branches and leaves of the mystical height it behooves us to be humble and practical. . . . Pick out five sisters, fill valises with linen and kitchen utensils, raise money for their train fare and send them to me. . . . In the meantime I will have managed (with His help) to rent a few rooms. Courage and forward in His love!"

Monsignor Serrati was overjoyed for her. His determined little angel must not be let down! He sent her every lira that he had and that he could solicit and borrow.

When she received the money she declared, "Neither men, circumstances, nor devils can stop me now! Every single lira for His children is bread and fish and shall do the work of a multitude of lire!"

With a few lire in advance—and smiling promises—she rented an unfurnished apartment on the Via Nomentana, then curried junkshops and auction sales for the cheapest furnishings.

When her five daughters arrived from Codogno with their shabby sacks and baggage, she greeted them as if they were a conquering army. To her, they were His first column of brides, that she had marshaled to His city eternal!

And they were as chattering doves. They are in Rome, Rome! How many questions they asked, how much news there was to tell!

By lamplight and from a table made of boards upon boxes they ate macaroni and sipped wine. How good it was for young nuns to be with their mother! What a joyous feast was their bit of food! And beds?—straw spread upon the clean floor, and hood and habit were sheet and blanket. And their poverty only made them laugh.

The cardinal-vicar silently observed her almost incredible

wisdom and industry in successfully establishing the schools at Porta Pia and Aspra with little funds. The cardinal saw that she instinctively put into practice the new tenets for Catholic education that the pope wished to promote, and that she was the kind of woman religious the church needed for the challenging future. She brought a vivid new torch to illumine His camp. Her passion for Christ burned new life into cautiously tired, static, and complacent clerics.

The apartment in Via Nomentana was now the Rome mother house for her institute. She and her daughters, with wood salvage, hammer, saw, square, nails, brush, and paint converted one of the rooms into a chapel. The needs of the day? They would make it with their own hands, no matter how inexpertly; they would eat less, for the spirit would nourish; they would wear and interchange their habits until they fell apart and could not be further repatched.

Wherever in Rome her feet gracefully darted, she revived love for Him. She combined naturally the clear qualities of early Christianity with a working spirit and high mentality to meet the modern age. Girls of every description, the rich, aristocratic, middle-class, poor, agnostic, once meeting her and listening to her, followed her into the missionary sisterhood and vowed their lives to being her daughters in His family.

She became dear to Cardinal-Vicar Parocchi. Unknown to her, he sang her praises to the lofty pillars of Saint Peter's. On March 12, 1888, the thirteenth child of Stella Cabrini and her farmer-husband, Agostino the Christian Tower, received from the Vatican, the *Decretum Laudis,* the recognition and approval of her institute.

The wisp of a golden-haired girl by the fireside in Sant'-Angelo who listened to her father read about missionary saints, the little girl who fell in love with the Son of God, the little Francesca who in the secret of night reached ecstatically to Him, would always be with her. Now that she was the bride

54

accepted for far missions, her passion for Him was a conflagration of love which nothing could contain.

During the course of opening a college at Castelsangiovanni in Piacenza she formed the friendship with Bishop Giovanni Scalabrini of Piacenza which was the harbinger of her life's true mission.

The dedicated aspiration of Bishop Scalabrini's heart and soul was to extend moral and spiritual aid to the vastly swelling stream of emigrants who made their way to America. Migration is an outstanding feature of human life, changing the ethnic composition of lands as the prehistoric glaciers once charged their physical composition. Moving from place to place in search of means of subsistence, or to escape a stronger foe, men from time immemorial have spread over the earth's surface. The unprecedented flow of emigrants to the New World during the latter half of the nineteenth century was primarily caused by painful conditions in Europe. Population growth in many countries, and the disparate ration between the number of inhabitants and the resources at their disposal were the strongest factors in the great migratory trend, hearkening in a vivid sense to the Bible's story of the separation of Abraham and Lot, "The land was not able to bear them, that they might dwell together." [Gen. XIII, 6.]

Not all European countries suffered to the same extent at the same time. Local conditions varied, and a particularly bad year, or even decade, would hit first one nation, then another. In Italy, there were even sharp differences between localities within the country. The north was industrialized, politically minded, ultranationalistic, and comparatively prosperous. The south, however, even before the unification of Italy, had suffered extreme poverty. Malarial conditions and centuries of misgovernment made for brutalization and a low standard of living. Illiteracy and poor system of communication in the south imposed on its inhabitants primitive ways of life and methods of agriculture. The south showed the influences of the days of Spanish and Moorish occupation, and northerners considered the south distinctly barbarous.

Liberalism, in the early years after the unification, did little to ease the fundamental social and economic problems. The dominant north, with its exaggerated nationalism, favored military development of the country as a whole, which imposed conscription and large taxes that were hateful to the south. The powerful central government, so new to Italy, harbored for a time unbridled political corruption. The system of absentee landlords so common in many parts of Europe, deprived the peasant of many rights. The loss of the country's foreign markets for agricultural produce resulting in part from competition from Russia and America, and similar hardships suffered by the wine and silk industries lowered the standard of living. Speculation resulted in scandalous bond failures. The price of food increased, and the opportunities for employment decreased. Whole masses of the Italian people were reduced to and below the starvation level. The economic crisis of 1887 was such that the government gladly encouraged emigration. Thus began the yearly outpouring of some quarter of a million emigrants from central and south Italy to labor-hungry Americans.

The government hoped that emigration would ease the problem of overpopulation and even expected the country to benefit from American dollars sent back home by emigrants to families and relatives and friends. It was truly only the Church that deeply concerned itself over the precious spiritual, moral, and social well-being of its emigrant flock gone to America.

Bishop Scalabrini made the emigrant cause his cause. He gathered factual information, wrote pamphlets, and lectured on the subject, seeking organized aid for the emigrants. After visiting America and seeing for himself the conditions of the emigrants, he returned to Rome and, in 1888, founded the

Congregation of St. Charles Borromeo, often referred to as the Scalabrinian Fathers, to render help to the emigrants. When he became friendly with Francesca Cabrini, he saw in her by an inspired direction the right woman for the American mission. He told her about the little church of San Gioacchino that a few of his Fathers of St. Charles had recently opened in the Italian section in New York City. He spoke passionately of the emigrant cause.

"Mother Cabrini, the spiritual and social plight of our people in America is beyond belief. Italian souls that have inherited many centuries of Christ's love are corroding and being seduced back to a dark pagan desert in the huge new America. America needs your Missionary Sisters of the Sacred Heart, for there are prodigious works of light to be done."

He hoped she would seriously consider going to New York to help his Fathers of St. Charles. But Mother Cabrini had never thought of missionary work in America. She could not answer him. Bishop Scalabrini was not discouraged by her silence. Some months passed, and one day, her friend came to her excitedly.

"I have spoken for your institute with an American prelate visiting Rome, Archbishop Corrigan of New York. He listened carefully, and then expressed a sincere wish that you bring your mission to New York and assist with Italian orphanage work!"

At last, at the age of thirty-eight, she was offered a mission across the ocean. Ever since her childhood she had longed for faraway religious ventures, like those described in the Annals of the Propagation of the Faith, and had had before her the image of brilliant dangers and probable martyrdom. But, America? Why America? Could America provide the test for a bride of Christ? Yes, she had studied the history and geography of America; it was populated mostly by Christian denominations and heralded as a civilized nation, the New World; it had a

57

humane constitution; it was not dominated by royalty, and championed equality; it had splendid democratic principles; it was mentioned with respect and admiration as the modern symbol of liberty, the refuge from feudalism. America was not the dark Christless realms of China, Japan, India, and Africa. After having for so long imbued her daughters with an ultimate heroism meet for jungles, steppes, wildernesses, and savages, could she turn about and say, "Let us go to safe America"?

But why did she feel a trembling, a timidity about even going to safe America? So then, it was one thing bravely to dream and contemplate missions to other lands, but now that the opportunity to leave her own country for a strange continent was nearing, her breast fluttered. Was she still a little girl, courageous only in fancy? She did not know just what to do. But it was not up to her to decide. What did He want her to do?

The night before she was summoned to the long-wished-for intimate audience with the pope, she had a vision as if in a dream, and whether vision or dream, she knew not. She was on the bank of the swift-moving Venera river placing flowers as her nuns in a large paper boat to waft across the ocean, but she feared to get into the boat herself. Her mother appeared and said emphatically, "Francesca mine, and what is it? Afraid? Daughter, courage is wanting! Why did you say, 'I am going to become a missionary!' Did you mean it, or were you pretending? And now why are you reluctant to leave the Christian soil of your people?" Then in silent procession appeared Saint Catherine, Saint Teresa, Saint Francis Xavier, and beautiful Virgin Mary. Finally, her Spouse came to her, and about His glowing Sacred Heart and impressed upon His white robe was his name, enwreathed with red roses. "My child and bride, what fear thee? Knowest thou not that thy prayer bringeth passion, and my love in return bringeth strength? I send thee to bear my name in a distant land. Then, be coura-

58

geous and fear not, for I am ever with thee, and with Me thou canst do all things."

The following morning as she was leaving the convent for the Vatican, Bishop Scalabrini arrived by carriage and alighted. Before he could open his mouth she told him of her dream.

He laughed with elation, took a letter from his pocket, waved it, and said, "Mother Cabrini . . . Francesca, you and your 'dreams.' Here now is the dream you speak of—just came—the letter from New York. Archbishop Corrigan has an orphanage waiting for you there. Now you can actually depart for America!"

Francesca entered Saint Peter's, that supreme temple of her faith. What dramas, bestial and sublime, had been enacted on this very spot! Here had stood Caligula's brazen circus. On this site sixty-four years after the cross had been raised on Calvary, Nero enjoyed martyring Christians. Two years later on this spot Peter was made to follow them in death. Here in the ground, under her softly treading feet, was the Fisherman entombed. There, enshrined in the basilica, was the veil of Veronica, blessedly stained. There also was Longinus' merciful lance, bathed with blood and water from His naked side.

And Francesca was going to the pope, the father of Christendom, whose word would be her direction. By the time she went to meet Leo XIII he was seventy-eight and had already been pontiff for ten years. She, like many other religious, was familiar with his activities and influenced by his extraordinarily dynamic principles.

The revitalizing originality of Leo's convictions, Francesca knew, lay in his real concern for the welfare of all classes of society, the poor and humble as well as the rich. Leo XIII had divined that the strength of the secular philosophies lay in their almost exclusive monopoly of the study of social questions. Since the 1840s not only intellectuals but also the mass of the

59

populace had been drifting away from the Church toward materialistic godlessness. To Leo, labor was a dignity, not a commodity without soul. The laboring man's human worth had to be safeguarded even as religion. He felt that it was everyone's duty to ensure that labor received its just reward, and he lent the profound authority of his approval, both as pope and as one of the most respected intellects of his day, to legislation designed to protect the laborer, as well as trade unions and cooperative organizations. He despised employers who behaved primarily as capitalists and only secondarily as Catholics. The great spiritual power and intellectual acumen of Leo XIII enabled him to reestablish the papacy's international prestige.

Tall, sinewy Leo XIII, the Shepherd of His children, the mountain of the common man, the light of the oppressed, the virile man of God, bade Francesca arise.

The pontiff courteously inquired about her family, village, childhood, dreams, and schooling. He interested himself in the details of her young womanhood and the founding of her institute. He discussed with her the spiritual and practical capacities of the Missionary Sisters of the Sacred Heart. From his manner he might have been her good father, the farmer Agostino Cabrini. She answered him lucidly. Chuckling, he informed her that he knew all about her but enjoyed hearing her voice tell of it.

"Sweet Daughter, Cardinal Parocchi and other of my good sons tell me you dream of bearing the light to the Orient."

Leo regarded her thoughtfully, then slowly shook his head.

"No," he said at last. "The house and family of western civilization must first be put in order. His love must conquer the West before we approach the East. There are sad truths you will learn by seeing with your own eyes. America, growing in titantic strides, will soon achieve world influence. If she becomes another soulless Babylon, she will topple, and with her

60

fall she will drag down lesser nations, and the Christian labors of centuries.

"Hundreds of thousands of our Italian souls in America have become lost and battered sheep, isolated from Christ, understanding, and ordinary decency. The New World cries for the warmth and the compassion of a mother's heart, a heart tempered by love and sacrifice, the heart of the apostle. Francesca Cabrini, you have that very heart. My Daughter, your field awaits you not in the East, but in the West. I desire very much a great missionary expansion in America. Francesca Cabrini, go to America. Plant there, and cultivate the beautiful fruit of Christ!"

Until then her work was of training her doves and building her cote in Saint Peter's. The time had come to wing across the ocean, and each passing moment filled Francesca with impatience. When her Spouse moved on His mission he did not waste time in elaborate preparations. He moved swiftly, bearing love as His sole possession, giving it as His single gift.

See the masterpieces of the Vatican? No, not now. Some other time. After she had done good work in America. She has already seen the Vatican's invaluable treasure, Pope Leo XIII. Quickly, credentials and steamship tickets for six daughters and herself. Rapid instructions to the superiors and daughters of her houses: "Be not ashamed to love our Spouse more intensely each day. . . . Take Him proudly, more closely, more possessively to your hearts night and day. . . . Guard the spiritual, mental, and bodily health of the orphans, students, and postulants. . . . Each House must stand on its own feet. . . . Watch the economy sharply! . . . Learn the English language and crafts of all useful kinds for missionary work in America. . . . Write to me and bare your very hearts and souls. . . . Regard every aspect of a problem, reach a decision, and then carry it through with expediency. . . . Never be satisfied with yourself

61

and your accomplishments. . . . Sacrifice more and more for our Spouse!"

At the Codogno house, Francesca attended an overjoyed Mass celebrated by Bishop Scalabrini and assisted by good Monsignor Serrati. She and the six daughters who were to accompany her lost little time in the hasty packing of the few personal articles. They supplied themselves with modest bags of food, to sustain them until they reached the steamship at Le Havre, France. Bishop Scalabrini, Monsignor Serrati, and relatives and friends of her six daughters accompanied them on the train to Milan. Before they parted, Bishop Scalabrini gave each of the emigrating missionaries a blessed Rosary and Crucifix.

With tears in his eyes old Monsignor Serrati said to her, "Mother Cabrini and missionary to the world, but always dearest child to me, I do not know what to say to thee, except to leave thee to the arms of thy Spouse, and I know He shall do with thee according to His will. Fare thee well. Adio."

4 ✛ ✛ ✛

IN THE PORT of Le Havre at nine o'clock on the morning of March 23, 1889, clutching their sacks and bags amid a confusing mass of emigrants, Francesca Cabrini and her six daughters ascended the gangplank of the old French liner Bourgogne. After they had been assigned their second-class cabin, they went out on deck. She stood at the ship's rail with her daughters by her side. She saw emigrants from various European nations, but the majority were Italians—men and women, young and old, girls and boys and swaddled infants. They wore sorry, bundled, ragged clothes, and carried their possessions in boxes, crates, bags, and occasional cardboard and straw valises.

Bewildered faces, sturdy faces, questioning faces, lost faces, tight-lipped faces, seemed to ask, "Are we going to a better or worse life? What fate is there awaiting in America? What is America? Why is America? Will I ever see my Sicily again? My Abruzzi? My Naples? My Bari? My Calabria? Will our Christ be with us in America? Will he leave our hearts, our flesh and bones, our dreams, our lives, under American earth?"

Each emigrating laborer was her dear brother. Each family was her family. They were His children and her children. A deep compassion for the emigrant pervaded her, and she bowed her head.

My Lord and Spouse, the crosses of these Thy children shall

63

be my crosses until it pleases Thee to take me from earth and to Thy realest embrace.

The ship's whistle blasted, and they throbbed away from the dock. It was the actual moment of physical parting from the old world, and a moment of sudden human loving. Tear-stained handkerchiefs, hats, shawls, papers, waved farewell. Friends and relatives called good-bye, and strangers waved to strangers.

One of her daughters asked, "Mother, although we do not know any of the people left behind, may we too wave fare-well?"

"Yes, dear Daughters. Wave to them with your handker-chiefs and the prayers of your pure hearts."

And as she and her daughters raised their voices tremulous but clear, and sang "Ave Maria Stella," her eyes moistened.

No sooner had the ship got underway than her daughters, one by one, became seasick and frightened. Was this the brave legion she was bringing to America? They ran for their very lives to the cabin. A few drops of rain and Sister Assunta perceived a hurricane. Sister Battistina became so dizzy that she could not stand. As for the rest, one was more woe-begone and miser-able than the other, thinking with every movement of the ship that they were in a great storm. How would they be when the sea was rough! Sister Assunta made Francesca laugh when she asked if the captain would please stop the ship during meal-time, and Francesca joked about sea-sickness so much that they laughed heartily despite their illness.

Of the 1,300 passengers on the ship, there were 900 emi-grants below deck in steerage, 700 Italians and 200 Swiss. Her daughters, though weak and stumbling with seasickness, went with her below among the emigrants. In the large prison-like hold the emigrants seemed to her like souls piled helplessly in purgatory. Almost all the emigrants were seasick and de-pressed. When she addressed them in their rich Italian lan-

64

guage they became animated and extremely friendly. A group of men gallantly worked with her to ease the distress of the very old and very young.

One of them, a staunch Sicilian, proudly informed her that his brother Giuseppe was a priest. "I am from Caccamo, Sicily," he said, "a village that existed before our Lord came to earth. I have been blessed with a Madonna of a wife, three toddling boys, two girls, a very old father and mother, five sisters, and my good priest of a brother, Giuseppe. On a steep, twisting lane among sun-scorched mountain rocks is my hut, and below in the valleys are orange groves and flowers."

"Pray tell me, Brother," she asked, "why did you leave Caccamo?"

"Ah, Mother, because of unremitting poverty and debt. I was a member of the municipal council and had a cobbler's shop of my own. Times were hard and became worse; people went barefoot, and my business failed. There was no work to be had. My brother Giuseppe, the priest, received an income of one and one-half lire a day; he starved himself so that all the relatives and my family could have a bit of bread and greens. Various *paesanos* had left for America to make money, and they were sending money back to Caccamo. My friend Romero wrote me and sent me the fare to join him, and work and live with him in a place called New Orleans. As much as I loved Caccamo I could not bear the hunger of my family and my business debt of 450 lire. Pray for me, pray that I will return someday to Caccamo with the money to pay off my debt and feed my family."

These were her people; they were dear to her, and smote her heart. She hoped at least they would arrived in a town or village where there would be someone who would break for them the bread of the word of God. God alone knew what would happen to the greater part of them!

On shipboard she wrote to the daughters left behind in Italy:

65

I rose early this morning and went on deck to view the sea. Oh! how beautiful is the sea in its great motion! It is Heaven's grand opera of rushing winds and water! How the waves gigantically swell and foam, seeming a righteous indignation of Moses! Enchanting! A single wave could submerge our ship as if it were a toy, but He who has created the sea and has commanded it to rear like a lofty mountain would not permit His beloved creatures, much less His loving Spouses, to be drowned. God loved us before He created the sea; nay, He created the sea itself for our use and pleasure. He had chosen us for His passionate brides, and we have answered His call, attracted by His beauty and infinite lovableness. Let us remain, my Daughters, entirely subject to our Master, conquered by His insatiable love; and let us run swiftly in His footsteps. He has perpetually loved us with the love of predilection, so let us love Him and serve Him with joy during the few days of our life. If you were all here with me, dear Daughters, you would exclaim, 'Oh, how great and loving is God in all His works!' But the ocean of graces, my Daughters, that our Spouse pours down upon us, in every instant of our life, is immensely superior to anything in nature.

All natural splendors are eclipsed by the abundance of riches which God showers upon His beloved brides. Let us venerate and love, then, our excellent state, and let us examine ourselves frequently and remove all defects unbecoming the virgins of Christ, so that our Beloved may quickly introduce us into the Holy of Holies and plant charity in our souls. May Jesus bless you and enclose you in His amorous Heart, where we will find the true Paradise, and may He make you always fervent in spirit, in the perfect abnegation of yourselves, and in detachment from all creatures and all passing fancies. Your affectionate Mother in the SS. C.J., FRANCES XAVERIO CABRINI.

On the morning of March 31, the passengers beheld the outline of American land, where the futures of these pilgrims, lay mutely locked. She watched the inarticulate commotion of the emigrants, and noted with compassion the battle of hope against fear on eager yet anxious faces. They were cuttings, plants with exposed roots for the new fields.

66

Awake, awake, put on thy strength; put on thy beautiful garments, O America, to welcome thy new orphans!

Would they receive the sincere milk of the Word, that they might grow thereby? And she mused: *Cristoforo Colombo, meaning, Christ-bearing dove, sought the eastern passage, but God's breath blew the Santa Maria westward. Colombo came ashore holding the cross of love before him, and with cross and lips blessed this earth newly promised.*

Amerigo Vespucci etched on map the sleeping vastness that awakened and said, I am America. *Does America remember its chrism of love? Is she building upon the rock of ages, or is she again the Plain of Shinar in dark wisdom raising accursed Babel? These all but naked pilgrims look to the expectant shore with hungry eyes. If they ask for bread, will they be given stones? What do these uprooted seek? Justice? Freedom? License? Gold? Hearth? For where thy treasure is, there is thy heart also. Of what treasure and heart does America dream?*

By dusk the ship entered New York bay. High above a floating forest of long-bellied wooden and iron ships, belching stacks, and slender masts, the Statue of Liberty silently upheld a burning torch.

Jammed with the emigrants of many nations, Ellis Island was a bedlam of tongues, a mart of dispersal from whence embodied spirits were assigned and despatched to the next Unknown: "Where Hoboken?" "Where New Orleans?" "A place, Chicago." "They say Colorado." "I do not know." "Where? Wherever there is work." "That is what 'they' told me." "Whatever they say." "Any place." "God bless you." "I beg you." "Anything, anything, thank you." "Yes, yes, yes." "Gratefully, happily, I will obey." "Somewhere." "Work from morning to night like a giant." "They were supposed to. . . ." "Maybe." "Someday." "They said, 'mines, docks, bridges, factories, railroads.' " "Big, big job." "I do not care how long it takes, but I will." "Most willing." "The paper has the address." "I do not know, but I was told they have vineyards there." "They did not inform me." "That's the place! That's the place!" "We will manage." "And could we walk to this Los Angeles?" "With utmost respect." "At last we are together again!" "How do I get there?" "With God's help!"

There were neither Scalabrinian Fathers nor representatives of Archbishop Corrigan there to meet her, and she thought it strange. It was late evening and raining when finally she and her group were ferried to the city. Her daughters looked with consternation at the city before them and clung to her. It was a phantasmagoria of noises, clanging horse-drawn trolleys, plunging rattling wagon trucks, fast carriages, whistles, bells, galloping horsemen, shouts, hustling, jostling figures, dizzying structures, glaring gaslights, and a tense doleful obscurity. What were people fleeing? What were they rushing to?

A policeman saw them to Roosevelt Street and the rectory of San Gioacchino's Church. They were cordially received by the three Scalabrinian Fathers, who covered their surprise, and put before them a simple Italian dinner.

"Thank you, good Fathers," she said, "We are weary from the sea and emotion. Now we wish to retire, and rise early to grasp our work. Would you be so kind as to direct us to our orphanage house and quarters?"

The fathers looked at each other with embarrassment. "But there is a mixed-up situation," said one meekly. "That is . . . we thought . . . surely Archbishop Corrigan's recent letter to you explained. . . ."

"Pray, what letter? Bishop Scalabrini asked me to take over the orphanage in New York. I am here to do that. Is the orphanage nearby?"

"It is neither near nor far, for at present the orphanage exists only in Bishop Scalabrini's wish for one. And we regret, but tonight at least, you sisters will have to stay at some public lodging."

The fathers explained the misunderstanding: A certain

68

Countess Cesnola, formerly Mary Reid, had donated 5,000 dollars toward an orphanage for homeless Italian children, and had chosen a house for the purpose. Thus, in their enthusiasm they had written Bishop Scalabrini, telling him that the orphanage had been initiated. But in the meantime the orphanage did not become a reality because Archbishop Corrigan disagreed with Countess Cesnola over its location. The fathers were downcast with chagrin.

"Now, Fathers," Francesca said cheeringly, "this confusion will not derail the planets. In the morning we will break fast with our Lord, and He will plan the orphanage for us."

The Scalabrinians, being miserably poor, counted their pennies for the nuns' lodgings. Then, through the late, raining darkness they searched and led the Sisters to the cheapest rooming house in the vicinity.

When she turned up the flaring light of the gas jet in their room, she and her daughters were repelled; the room was stenchful and filthy beyond hope, and over the soiled unmade beds scurried bugs and roaches. They barricaded the door with a broken dresser, and spent the night taking turns sitting on the one chair in the room. As her disconcerted daughters prayed strenuously for their mission, she could not help smiling at their predicament. Anyone could do the easy and unchallenging. She had come to America because its people were insufficiently Christian and heroic to protect the weak and the poor, the sick and the orphaned. What credit would it be to the brides of Christ if the paths of their mission were easy and not difficult?

Mice ran arrogantly about the room, terrorizing her daughters.

"Daughters, Daughters," she chuckled, "what manner of missionaries are we?" To which Sister Eletta cried, "Mother, forgive me, but a thousand times would I rather brave the heathens than these awful mice. Oh, forgive me, Mother!"

In the morning, they were more tired than they had been

69

the night before. But after they had received the grace of their first Holy Communion in America at the altar of San Gioacchino, they were refreshed and ready to confront all difficulties. They proceeded to Archbishop Corrigan's residence.

The archbishop received them with paternal benevolence, but could not disguise his uneasiness. "Mother Cabrini, I had written you a letter asking you to defer your departure from Rome, for as yet we have no house for Italian orphans. It is a great pity that you crossed the ocean for nothing. You cannot possibly know the complexity of prejudices and obstacles here that stand in the way of organized aid for Italian immigrants. It may be a long time before we are in a position to open an orphanage. The problem is too big for you. I see no other and better solution than for you to return to Italy. I am sorry."

Her daughters looked shocked. One turned to her and murmured. "Dear Mother, must we turn about and recross the ocean?" Another said, "And what shall we say to our sisters at home?"

Francesca paled at the archbishop's verdict. Did her Spouse let a nay deter Him? Did He ever retreat and flee from His suffering children? She breathed in deeply. Calmly, most respectfully, but firmly she said, "Excellence, I came to America by order from Saint Peter's sacred seat. America is my ordained mission. Excellence, in all humbleness I must say, in America I stay."

The archbishop gasped within himself. To his knowledge, not even an Italian prelate had ever shown such adamant will in America. He could not deny the strong light of this woman religious. He smiled.

"Very well, young Mother, somehow or other, you may begin with a small school for Italian children in the church of San Gioacchino. In the meantime I shall make arrangements for you and your group to stay with the Irish Sisters of Charity on Fifty-first Street and Madison Avenue. God bless you,

Mother Cabrini." And he gallantly escorted her and her Daughters to the nearby convent.

There was truth in Archbishop Corrigan's assertion that Francesca could not possibly know the problems of the Italian immigrants, and how America thought of Italians. The majority were illiterate peasants who in Italy had known only slow-going toil, the edge of hunger, a hut, and the stern hand of authority in any form. When they came to America, their possessions, other than the quaint clothes they wore, were their health, their profound love of God and family, and their solemn respect for labor. All they sought was a little more food and the possible future America promised.

No descriptions, however horrible, could exaggerate the injustices and miseries the docile Italian immigrants had to undergo. But a basic wisdom, an instinct told them the Old World was the past, and they could feel in the electric air of America its expanding destiny, and a different and better future for their children. So, come what may, they stayed. They were the ones, who, totally unfamiliar with a sentence of the Constitution, had a mute and dogged faith in the New World.

The steamship agencies played an important role in the netting of immigrant labor. They often worked hand in hand with giant corporations, Italo-American contractors and jobbers, the corrupt Italian government, and mulcting private employment agencies. The hungry unemployed and unskilled were enticed from their cities and villages by golden-tongued agents with glowing accounts of America. They were conveyed to ports of embarkation, and in droves they were herded into steerage and brought across the ocean to the voracious American labor market. The expression about the streets of America being, "paved with gold" was commonplace. Commerce, distribution, and speculation were chiefly in the hands of those who appointed themselves birthright owners and rulers of the

New World, and bragged that they were "real Americans."

They had no human, spiritual, cultural or democratic interest in the "foreigner." The immigrant was an exploitable and expendable living commodity. The twelve-hour day and six-day week were universally applied to the immigrant. Child labor was a commonplace, and working conditions were criminally hazardous. Pay was low, and the cost of living high. Rent-gouging was a flourishing institution. The immigrant was the inarticulate beast of burden in the New World jungle, where the ideal of freedom was a trap manipulated by the predatory. Trade Unions, Workmen's Compensation, unemployment and medical insurance, compulsory education, safety laws and child labor laws, and low-income public housing, would have been considered the wildest of radicalism and subversion. Fire escapes and adequate sanitary facilities were unknown, and humane working hours were unthought of.

Social workers periodically probed the immigrant masses through dispassionate interpreters. On the other hand American journalists and authors slum-dabbled and wrote melodramatically about, ". . . these emotional child-like *paesani* from sunny Italy for whom poverty is traditional, and a somewhat gay art at that. . . ." Italian women were portrayed as stout, cheerful, rosy-cheeked "Marias," singing at their chores, and the men caricatured as squat, burning-eyed romantic " 'Tonios" loving the pick and shovel, wine, macaroni, and fiestas—or, as swarthy born killers committed to such nebulous, often mythical societies as the "Black Hand," the "Camorra," and the "Mafia."

Wretchedness was the fruit of the emigrants' ignorance, even though their behavior in the main was virtuous. The emigrants hurt themselves in many ways. They brought with them regional prejudices which were added to unforseen new problems. Northern Italians were contemptuous of central and southern Italians. The social and political animosities of the Italy they left remained open wounds. Among the ambitious

Italians there was indiscriminate jockeying for the American dollar, at the expense of their undirected fellow countrymen. Most of the literate Italians were headily antireligious. The first step toward redeeming this situation could only come from Italian-speaking priests and organized Italian parishes, and they were sadly lacking. Without the practice and comfort of his religion the Italian immigrant in America felt himself an outcast. Leo XIII and Bishop Scalabrini were aware of these conditions, and fervently desired to remedy them. It was for this that the pontiff had sent Francesca to America, armed with his prayers and blessings. The morning after her meeting with Archbishop Corrigan, after a good night's rest and the hospitality and companionship of the Irish sisters, she and her daughters attended Mass and received Holy Communion in the recently completed Saint Patrick's Cathedral opposite the refuge of the Irish sisters' convent. Immediately thereafter, Francesca marched her daughters at rapid pace from Fifty-first Street downtown to Little Italy.

"Come, my daughters, our Spouse strengthens our legs toward His children. At the same time we will get a taste of this king of cities. Now then, money we have not, but from our faith will spring forth miracles."

Along Mulberry Bend, Italian hearts opened at the sight of seven young nuns of their own blood who came to them, and their presence and purpose was gladly spread amongst the thousands of Italian families. Parents brought children in droves to her religious and educational classes that occupied the nave, the sacristy, the basement and choir loft of little San Gioacchino's Church. Daily she and her daughters visited the homes in the congested tenement rookeries. Her acute intuition immediately and sadly appraised their material, moral, and spiritual misery, their despairing problems. An old Abruzzean couple on Mott Street lived in three rooms with five parentless children: "Our son ran away with the Neapolitan widow next door. His wife lost her senses and is in the asylum for the crazy. Mother Cabrini, what shall we do with these children?" The father of a Calabrian family had been blinded by acid in a factory. A Sicilian woman bitten by a rat has died from gangrene and left eight children, who roamed the streets like wild animals while the father worked as a construction laborer. Many sons and husbands, who had been lured by employment agencies to help build railroads in the west, died of disease in the camps or were killed by accidents, leaving helpless widows and children. Nicoletta, a lovelorn peasant girl from Bari, had shot her frivolous betrothed and was being held for murder.

Who would plead for these illiterate people? Who would tend the sick and crippled, feed and shelter the destitute, guide the growing children, console the dying, and bury the dead?

Francesca had hardly time for meditation, prayer, and lyricizing love to her Spouse. In every direction before her eyes were His children crushed, twisted, and torn in the giant machine of the New World. It was lack of money that crowded ten laborers in one room, that obliged large families living in three rooms to take in lodgers, so that beds were slept in around the clock. Housing conditions alone were enough to breed immorality and violence. Sanitation was utterly impossible when there were non-draining sinks and twenty families attempting to use an unworkable cellar latrine.

Each day she steeled her daughters: "Observe unflinchingly the realities of that which causes want, pain, misunderstanding, and tragedy. Let us put courageous and probing hands to these injustices and social wounds inflicted upon our dear good people. To grapple with their many problems, we must be close to them. We must keep in close contact with the evil sores of this world. Though we are not of this world, we must clutch its evils by the throat."

Her catechism classes in the church of San Gioacchino became the purifying beacon of the Italian quarter. Men and women who had been deprived of God's house for ten, twenty,

74

thirty, and forty years were able to renew their Christian exercises. Within weeks she had gathered 200 children to the love of Christ. Often the classes had to be interrupted to permit weddings, funerals, and baptisms; yet still the people flocked to her.

How did she regard the New World, with its compelling energy that meant so much for good or evil? Viewing the unrestrainable industrial tempo, the buildings daily rising to the sky, streams of work wagons and horsecars, roaring trains and puffing mills, and the hurriedness of open-faced masses teeming the streets and thoroughfares, perceiving the absence of kings and queens and their entourages, seeing instead the active pushing jaunty human beings, with their rough unguarded friendliness, who were Americans, she felt the pulsing stride and challenge of America.

"Daughters," she said, "in our mission here we will find more who will be with us than against us. We shall produce the beautiful fruit of Christ's love in America. We must beware of two temptations, that of failure and that of success; and often prosperity will be more dangerous than adversity. The money that is the immigrants' blood and tears converted into the gold of banks must be redirected to labor for their wellbeing. With the love of Christ, the earth's wealth of this new field shall be as servant to its soul."

On Palm Sunday, Francesca and Countess Cesnola pressed Archbishop Corrigan to let her open an orphanage in the large building on Fifty-ninth Street that the Countess had provided. He feared they would begin an orphanage they could not support.

"The 5,000 dollars you have raised, how long do you think it will feed and care for the orphans, and pay the gas bill, taxes, and maintenance?"

The Countess knelt before him imploringly.

"Your Excellency, remember, in the *Pater Noster* we ask God for the bread of a day, and not a year."

75

The archbishop was moved. He left the room and returned with a blessed palm frond. "Mother Cabrini," he said heartily, "accept this palm as the blessed sceptre for your mission in America."

With Mother Cabrini to inspire her, Countess Cesnola rallied family and friends, rich and poor to equip the orphanage.

"Oh!" Francesca exclaimed when she beheld the beds and furniture and utensils for the orphanage, "who cannot recognize the goodness of the American soul? We must make it grow as great as its continent—greater!—and closer to the love of Christ!"

On April 21 she and her daughters left the hospitality of the Irish nuns and walked to their new home on Fifty-ninth street. A surprise, brought there by an unknown person, awaited her. In the alcove by the entrance she found a beautiful statue of the Sacred Heart. Upon the base, at the feet of Christ, was a fragant loaf of bread. She kissed the bread.

"Bread of heaven, bread of love, bread of life, shall never be lacking from His little orphaned girls!"

She was about to unlock the door, but she reflected, and placed one of the entrance keys into the outstretched hand of the Sacred Heart.

"Thou, sweet Spouse, art Master of brides, children and house."

As in every one of her houses, she and her daughters improvised a tiny chapel, and on May 3, 1889, to their joy, Archbishop Corrigan celebrated Holy Mass in the first American orphanage opened by the Missionary Sisters of the Sacred Heart. The following day the work of gathering abandoned little girls began. The very first girl brought to her, who in later years became one of her missionary daughters, was in pitiful rags. Francesca cut apart her extra habit and made a sturdy neat dress for the girl; she bathed the child, brushed her

76

tresses, transformed her appearance, and embraced her with the supreme tenderness of the mother.

The immediate necessities, the tasks before Francesca became staggering and seemingly insurmountable. Where and when and how would she get the funds to keep body and soul together for her daughters and the growing number of orphans? She kept her feet on earth, and raised her eyes to Him. "With Thee all things I can do!"

Her conviction of love as the reason for being, her daring, her eagerness, set into constructive motion everyone she appealed to. She endowed her little orphans and pupils with the spirit and competence to help each other and themselves. Her unconditional love brought forth from the innocent orphans their pure love in return, and they became her junior co-founders of the House.

The children of her classes downtown in the church of San Gioacchino had parents who felt for her orphans. The little students became small, eager angels, bringing to her for her orphans pennies and candies and bags of food and clothing from their own precariously poor homes.

To the poor she went and presented the even greater hunger and need of her orphans, for who better than the laboring masses would understand the gnawing pain of want? Eyes that beheld the seven young nuns begging through the tenement passageways that orphaned girls might live to become confident Christian women lowered in silent respect.

Who are these humble serving maids of God? Are they women in any of the senses that construe the female image? They are obedient daughters, knowing sisters, virgin mothers, and wives whose passion cannot be equalled. They are the crown of womankind.

In the month of May, 1889, a New York newspaper carried the following item: "This week young ladies with radiant faces dressed in plain black religious hoods and robes were seen coursing the overcrowded streets of Little Italy between the Ghetto and Chinatown, befriending and soliciting the Italians. They left no stones unturned, climbing the dark narrow hallways of poverty to the top floors, descending murky cellar-ways into filthy basement flats, boldly entering questionable alleys, backyards and obscure areas into which not even the police would venture. They speak very little English, and except for one, these young nuns are slender and delicate. They are the pioneers of a congregation called the Missionary Sisters of the Sacred Heart, and in the short period of a month have already founded a school and orphanage. It is not unlikely that after their devoted rounds these young religious ladies are rewarded with scant alms and the care of more of our vaunted city's shamefully neglected orphans.

"These young nuns hardly speak English. The Directoress of their congregation is 'Madre Francesca Cabrini,' a diminutive, youthful lady with great eyes and an attractive smiling face. She does not know the English language, but she knows the universal language of the human spirit."

How do the many million souls of the New World greet the day? With love or with hate? To give or to take? Do their lips bless or curse? Will their hands aid or smite, build or destroy? Will their day be a service to their brothers and sisters, celebrating the glories of His gift? Or will they violate the sun and profane His bounty with greed, neglect, and death heaped upon the weak, the innocent?

"Good morning, Lord. My passion is the flower opening in Thy hand. This day, again, consume me with Thy love. Teach my lips to guide Thy brides, strengthen my arms to lift Thy children. Oh, Spouse, make Thy children also mine."

Soft is the Sisters' stepping to the Chapel. Before candle-lighted altar they sit upon benches and read silently from missals.

The ringing of a hand bell calls the children from their beds.

78

They scramble up, twittering and chattering and balking and shrilling, the younger girls monitored by the older. Who stokes the big coal stove in the kitchen, stirs the porridge in the pots, sets the long tables, and pours the hundred glasses of milk? What has to be done will be done, and is done. Little faces have lingering sleep washed away and are brightened. On the way to the dining hall, the children genuflect as they file past the chapel, sign His cross, and say, "Good morning, our dear Lord Jesus."

Francesca sits with the children at the breakfast table, and their prayer of thanks is the song of birds. Later, alone in her room, she quickly scans the Italian newspaper, *Il Progresso,* the New York *Herald,* the *Times,* and the *Evening Sun* of the previous day, learning English by comparing stories of the same events.

Il Progresso portrayed emotionally, in rich Italian and with appalling facts, the immigrants' unequal struggle in New York and New Orleans, on the docks and railroads, in near and distant states, in mines, tenements, courts, prisons, and asylums.

The American newspapers, aside from their garish and blatant advertising, were honest, sympathetic, robust, dynamic, and flamboyant, depicting alike the good and evil of life in the New World. Those were the times of the fearless Seth Low and the *Evening Sun's* crusading reporter Jacob Riis, who revealed shameful social conditions through the eyes of an intelligent idealistic immigrant. Daily, Riis exposed Croker's Tammany-machine boss rule of New York. New York was then perhaps the worst run city in the world, with overt thievery flourishing in every municipal department. Favors and contracts for the city's services were crudely bought and sold by politicians in saloons. Clean-up administrations were short-lived. New York was greatest in everything, including the basest forms of corruption. It was an open secret that boss rule was protected by both temporal and clerical powers. Tammany Hall, representing collusion between politicians, police, and criminal elements, became the prototype of political organization for many American cities.

For Francesca, the newspapers were her extra eyes and ears. Through them she learned of trends, currents, rhythms, and cross currents that broadened her grasp of the compulsively growing America. In Italy, unlike America, the government was vigorously anticlerical. Even so, in America, the uprooted immigrant, besides being inhumanly exploited, was also in the greatest danger of losing his soul. With Him Francesca would in her lifetime meet this challenge and help to conquer it.

Each day there was also mail to read from her daughters and children in Italy. She wrote thoughtful letters in return, requesting more missionaries for the New York school and orphanage, advising the study of English, describing the features of democracy and the cosmopolitan American personality. She thus renewed their initiative for the ever-increasing development of the institute, reaffirming her motherly affection, and inciting more love for her Spouse.

Her correspondence completed, she must out and forage for this evening's supper. With a few daughters and orphans, she sets out for Little Italy, to sell subscriptions, beg, gather food, and teach school at San Gioacchino's.

One day she brought back with her little Yolande, her sister Loredana, and a Chinese orphan, Mary. A storekeeper on Mott Street had told her about the homeless tikes, and she found them living like kittens in a cellar bin. The resourceful eight-year-old Yolande had been keeping her sister and the Chinese girl alive by shining shoes and pilfering food from pushcarts. The first evening, Francesca had her hands full. After she had stripped them of their verminous rags, nudged them into the shower, and began to scrub away the stubborn layers of filth, they rebelled furiously at the strange new experience, screaming as though mortally wounded, stamping their feet, and squirming.

80

Yolande kept crying, "What are you doing to me? I thought you were a nice lady. Why are you so mean to me?" There followed another long slippery struggle while she snipped, combed, and brushed their overlong, matted hair. But after she had liberated them from itching filth, dressed them in nightclothes, fed them, and tucked them into clean soft beds, one by one they threw their arms about her and kissed her.

The burly, humorous, tobacco-chewing drivers of the long, yellow Broadway horsecars, mostly aggressive open-hearted Irish, gallantly let her missionaries and orphans ride free.

How different traffic on this thoroughfare was from the casually paced movement of the Old World. Muddy, cobbled Broadway is a circus course, filled with team-pulled drays, red-and-brass fire wagons, ambulances, police wagons, trams with horses nosing the cars ahead, omnibuses, postal wagons, gigs, traps, barouches, cabriolets, finely seated horsemen and splendid horses, cyclists, cart pushers, and barrows, and pedestrians nimbly skipping away from hoofs and wheels.

At Mulberry Bend Francesca musters all her strength to beseech her orphans' keep. It is difficult for her to beg.... Why, oh why, is a rich world so deliberately blind? But she smiles within as her daughters attune themselves with cheerful humility to the chore. Their dealings with the store owners and pushcart peddlers gives rise to a vivacious excitement. They gather into their purses pennies, dimes, quarters, and occasionally, crumpled paper money. In many a coffin-like flat, instead of receiving, they give of purse or food.

The presence of the orphans by their side tells of their mission better than words; Yolande, Loredana, and the little Chinese girl Mary, were the former abandoned tatterdemalions in the street. The people of Mott Street recognize Yolande. Yolande now has a home; Christ is now her father and the nuns are her mothers. She hungers and steals no more; she is loved, is taught, has a future, and is proud to keep the nuns' shoes at the orphanage polished and shining.

"Hey, Yolande," one calls to her, "fortune has found you, and now you look the little Christian lady!"

"Yes, Signora proprietress. Fill this bag with bread and biscuits and prove yourself a Christian for Mother Cabrini!"

Oh, the quick warmth, the felicity of helping one's own kind in a new and strange land! The man from Asti who has the dried-bean shop, he from Palermo with the fish cart, the herb woman from Vasto, the various vendors and storekeepers from Bergamo, Genoa, Venice, Pisa, San Marino, Naples, Spoleto, Salerno, Anzio, the Abruzzi, and elsewhere.

"God's benedictions to you, good sir; we are Sisters of the Sacred Heart seeking contributions for our orphans. Will you not help to feed them as you do your own blessed children? We are grateful for anything it pleases you to give."

"Dear Sisters, raise your voices, speak up boldly. What do you need most? What will serve you best today? Oil, cheese, garlic, sugar? Mention my name to the Lord. Remember a bit of me in your prayers."

"Mother Cabrini, when you enter, you bless my little market. Here, this is no cause for modesty, load your bags to the brim with whatever you wish. We are Italians! Nay, first we are Christians!"

"True Sisters of ours, do you mind taking yesterday's squid, whiting, and dog fish? But be sure you cook it tonight! Listen, go to Giacomo Chambruno's bakery early Monday mornings, for he generally has much leftover bread."

"Ah Sisters of the Sacred Heart, I am overstocked today with kale and broccoli; take all you want. We might as well add some artichokes, and escarol, and why not these nice big zucchini? Do you think the orphans would like sticks of Saint John's bread? Take, take and don't be bashful!"

They go into store after store and come out with gifts; the pastry shop, dairy market, wine shop, sausage shop, the novelty store with kitchen utensils, the grocery. There are days when the haul is so large that a kindly store man drives them and

82

the collected gifts back to the orphanage in his work wagon. One way or another the orphans shall eat, and well!

Then to the dilapidated old building on White Street that Archbishop Corrigan rented for her, so that she can move the classes from the church, and house more daughters. She has much work to do to make it habitable for classes and daughters. She does not wait for help, but with daughters and orphans and pupils, sets to work to clean it and repair the broken windows and doors.

Dust and garbage must be disposed of, bugs, mice, and roaches banished. Again the daughters who will live and work in this new house will start in abject poverty, with straw on the floor for beds, benches for tables, and a useless stove. But at least there will be cleanliness.

What is for supper at the orphanage? Whatever the day's begging brought. But grace is the same. Francesca prays as a child with the children, and they go to their beds. For a while she and her daughters sit, relax, and tell each other of their day. Breezes of humor play over their fatigue. They laugh over the Irish policeman who once apprehended Yolande pilfering park flowers for the chapel, and who now each day comes proudly by with park flowers for their altar; over the time Sister Agostina tried to fire the broken stove of the White Street House and then, completely unaware of her sooted face, rode the horsecar serenely uptown to the mirth of the passengers, as she looked for all the world like a blackamoor missionary.

In the sanctuary of the chapel she and her daughters sing hymns of love to the Spouse, and close with prayer the day lived for His children.

As soon as her school and orphanage were established, Francesca sought out the other and smaller Italys uptown on the east and west sides, and found colonies of them also in Brooklyn, Staten Island, and Hoboken. In the course of

83

her travels to beg, she saw all the economic sins of the New World, and the tragic toll taken by its prejudices. Adjacent to Mulberry Bend's Little Italy were street after street of tenements crammed from cellar to garret with Jewish families, with ten to twenty human beings of both sexes and all ages occupying every room. In these quarters the bulk of the city's tailoring and garment making was done, but the income from such work was barely enough for the inhabitants to keep absolute starvation at bay. The air was unendurable with the odor of ill-cared-for bodies mingling with the odor of spoiled food.

In the hallway of many a tenement, Francesca would see a crucifix upon one door jamb, and on the adjacent door jamb, a small parchment scroll. As she knocked on doors and begged in the dark hallways, she often passed a reverent Jew with beard, skullcap and long-skirted caftan, who would kiss the scrolled laws of his faith in his coming and going.

Francesca did not need to be in New York long to realize that Archbishop Corrigan had in fact been right about the orphanage building. It was badly located. Politicians, real estate men, and the complacent rich resented an orphanage in the heart of an exclusive district and threatened it with legal restrictions. Francesca was determined that her orphanage must survive and grow. She saw it as not just one refuge, but the cornerstone from which she would build others. No circumstance, she vowed, would destroy it.

She herself was not satisfied with its location. In her mind, she visualized an estate in the country for the children, like her father's farm in Sant'Angelo, but far vaster. She wanted acres and acres of hills and plains, streams, woods, orchards, and vegetable gardens, and cows, chickens, goats, birds, and flowers everywhere. Orphans should have the best!

Francesca longed to move her establishment, but not until she had had one of her prophetic dreams did she broach the subject to Archbishop Corrigan.

84

"Excellence, I confess that you were right regarding the location of the orphanage. In fact, no part of the city is a place for my orphans. In a dream I saw the site for our orphanage." And she described her dream in detail.

"Mother Cabrini," mused the Archbishop, "by chance has anyone taken you for a drive along the Hudson River?"

"No, Excellence."

"That is very interesting. The place you saw in your dream sounds to me like an estate among the hills up the Hudson. I have an idea. Come, let us drive up there in my carriage!"

They paused at Peekskill and viewed the majestic river and hills. She pointed to the opposite shore, where there were a group of charming buildings atop a hill. "Ah, Excellence," she exclaimed, "there, that is the place where our orphans should be!"

The Archbishop smiled in wonder. "Mother Cabrini, that is a large estate belonging to the Jesuits. Shall I look into the matter? Could it be . . . is it possible Our Lord wants them to sell?"

She nodded. "It may be Our Lord's wish . . . and He may be waiting for Your Excellence to suggest His wish to the Jesuits—and at a bargain of course!"

5 ✠ ✠ ✠

HAVING established a school and an orphanage within four months, Francesca was obliged to return to Italy for more Daughters to help expand the American mission. On July 20, she boarded ship with two young Irish-American postulants, Loretta and Elizabeth. The whistle warning visitors was a blow to the daughters she was leaving behind. They wept, and kissed her hands and her wedding ring. They were still young and felt truly secure only when she was with them. She smiled understandingly, but she wanted them to rely completely upon their Spouse and not upon her.

"My dear daughters, weeping? The bride of heaven is not supposed to weep. Why do you weep when my spirit is always with you no matter where I am? Now go each of you as a great mother and do your duty. Make your beloved Spouse proud of you. I shall not be gone long."

When she returned to Codogno, her first house seemed to her a delicious oasis that she had come back to after a long walk in the desert. There were joyful reunions with her Codogno daughters, whom she called "the elect of my garden, my flowers of virtue." There was time for refreshing spiritual retreat.

One of the extraordinarily providential episodes that dotted her career took place while she was at Codogno. A local citizen, a poor demented creature, set fire to the woodshed at the convent. The wind was high and the flames slashed the night, threatening at any moment to destroy the convent and all its buildings. Daughters, orphans and villagers looked on in fright. Without a sign of fear or confusion, Francesca went to the blaze, lifted her eyes to heaven and prayed. As she signed the cross, the wind slowly changed direction and veered the flames away from the buildings. Then a heavy rain came to smother the fire. Later, when the arsonist was caught, it was she who saved him from the violence of the people.

While she was at Codogno, her daughters in New York wrote to her that the vast Jesuit estate on the hill across the Hudson from Peekskill was, as she had hoped it might be, for sale.

She visited her houses in Lombardy and Rome briefly. She went again for strength and blessing from Pope Leo, who was delighted to see her and was keenly interested by her report about what she had seen in the New World. Then, taking a group of seven daughters, Francesca sailed back to New York.

This time, dear to her as the land of her birth was, she felt on approaching the American shore that she belonged less to the historical, slow-moving Old World than to the racing, open New World. An urgent pulsing told her this far-spread field would be hers. Here she would accomplish her greatest work of love for Christ, and in this new earth she would leave her mortal self.

She lost no time, upon her return, before taking in hand the matter of the new estate on the Hudson.

Upon seeing the magnificent houses and the 450-acre property of the Jesuits in West Park, she exclaimed, "This is the very place I saw in my dream—the large country houses, the cliff and river, the trees and bushes, the barns and stables, the mountain on the other side of the highway. Oh, how my heart desires this for the hurt children of my Lord!" And pensively she said to Sister Aurelia, who had accompanied her on her inspection trip, "Here will I be buried, on the gentle slope overlooking the river. And you, Daughter Aurelia, when aged, must come to my tomb unweeping, nay, smiling, for I will have prepared for you a niche in the arms of my Spouse."

The Jesuits explained that they were willing to part with the estate because of their hopeless water problem. Their well had gone dry, and one well-driller after another had failed to locate water. The only source of supply was the river far below, and the water obtained from the river with strenuous hauling of buckets, was unsuitable.

Even though they brought the sale price down to a fraction of what the property had cost them, and gave her easy long terms, the Jesuits shook their heads in pity for her.

"Mother Cabrini, how can you keep hundreds of children here without water?"

She smiled confidently and answered, "Dear Brothers, remove that concern from your conscience and let it rest upon my shoulders. If our Lord wants me to raise His children here in West Park, He will have to bring water."

She dragged young, strong Sister Aurelia over the Jesuits' land for hours, up and down the slopes and all over the many acres. They examined the terrain foot by foot and arrived back at the orphanage late in the evening and exhausted. Her daughters gathered eagerly about her.

"Mother, did you get the beautiful land and houses?"

"Of course, my daughters. I had made up my mind to do so even before I got there."

"Forgive me, Mother, but where is the money to put down? We have not a cent in the bank!"

"The Jesuits are packing and going to another monastery they have built in Peekskill. I told them Our Lord is my banker and will not fail to help me find the money. These problems overcome my naturally weak condition and make me strong! The bigger the problem, the stronger I become! And now, I would like nothing better than a plate of rice *à la Milanese* and a glass of cool beer!"

88

She enlisted carriages from the rich, work wagons from the storekeepers of Mulberry Bend, drays from Italian contractors, and moved the furnishings and her hundreds of orphans to West Park. The children had never seen the country before, and went delirious with joy, and who better than Francesca, the farmer's daughter, could demonstrate to the gaping girls how to treat the livestock that the good and generous Jesuits left for her. She taught them to saddle and harness the horses, to milk cows and goats, to call and feed the pigeons and chickens and pigs and sheep. Sister Eletta, who had sentimentally collected all the stray dogs and cats in New York City, much to everyone's amusement, was triumphantly gratified to see how proper they were in the barns and stables, romping with the gleeful girls!

The girls knew that these fine buildings and handsome hills were theirs, and they plied themselves with a proud and cooperative sense of ownership to painting, waxing, gardening, cooking, and cleaning. They washed the linen on the banks of the river, and sent water up from the river with the many willing hands of a bucket brigade.

By now Archbishop Corrigan had a most profound affection for this mystical yet practical bride of Christ. When he visited and saw the orphans so perfectly happy in their West Park paradise, he celebrated Mass there with moistened eyes. He fervently thanked God for Mother Cabrini and vowed to do all in his power to help her expand her American mission.

She invited her benefactors big and small, high and low, to share the pastoral beauty of West Park, and they came on weekends with their carriages and wagons and bags loaded with food and gifts.

The golden summer Sundays saw the friends of the orphanage gathered in the grove overlooking the stately Hudson, surrounded by the soft green hills. The wealthy came, along with the respectable poor from Mulberry Bend and the Irish horsecar drivers and policemen. The Archbishop and lesser men of the cloth visited often. The guests all mingled, playing games

89

with the orphans. The old Italians with musical instruments played nostalgic melodies. There were picnic tables laden with good food, with a glass of wine for the adults and ice cream and sweets for the children.

She prayed to Our Lady of Graces to help her locate water, and as if in answer to her prayer, Our Lady appeared to her in a dream and indicated where the well should be dug. She obeyed the dream and lead the well driller up the hillside to a thickly wooded area. With a stick she tapped a damp spot on the ground amongst the rocks where the man was to dig. Exactly there, the man uncovered a mountain spring that assured the orphanage an inexhaustible supply of crystal clear water. With her own hands she placed at the site of the well a statue of the Blessed Virgin.

By this time her ability had become well known in the Roman ecclesiastical world, and requests came to her to found schools and orphanages in France, Spain, England, and Latin America. Soon after the opening of West Park, she made another trip back to Rome to enlarge the facilities of her institute and to bring back more nuns. The two American daughters, Ann and Elizabeth, who accompanied her on this trip were quiet and sweet. The calm sea they enjoyed on the voyage seemed to reflect the peace and features of a soul adorned with sanctifying grace. Francesca did not feel well and had no desire to do anything. Nevertheless she was happy, for she was able to meditate freely. The letters she wrote on this trip give eloquent testimony to her spiritual pleasure.

Oh, Love is not loved, my Daughters! Love is not loved! And how can we remain cold, indifferent and almost without heart at this thought? How can we forget ourselves in folly and nonsense? How can we put a limit to our affection and to our energy when we consider the interests of Jesus? Oh! how beautiful is the hymn of that fortunate bride who can say, 'Jesus loves me, and I love Him! He is the only object of my thoughts. I have printed Him on my hands and in the deepest recess of my heart.' Be wise, then, Daughters. Let us please our Husband by doing more good for His mystic members, the souls redeemed by His great sufferings and death.

Let us not be deterred by blind men's laws. Let us not shirk and dream and wait to help His children who are this moment in pain, in want, crushed and abandoned by the society of men who are mortal microscopic things compared to Christ! Let our bride's small hands do the work of a hundred hands and bring His love and aid to the lost souls, to the poor in prisons, tenements, streets, mines, hospitals, fields, and wherever is suffering! Missionary Daughters! if, then, we do not burn with intoxicating love, we do not deserve the beautiful title, 'Bride of Heaven' which ennobles us, elevates us, makes us great, and even a spectacle to the angels!

In Rome, despite her ill health, she set to work vigorously to expand her institute. She elaborated higher methods of education and undertook the founding of a teachers college to train laywomen as teachers. She appointed more daughters to responsible offices, recruited postulants, and began to raise funds toward one of her fondest dreams, an American convent and novitiate, to be located at West Park.

At Christmastime she was in Rome and was one of a select group lovingly received by Pope Leo during the Natal Novena. When the group came before his throne he recognized her. His face lighted, and he beckoned to her and said with paternal affability, "Ah, Mother General, we have been together before, is it not true?" At his feet she prostrated herself and proffered him a graceful little statuette. "What have you, Cabrini my child?"

"The Madonna of Victory," she responded. "She is the bearer to your sanctity of the complete victory we so much wish for you, we who are your small branches."

Moved by her words, he accepted her offering, clasped her hands tightly and said, "Thank you, thank you child for thy gift and good augury."

"Oh, Father, day and night we pray for the triumph of your sanctity."

He put his arm about her and said warmly, "My capable missionary to the West, let us have a long talk. Are you doing your duty well in America? Tell me about your school and orphanage, the American girls who are following you into your institute, for I love your congregation and every one of your Missionary Sisters of His Sacred Heart!"

She wrote to her daughters in New York: "Oh! the benediction of the Pope! How potent it is! His mouth is the mouth of Our Lord, his words the words of our Spouse. He is the illumination of divine wisdom, and therefore his words and benedictions, for me, is the true column of fire that guides me through every difficulty and danger."

Her work in Rome absorbed her for a number of months. During her stay there, she had opportunities for other audiences with the pope, and each was for her a supremely inspiring experience. In the light of his personal interest in her work, she herself became ever more enthusiastic about the American mission. She delighted in conveying to him her profound faith in the fundamental goodness of the American character, and telling him what a fertile field America was to be.

On Sunday evening, March 15, 1891, she left the Vatican exhilarated after a long interview with Leo. Before she arrived at her Via Nomentana house, newsboys were shouting, "America kills our people!" "Read now the horror for Italian people in America!" "The King has severed relations with murdering America!" The street throngs, while reading the hastily printed extra, roared aloud, crying oaths and curses of revenge. She bought a copy, and read it in the convent. The main article was a translation of a New York *Herald* correspondent's on-the-spot report, filed from New Orleans, La., March 14, 1891. It was headed: STUNG BY LAW'S FAILURE TO CONVICT ITALIAN SUSPECTS ACCUSED REGARDING POLICE CHIEF HENNESSEY'S

MURDER, THE CITIZENS OF NEW ORLEANS TAKE MATTERS INTO THEIR OWN HANDS.

Leading lawyers, merchants, and editors of New Orleans, the story explained, had reacted bitterly when a group of Italian laborers who had been accused of murder were acquitted in a jury trial. In their own minds, they had convicted the Italians, and determined to see them punished, they had signed a call to the citizens of New Orleans demanding a mass meeting at the Clay monument. The meeting quickly degenerated into a riot, and a hysterical mob marched from the monument to the jail to take charge of the prisoners. The authorities, whether out of terror or complicity, offered only passive resistance.

With clubs and axes, five thousand raging citizens battered down the doors to the parish jail. Nine Italian immigrants were shot down, riddled with buckshot and bullets. Two were publicly hanged.

Politicians and influential citizens failed, it seemed, to condemn the action of the mob.

The *Herald* correspondent told all the sickening details, and concluded,

Dr. Luigi Raversi, a well known Italian journalist, editor of *Il Progresso Italo-Americano,* a daily Italian newspaper published in this city, expressed himself in this wise concerning the lynching:

"It is a horrible crime, a massacre of innocents, unworthy of civilized and republican America, a lasting disgrace to a Christian and progressive people. It is a crime a thousand times worse than the unsolved murder of Chief Hennessey because Hennessey was an armed free man and able to defend himself, but the poor acquitted prisoners were unarmed, and fell victims like helpless lambs under the knife of the butchers. Remember that these men had been proclaimed to all the world innocent by an American jury, and further, that the persons of these men, who were in the prison under the aegis of the law, should have been sacred. And remember that these men were no longer under the accusation of

93

murder, but that they were free men; that they had been declared innocent. When we look upon the occurrence in the light of these facts the lynching becomes a crime against civilization of the deepest dye.

"Coroner Lemmier reached the prison at half-past twelve o'clock noon, and with his jury viewed the bodies. The coroner's jury decided that death in all the cases but Pietro Monastero's resulted from gunshot wounds at the hands of parties unknown.

"The dead Italians leave wives and quite a few children."

That night Francesca and her daughters prayed for the immigrants slain in New Orleans and for their bereaved families, and asked Christ's mercy for their killers. There was a cruel man-made cross for the immigrants in New Orleans, and she resolved to found a house there, to help bear that cross and lighten their burden with His love.

In September, taking a group of twenty-nine young new brides of Christ she again sailed west.

She remained in New York for a few intense weeks, improving the school in Little Italy and preparing West Park as the novitiate for America. The beauty of the chapel and villa, the order and tranquillity of West Park pleased her so that she told her daughters, "Every time I find myself at West Park I think that, perhaps, when I have worked sufficiently for the institute, this will be the place of my retreat and retirement to prepare myself for the journey to eternity. Ah . . . but this is an illusive dream, a childish feeling. Let us leave to Providence all thought of our future."

Well might she leave thoughts of the remote future to Providence, for the immediate future, as she had planned it, called for exploits demanding enough to require all her attention. Before her last trip to Rome, a well-to-do Nicaraguan lady, Donna Elena Arrelano had come to her at West Park and implored her to open a school in Granada. Donna Elena graciously offered to contribute a building to house the school, and spoke eloquently of the need for Catholic institutions in

94

Nicaragua. Francesca knew that the school Donna Elena had in mind would not be a charitable institution, but a private academy for the daughters of the wealthy. But she had reasons for accepting the invitation. She was never one to construe her mission narrowly, and though the most urgent field for her labors lay in the United States, she saw no reason to exclude Latin America. Moreover, the wealthy, she knew, might not need physical assistance, but they could be and often were sorely in need of spiritual guidance. Too, a private school could easily support itself, and once her Missionary Sisters had established themselves in a large city for any purpose, no doubt they would find ways to ease the burdens of its poor.

Accordingly, she chose fourteen daughters, borrowed passage money from Archbishop Corrigan, and set sail for Nicaragua on October 10, 1891.

Had timid Sister Eletta accompanied Francesca on this voyage, her worst fears would have been realized, for hardly had the ship left New York than a storm came up. This was no moderate rainfall, such as those that had struck terror into her inexperienced daughters on the first voyage to the New World. The sea began to swell extraordinarily, the windswept waves formed mountains, with deep valleys between. The steamer seemed lost amid precipices of water. Even to the least experienced of travelers, it was soon apparent that this was a hurricane.

Francesca arose and dressed in haste to save her daughters, or at least die together with them. In their cabins she found them fully dressed and quietly in their berths, ready to perish, but completely covered and hiding under their blankets. Throughout that night and the next day, the sea continuously threatened to dash the ship to pieces. Her daughters were so ill that they acted more like children than religious, which fact disheartened her so that she almost repented having chosen them for so difficult a mission. But within a few days the storm exhausted itself, and she had reason to be glad that

95

she had not disclosed her misgivings, for her daughters at length showed themselves as really sensible young women quite willing to undertake any arduous venture. To Francesca, the uneasily tamed sea after the storm looked like a soul agitated by remorse and pride, who never finds peace with God.

The ship anchored for a day near some small isles a short distance from Panama City. She hired a small boat, and she and her daughters rowed ashore, singing hymns the while in preparation for Holy Communion. When they got back, the sea was at low tide, and they had to walk a half mile over the wet beach to get to their rowboat. As they rowed to inspect one of the gemlike isles before returning to the ship, a flight of sea gulls hovered over them. Wrote Francesca: "The birds were drawn to us, either by the hoarseness or sweetness of our voices, to adore and praise their Creator Whom we carried in our hearts as living Tabernacles.

"Some of the Sisters wanted to know what this procession of birds meant, and I replied that they represented the Religious of those countries who might enter our Institute some day, but one of the Sisters was not convinced of my interpretation, and answered, 'They rather represent the souls that shall be saved by us.' I still argued, when another flight of other aquatic birds appeared, a thousand or more, and eventually we decided that they represented the souls which were to be saved by us in the course of time. Sitting at the stern of the rowboat, I put my hands into the sea and bathed them, but I withdrew them quickly when I felt one of them being drawn down vigorously by a crab. I admit my weakness, I am afraid of the sea, and I have no courage to go where I fear danger, unless I were sent by obedience, when, of course, one's actions are blessed by God. Oh, blessed voice of obedience! When that speaks, the Missionary crosses the ocean and gives no thought to the roaring waters, the rising and lowering of the billows, but the ocean becomes to her a sublime and magnificent sight that fills her with admiration, and induces her

96

to praise the Creator for the beauty and wonder of His works. We enjoyed ourselves like happy children on the isles and under shady trees, and came back aboard with pretty shells."

On Saint Raphael's day the ship entered the stunning gulf of Nicaragua, off the coast of Corinto. The sisters were met by dignitaries and prelates who escorted them inland by train to Leon, Momotambo, across the lovely Nicaragua lake and again by train to Granada. Francesca faithfully described their arrival, for the benefit of the daughters left behind.

"The whole population awaited us. The crowd prevented the carriages from coming up to us, such was their enthusiasm, and I feared we would be suffocated. I was particularly anxious, as some of the Sisters were not feeling well. I thought they would make martyrs of us through excessive friendliness. I therefore prayed the soldiers to make room for us, and as soon as I called them they drew near and put the people in order, forming a procession to the church, where the Parish priest, accompanied by other priests, awaited us to sing the Te Deum."

That evening the nuns were dinner guests at the palatial table of Donna Elena Arellano. But at the sight of the Indian women servants who were naked to the waist, Francesca arose from the table and said, "Donna Elena, no daughter of mine will eat a mouthful until these women make themselves modest!"

Donna Elena begged a thousand pardons and blushingly explained that it was the mark of the half-breed and lower-class women to go about naturally exposed. It was, she said, their inveterate tradition, and one not to be corrected in a moment.

"Donna Elena, I recognize neither higher nor lower classes. These women also are children of God, and daughters of Mary, Who elevates woman to the Heavens. As of this moment they must raise themselves by being shown, and observing, the honor of womanhood."

Only after the half-breed women, much to their surprise, were made to cover themselves with towels, shawls and sheeting, did she signal her daughters to begin eating.

Francesca's letters described her work in detail.

All the children of the town want to attend our school, and boarders from the neighboring districts are asking admittance, but for the present, we can only take fifty boarding girls, for although the house is big, it is not big enough for this tropical climate where the heat is prostrating. Now and then we have a providential breeze which, pure and fresh, restores us a little. We have large enclosures with a variety of orange trees and other smaller plants, and flowers of all colors and kinds.

The good Lady Elena Arellano had all the dormitories in order for the Sisters, and a very nice airy Chapel. At present Donna Elena is preparing the desks and arranging the prospectus, which will be approved by the heads of families, for they say we have brought them true progress. We hope this will result in good to their souls. For this alone have we undertaken such a long voyage.

All the Sisters are well and working hard to open the Academy very soon. Perhaps they will begin about the middle of December. Those Sisters who feared earthquakes fear nothing now, though we experience some shaking. We have an active volcano quite near. Some people want us to visit the country, which offer I intend to accept later on before I leave for poor, wretched New Orleans, so I shall have something to write and tell you, and not be like those who go to Rome without going to see the Pope.

I beg of you to become true Missionaries. Seek to perfect your spirit and the observance of the Holy Rules. Our great Patron, Saint Francis Xavier, said, 'He who goes holy to the Missions will find many occasions to sanctify himself more, but he who goes poorly provided with holiness, runs the risk of losing what he has and of falling away.' I become more convinced of this truth every day, and as experience is a great master, let us take advantage of the lessons it teaches and never let a day pass without examining our conscience and making serious resolutions to acquire the virtues we need. May our Spouse bless and enclose you in His sweet Heart,

98

imprinting His love on yours, and giving you perfect detachment of yourselves.

Your affectionate Mother in the
Sacred Heart of Jesus,
FRANCES XAVERIO CABRINI
Granada, Nov. 3, 1891.

She did not delude herself about the clamorous and festive reception accorded her. Perceiving the volcanic nature of the people and their inconstant politics, she saw that they could, without reason, suddenly turn to insults.

With her acute mind and eminent practicality she studied the people, their ways and needs. Soon she was painfully aware of widespread moral license, particularly the plague of illegitimate children of every class and color. She would not permit the admission of these children until their fathers had made them legitimate by law, Church, and spirit.

Her girls had to be equal in the eyes of God and society. Only then could she cultivate their souls. Individuals of local renown who had illegitimate offspring opposed her rule. They attempted first to evade it by means of bribery. When that failed, they turned to threats and disconcerting acts of intimidation. But she had not traversed oceans only to compromise with corruption. She remained adamant, and won. She firmly established and directed her school, and in spite of the wellnigh insupportable heat, worked along with her daughters, teaching, educating, instructing, and playing games with the girls, and at the many manual and domestic duties of cooking, serving, cleaning, and caring for the children. The nights were intolerably hot, and alive with armies of toads, scorpions, insects, and not infrequently, snakes, which she dreaded. The nearby volcano rumbled repeatedly, and the earth was susceptible to unnerving tremors. Three of her daughters fell gravely ill with typhoid fever. For days and nights she was with them during their delirium, and did not leave their side until the crisis had passed.

Her cross was not without the light of laughter. Someone

presented the school with a parrot of splendid colors and rare abilities. He was everywhere and mimicked all with uncanny accuracy.

She named him, "Professor Talk-Talk," and most pious was the feathery creature, often startling her and squawking, "Ah! dear Mother Cabrini! Laudations! Benedictions!" She would admonish him as a "winged little hypocrite." He would follow her about, causing her and her daughters and the pupils much laughter. At times he would slyly hide to overhear her orations, then flap to the top of a palm tree, and repeat them with fine fervor, even to her Lombard accent. At last she decided to return the loquacious bird to the donor. Her daughters were becoming unduly attached to him, and he showed a definite enthusiasm for disrupting classes.

The Granada private school was now established. The tuition from its paying pupils was carrying the school, and permitted her, as she had hoped, to also take some girls of poor families as pupils. Yes, the Granada mission was going well, but inwardly she had misgivings.

New Orleans was her next mission. She chose Sister Cepeda as her traveling companion. To leave fourteen daughters in temperamental Granada was a maternal sacrifice. She had forebodings about their future. But the day she left was too lovely for her to remain depressed, as she explained later in a letter, "... for it was a day dedicated to Him Who comes upon the desert of this world as surging dawn, peaceful as the moon, elect as the sun, and beautifully terrible as righteous forces in battle order."

At the solemn moment of departure she embraced her daughters and prayed of them to be strong and to sustain themselves above human weaknesses.

Sailing across Lake Nicaragua she exulted at the vista of the Cordillera with its cascading streams, plains, mountain

100

peaks, thick forests, and tropical vegetation. Who but her Spouse had made these natural wonders? During her twelve day voyage along the treacherous San Juan river she and Sister Cepeda had to transfer many times from one open small boat to another. They were caught in a rainstorm and drenched for five hours. Francesca described the ordeal with her usual wit and good humor.

"We had as fellow passengers rats and all sorts of cheeky rodents. As Sister Cepeda and I had not much confidence in the designs of these small adventurers, we passed the nights dodging them, standing on boxes, and cheerfully finding motives in our fright to laugh at their antics."

By the time they got to San Juan she was gripped with a high fever that robbed her of energy and will. Feeling that she was dying, she dutifully offered her soul to God. At the same time the thought that she was leaving the earth with her work undone distressed her, and she felt sorry about dying without bidding her beloved daughters a final farewell. "I confidentially asked my Spouse to at least let me reach the United States," she wrote, "and He benignly listened, and now I am beginning to feel somewhat well again."

In Bluefields, while waiting for a steamer to take her to New Orleans, she went among the natives. There was no church, no priest to visit the Indians of the Mosquitia Riviera, whom the Government considered little better than beasts. With sign language and a few Spanish words she spoke kindly to them, until they forgot their shyness and yielded to their respect for the "Black Robes." Then they begged her to send them sisters and priests. She felt for them, and would have opened a house there at once had she the means to do so. "Oh, if I could but loosen the purse-strings of the rich to whom God has so liberally given of this earth's wealth!"

On Holy Tuesday, 1892, she arrived in New Orleans, and was paternally welcomed by Archbishop Janssens and Scalabrinian Father Gambera.

The Italians still vividly bore the raw stigmata of the atrocity inflicted upon them the year before—the lynching of the eleven immigrants. With towering indignation she heard the particulars of the slaughter from the tearful widows, children, and friends of the murdered men, and she firmly resolved to uplift the Italians of New Orleans.

She found New Orleans a flamboyant mixture of nationalities and color, white, black, mulatto, and creole. In the large Italian colony were many Sicilians, and quite a few of them had been there since the Civil War years. The ruling citizens regarded them as cruelly as they did Negroes. They were treated like beasts of burden, and referred to as "dagoes" "wops" and "guineas." More tragic than this degrading treatment was the almost complete absence of their Mother Church and religion. Growing at a prodigious material speed, the New World did not find time to appraise the state of its soul, or care to provide temples of worship for aliens. Immigrants were to be used while they were useful and then discarded. Then again, it profited power groups to hinder religious planting and development. Parishes, especially Catholic ones, meant immigrant community, literacy, Christian independence, and organized bulwarks against total and ruthless exploitation.

Archbishop Janssens clearly recognized in Francesca Cabrini an inspired woman who would accomplish much in New Orleans, and he pledged all cooperation for her Mission.

She had to continue to New York, but soon returned with a group of daughters. She rented three rooms in an old tenement in the slums on St. Philip's Street, where she and her daughters could live least expensively, and could be in constant contact with the immigrants. Most of the twenty families crowded into the building were Negroes and mulattoes who used the courtyard as their living stage day and night.

The scene in the courtyard below gave the nuns the impression of being in the African jungle. At night while they tried to sing their hymns, meditate, and rest, scarred ex-

102

slaves and their indiscriminate generations drank whiskey, fought, screamed, and cursed in the courtyard, by the light of the bonfires. They sang with guttural and shrill voices, and danced to the beating of hands and sticks upon empty oil drums, bottles, and cans.

Sanitation and cooking facilities were primitive. Until the sisters were able to acquire a filter for the city water piped from the Mississippi, they had to fetch safe drinking water from friendly families. As the seminaked Negroes swarmed curiously about, they made a stove in an angle of the courtyard with bricks and a grate, and cooked their pasta and vegetables over charcoal. While sitting for meals upon boxes before a table of boards, they were harassed by hungry cats and large bold rats.

She searched in vain for an adequate house, and as the tenement on St. Philip's Street was for sale at a low price, she negotiated purchase. To raise the down payment she had to solicit the few wealthy, and the thousands of poor Italians. She was tired and ill, and her daughters implored her not to go begging with them in the suffocating heat.

"My daughters," she answered, "I also shall beg with you from door to door. Would you know the truth? Begging is disgusting to me! But I must conquer that disgust. I will not ask my daughters to attempt any duty that their mother cannot perform."

As soon as the tenants vacated, she, her daughters, and the enthusiastic Italians, began sweeping, fumigating, and scrubbing their building. They repaired plaster, painted and glazed, and carted the mounds of refuse out of the courtyard. On the ground floor partitions were removed and the enlarged space was made into the convent chapel.

It was a signal day for the oppressed Italians of New Orleans when the statue of the Sacred Heart arrived from New York. They uncrated the statue at the railroad station. Under a boiling sun, young and old, the women wearing shawls, the

103

men hatless, formed a procession, proudly carrying the statue upon a lavish litter.

As they bore the statue through the streets to the new church, they argued for the honor of shouldering the Sacred Heart a bit of the way. They gazed upon it with profound love, and joyous tears flowed unashamedly down their cheeks.

The immigrants came to the new little church in such numbers that not even the whole building could contain them, and it became necessary to celebrate Mass under a canopy out in the large courtyard. The courtyard was also used for the religious instruction and recreation of the hundreds of immigrants' children. Where a few weeks before, bloody fights and profane amusements held sway, children now recited litanies, prepared for Holy Communion and Confirmation, and played happy, innocent games.

Her fruitful labors endeared her to Archbishop Janssens. When visiting the St. Philip's Street house, he did not pull the bell cord, but tapped softly with his cane on the door, and the nuns and the children knew that not a stranger, but their good father, had arrived.

Within a matter of weeks the St. Philip's Street house, besides incorporating convent and church, was working efficiently as a day school and orphanage, and placed at the entrance for passersby was a fountain of cool, pure, blessed water for thirst of body and soul.

At any hour and in all weather she and her daughters immediately answered the calls of the distressed; they baptized mortally or dangerously ill infants and children and assisted the dying when a priest was not available; they brought food and clothes to the destitute, nursed the sick, assisted women in labor and after delivery; they ventured into sordid sections to return an abashed erring husband to wife and children, to reconcile families, feuds, and enemies, to lead back to virtuous paths a straying girl.

Outside the city there was a settlement of fifty families exposed to the perverted influence of an excommunicated preacher, a priest who had degenerated into a veritable devil's disciple. She went boldly to the settlement, visiting the families one by one. On the Feast of Saint Joseph, all fifty of the families came to church.

Saturday evenings she and her daughters would wait on the Mississippi docks for the workers on rice, sugar, and cotton plantations to come ashore, and they would sweetly greet them.

"God bless you, good brothers. May we speak together in the name of our Christ?"

How dear was the sight of Italian nuns! The callous-handed simple men would talk eagerly with the sisters. While the sisters listened with patience and sympathy, the men, like children, unburdened their tribulations, fears, and hopes.

Francesca would gently ask, "Sirs, how long is it since you have been to Confession and received the Holy Communion?"

They would shyly reveal that it had been many years, that for the absence of Italian-speaking priests they had wed unsacramentally, and that their children had not been baptized.

"It is never too late to seek again your Lord, dear brothers. We are here now to help you and your families. Bring yourselves back to Christ. Be at peace with your Jesus."

They would trail her to the little church on St. Philip's Street and humbly go to Confession. The next morning they and their families, sparkling clean and wearing their best clothes, would appear for the Holy Mass and receive the Lord. She would present them with blessed articles of faith, and they would leave with purging tears, strengthened, and better able to confront their hardships.

She arranged for Father Paroli to say Mass for groups of families on isolated plantations, and before improvised altars they received the Bread of Angels. Sometimes Archbishop Janssens would graciously accompany her and the sisters to

105

poor families on the plantations and administer the Holy Chrism, having for baldachin the blue sky, for carpet the green meadow, and for bishop's stool a tree stump.

She initiated Christ's works of mercy in the torrid city. An immigrant who had been in New Orleans more than forty years, had been blinded in an industrial accident and was left to wander the streets, a forlorn beggar. She succeeded in placing him in a home for the blind, and traveled an hour's trip to him each day for weeks, preparing the old man for his First Holy Communion.

She had her daughters bring the fresh fragrance of Christ to the desolate sick and dying in the public hospitals, and to the unfortunate incarcerated in prisons.

In every city where Francesca founded a house, she and her daughters went to the prisons to console and convert. When they entered a jail peace came over the disturbed men. They wrote and answered letters for the men, brought them news of family, and sought to help them in every possible way. In the New Orleans prison they brought the message of Christ to seven condemned men. On the morning when the hateful barbarism of execution was to take place, the first to mount the scaffold was a twenty-year-old Negro whom the sisters had converted. Having embraced the faith, he faced destruction calmly. As the noose was placed about his neck, he cried to his doomed companions, "I pray that you too repent our crime. Oh, how easy it is to die knowing that our sins are forgiven by our creator who awaits us in Heaven!"

Forgotten by society but recorded in the Sacred Heart are the many merciful acts of Francesca Cabrini and her daughters. Sing Sing, in New York, was the first prison that they visited. Francesca saw to it that Italian priests brought the Sacrament to immigrant prisoners. Victims of circumstances, scapegoats, or betrayed by their own violence, how many lives had been twisted and broken by one rash deed! How many misguided pilgrims in a blind, new, gold-worshipping world were enmeshed, hopelessly trapped, and judged not by God but by fallible mortals!

A twenty-nine-year-old Italian widower condemned to the electric chair, in those days called "the dynamo," did not want to die, protesting his death sentence as he claimed himself innocent. In despair he attempted suicide. Francesca Cabrini obtained from the governor a month's stay of his execution. She brought his little girl to see him, assured him a protected Christian life for her, and placed her in the loving care of the West Park orphanage, which was not far from Sing Sing. The father proclaimed himself as guiltless as Christ; he may very well have been. He placed his soul in His hands, and resigned himself to an immutable fate. On the dawn of his execution Francesca wept and prayed with him, and together, they recited the rosary.

Some years later, in the Chicago prison, the sisters gave the solace of Christ to five condemned men, and prayed with them the entire night before their execution. When the fatal moment came the men were overcome with fear. The youngest, only twenty, clung to the robe of a sister, supplicating, "Oh, Sister Della Casa, accompany me at least to the death door! Give me your strength of Christ to the end!" He asked the warden that only she be allowed to slip the dread black hood over his eyes. Sister Della Casa did so with trembling hands and quivering lips of benediction. As he was led along the corridor to the gibbet, he turned, raised his mask, and sent her one last appeal for his soul. With heart crushed for him and his executioners, she signed the cross. In minutes, the boy was hanged. The cruel and tragic ordeal left Sister Della Casa ill for many days.

6 ✠ ✠ ✠

AMONGST the immigrants herded in the tenements, contagious diseases, once they had started, spread rapidly to most families. There was no one to medicate the ill, to teach hygiene and sanitation, to perform emergency operations. There was no one to care for those injured in the tenements, on the streets, and in hazardous occupations.

An infant pierces an eye while playing with scissors, a mother slicing bread for the family severs an artery of her wrist, a falling rock smashes a ditch-digger's legs, a child tumbles from a clothes pole and breaks his arm, a bread-winner is paralyzed, a rat bite causes gangrene, a fire cracker explodes and shatters a girl's face, a mother becomes infected by the germ-laden fingers of a midwife, the wintry damp walls hasten a cold into pneumonia.

The need of hospitals for the immigrant hordes was extreme. Public hospitals were all too few, and usually only the cleverest English-speaking Italians would go to those there were.

The death rate was enormous, and only mysterious good luck could keep the immigrants healthy. When immigrants were injured or seriously ill, the language barrier, poverty, pride, ignorance, timidity, and the utter indifference of public officials denied them the aid that might have saved their

108

lives. They simply remained stoically in the miserable beds of their dark squalid rooms. When primitive treatments of herbs, poultices, and leeches failed they turned to prayers and votive lights, witchcraft and cabalistic incantations. Too often, death followed in the wake of agonies.

In 1891, the valiant friend of immigrants, good Bishop Scalabrini, during a brief stay in New York, opened a small crude hospital for Italians on East 109th Street. Before returning to Rome he solicited and received the services of ten of Mother Cabrini's daughters for the little hospital.

Two incidents decided Francesca to extend her mission to hospitals. Two of her daughters told her of an illiterate Italian they had befriended in the course of their merciful visits to a public charity ward. He had received a letter from Italy written in the scholarly hand of a professional letter writer. In the months he had lain sick in the ward he could find no one to read it to him. The letter was precious to him, for he thought it must contain a heartening message from his beloved mother. She was his Madonna, his world, and he lived for the day he could bring her to America. A sister read the letter, and blanched. It was a notification of his mother's death. His sorrow was inconsolable. Upon hearing the story, Francesca Cabrini wept.

Being extraordinarily sensitive to the sight of pain, by nature seeking beauty and not the grotesque, and helplessly nauseated by hospital smells, how could she obediently put her hands to grim, revolting hospital labors? A dream relieved her of her repugnance. In the dream she was in a hospital and beheld a most beautiful and delicate lady who, with sleeves uprolled, was cheerfully changing the repulsive bedsheets, and tenderly cleansing the ghastly wounds of patients. Recognizing the Lady as the Virgin Mary, she rushed to help her. But the Mother of Christ smilingly waved her away, and softly said, "Francesca Cabrini, I, I will do this urgent work for you!"

"Madonna," Francesca answered, "whatever is worthy of thy hands, I shall not deem beneath my efforts."

The Scalabrinian Fathers, though zealous, were grossly inept with the management of the little 109th Street hospital. They provided their occasional eloquent presence and little else, quite expecting the Missionary Sisters of the Sacred Heart, and heaven, to do all the work and pay all the bills. The sisters were under the impossible handicap of having to take unconstructive orders, and besides actually working and running the hospital, were obliged to go out in the streets to beg for the means to live and try to pay the hospital's mounting expenses.

Upon arriving from New Orleans Francesca found the hospital in bankruptcy and about to be discontinued. She would not abandon the merciful project begun by the Scalabrinian Fathers, nor would she submit to their incompetent authority. She sternly refused to assume the debts incurred by them.

A hospital for immigrants was a stark, crying necessity. God wanted this work done for His suffering children. But, where others drew back or failed, she knew she would be victorious, for, "With my Christ, I can do all good works!"

Debts were forcing the closing of the hospital. Even furnishings that her daughters had accumulated by sacrifice and deprivation were claimed by the creditors. Two real Christians, though not men of means, gave Francesca 250 dollars. Every dollar of that donation was to be a proverbial mustard seed.

She quickly rented two old attached residential buildings on Twelfth Street. After paying the first month's rent she had enough money left to buy ten beds and the materials to make mattresses and sheets. She could not keep all of the twenty-five patients who wanted to be under her care, and temporarily transferred fifteen of them to public hospitals. She decided to name her first hospital after Columbus—the first Christian, the first emigrant, the first pilgrim to plant the cross of Christ in America. The creditors tried to confiscate and sell the horse-drawn ambulance wagon of the defunct 109th Street hospital,

110

but the man who had donated the horse and conveyance indignantly reclaimed it and signed it over to her.

On October 17, 1892, she moved her ten patients to 12th Street. The patients, some of whom were incurably ill, were jovial and festive in spite of the absolutely straitened circumstances of their new hospital. To foil the watching creditors, they crammed all the towels, sheets, and other small articles they could appropriate into their hospital gowns and under the blankets of the stretchers, to take to their new haven.

Columbus Hospital was a hospital only in name and spirit; its rooms, in need of repair and alteration, were empty and cold. Before she was able to raise the money to have the gas and water turned on, prayers and bundling blankets kept the patients warm, water was toted in in containers, and soup brought from a nearby restaurant was reheated on a faulty coal stove. She and her daughters made mattresses and sheets for their patients. They themselves had to sleep in their habits on the cold bare floor.

Her pharmacy? Is there anyone today in America who has the greatness of soul to start a hospital with some twenty bottles of antiseptic, and a few packages of gauze, cotton, and adhesive arranged on a kitchen table?

A Doctor Villardi technically baptized her hospital with a desk and a small glass case filled with basic surgical instruments. The ten patients behaved as though they were in paradise; they responded to her kindness with all their affection and were her enthusiastic collaborators, helping in every way they could.

Francesca had no illusions about the tasks before her and knew that her hospital would have to wrestle strenuously to survive. Her audacity was markedly an affront to the powers of the day. The fact that the well-meaning Scalabrinian Fathers had attempted to found an Italian hospital and had failed was an embarrassment to Francesca, and their inability to meet expenses discouraged potential benefactors. With the launch-

111

ing of her own hospital, the Scalabrinian Fathers offered no help, but kept away from her. The Italian immigrants were not the only Catholics who needed such facilities as hospitals, and church authorities could not help favoring their own nationals. Not an encouraging word came, not a helping hand. Even those who admired Francesca herself feared associating themselves with another hospital that would probably fail. True, the work needed to be done, but a series of failures would hardly solve the problem.

The archbishop told her sincerely that he feared that, on top of the responsibilities of her other houses, the hospital mission would prove beyond her capacities and health. He suggested that she give herself ten days to back out of the venture and forget all about the work of hospitals. She answered that it was her custom to change her approach to problems but never to retreat. She communicated immediately to the Prefect of Propaganda, Cardinal Simeoni, in Rome. Without resentment or complaint she sent him a simple exposition of the facts and stated that she would abide by his advice.

The cardinal cabled back, "Mother General, the Fathers should attend to the affairs of their church, as the care of hospitals is indicated more for your Missionary Sisters of the Sacred Heart."

Timid well-wishers and conservative clericals might fail to help. They might even obstruct her way. She did not permit herself for a moment to be disconcerted. She went imperturbably ahead. God made all kinds of people. Charitable organizations would not help her? Very well. She went to businessmen. After talking with her, they would recognize her practical acumen. She was, above all, an executive herself. She realistically envisioned the inevitably changing and expanding future. Hard-headed investors saw what Francesca's colleagues in merciful humanity had failed to see: that she was a strong woman, that her project was seriously needed, and that it would sooner or later succeed and pay for itself. The business-

112

men respected her judgments and supplied her hospital needs on flexible long-term credit.

The poor, nearer to her struggle, felt for her and offered what they could. "Send a sister on such and such a day of the week," they would say, "when I have received my wages, and I shall give so much and so much to Mother Cabrini for our hospital." There was the old retired ravioli manufacturer from Long Island City who came to work gratis in the hospital and who put his purse at her disposal when "final notice" for payments hounded her. She called him, "my sweet old uncle, who does not fail his Lord." An eminent doctor, named Keane, was drawn to her and offered himself as head of staff, donating his services, money, and instruments.

In her hospital he could practice his dedicated calling in an atmosphere that radiated love. His truly American character set an example. Soon other Catholic doctors, and also Jewish and Protestant medical men joined him with noble gallantry. Then Italians of all classes awakened and were proud of her, and spontaneously and emotionally rallied to her side. They sold subscriptions for the hospital and held paying banquets to raise money. They began to shame one another into generosity. Some brought checks, some brought coins or wrinkled hard-earned dollar bills, some brought wagon loads of food-stuffs and wines, some brought beds and linen, some brought utensils. Among the gifts were statues of the Sacred Heart and of the Madonna of Graces to place as Guardian in the sick-rooms. Flowers were contributed in abundance. Soon, the two attached buildings began to look and feel like a hospital.

It was far more than a medical, surgical, and convalescent institution. It was a home where the afflicted were loved and refreshed, physically and morally. No one was turned away; the wealthy gladly paid their bills, and often added handsome donations that carried the expenses of the free wards. The poor were cared for without charge or onus and treated as though they too paid their way. They were served all kinds of

113

the incomparable home-style Italian meals and tonic wines. While they recovered, they enjoyed joking in the rich mother tongue with Francesca and her daughters. They played musical instruments and cards and games, sang hymns and recited prayers and litanies with the sisters. The nuns read newspapers and letters aloud to those who were illiterate, and encouraged the patients to help one another and develop friendships among themselves. The sick men and women enjoyed talking of their villages in Italy, of their experiences and problems in America, and of the future. Each Sunday morning, after Confession, they received Holy Communion and the benediction of Mass from a visiting priest, Father Rinaldi. Many of the patients were so happy there that after recovery it became a problem to get them to go home.

Columbus Hospital was firmly under way and in the secure trust of Doctor Keane, his staff, and Francesca's daughters, who had rapidly become natural and wonderful nurses.

At that time Monsignor Charles McDonnel, Archbishop Corrigan's secretary, was elevated to Bishop of the Brooklyn diocese. He was a discerning cleric who had silently befriended Mother Cabrini. Upon becoming bishop he honored her with a signal invitation to open a parochial school for him in Brooklyn. Within weeks she had carried out the new bishop's wish.

Her institute was now twelve vibrant years old, with fourteen houses and 200 daughters. "Like Saint Teresa," she said, "with five pennies and God, I can accomplish many great things." Such a statement was fundamental to her faith and modesty. She never acknowledged her exceptional talents for organization, her aptitude for financial wizardry, or her personal charm and inspiring character. But she knew enough herself about her ability to inspire others so that it was high among her motives for visiting all her houses as often as possible. Though she was in constant correspondence with her daughters everywhere, she felt that there was no substitute for

114

personal contact. Whenever she felt that she could safely leave a completed new project in the hands of a competent superior, and of course, whenever her purse allowed her to travel she would begin to think of visiting other houses. With the new Columbus Hospital under way, and her parochial school in Brooklyn running smoothly, there seemed to be nothing to keep her in New York.

Again she returned to Italy and visited each house. She did not burden her daughters in Italy with tales of the grave financial situations she faced, or of the unforeseen obstacles that would arise, nor did she talk of her chronic, demanding illnesses. Instead, she was serene and smiling. She was determined that her presence as foundress and mother general should not make her daughters feel nervous or inadequate. Never austere or rigid, she moved among them with an amiable and humble simplicity that inspired respect and confidence. When she had to admonish a sister, she did so with the gentlest smile. She was careful not to restrict their individual personalities, or impede their dispositions, and she gathered them closer to her by allowing them to expand upon their sentiments, and encouraging freedom of conversation. She especially enjoyed the young and vivacious daughters. She liked to hear their honest, varying opinions, and help them to form sound judgments. It was of little importance to her if their animated discourses were not spiritual, so long as their arguments were constructive. She particularly delighted in anything humorous, and no daughter could surpass her in the art of the comic.

Presiding at the dinner table, while sipping her wine, she regaled them with funny stories of work in the mission field. She described the cunning parrot in Granada and made light of the privations of their poverty. She told how, on a day when they were ravenously hungry, a kind American woman brought them a savory pot of clam chowder, and they spooned away with pleasure until Sister Maria bit into a tiny piece of salt pork, and then spat it out, signed the cross and exclaimed,

115

"Today is Friday! Oh, Lord, forgive us!" She joked about the ludicrous mistakes she made with the English language. And she mimicked the characters of her tales with such delightful gestures, facial expressions, and tones of voice, that her daughters would put their kerchiefs to their faces and laugh until they were faint.

In her study, poring over business papers and multitudinous details, she was always available to her daughters, even to the least postulant. However inopportune the moment, she patiently listened, advised, and consoled with a cheerful "God bless you, my Daughter."

After all were in bed, and the lamplight out, she would go to her room, lock the door, "and sleep like a baby, for when I lay my head on the pillow, Jesus my Spouse, comes and takes from me to solve for me during the night, the cares of our Missionary Sisters."

During her stay in Italy she enlarged the Rome house to provide a school of advanced education, opened a house near Frascati in Montecompatri, and founded a college in Genoa. In the country of her birth there were two fountainheads of mystic strength for her, the deep meditative well and cloistered quiet of her first House, in Codogno, and the personal affection for her of Christ's Vicar on earth, great Leo XIII, who had reached his episcopal jubilee. Learning from Cardinal Rampolla that she had her heart set upon obtaining a gift from him, Pope Leo sent her a 1,000-lire bill from his private bank. On one occasion, the grand old man, while blessing her with his right hand, pulled her to him with his left, and embraced her. And she said, "Holiness, 'tis the arms of the Church who takes to his bosom the Missionary Sisters of the Sacred Heart."

Two young American girls who had taken their vows in the Codogno convent and were destined for mission in the United States, dearly desired to see the Holy Father. It was the high heat of summer and private audiences had been temporarily suspended. Through Cardinal Rampolla, Francesca arranged to bring her two American daughters to the Vatican gardens, thinking that there they could content themselves by seeing the pope from a distance.

When the aged pontiff was being borne on his litter through the gardens he recognized her, and called out sonorously, "Cabrini! My child, come to me!"

She presented her American daughters to kiss his hand and receive benediction. As she knelt before him, he lovingly put his hand under her chin, raised her eyes to his, and then ardently embraced and blessed her.

"When do you leave for America?"

"In September, Holy Father."

"How many daughters are you taking with you?"

"Twenty-nine this time, and more later."

"And after America, where do you go?"

"I have been asked to open a House in Brazil, Holy Father."

"Brazil! Child, you will then see what a vast field for Christ South America is! Let us labor, Cabrini, let us labor, for paradise awaits!"

"It pleases me to labor for Our Lord, Holy Father." She hesitated, and then asked in a whisper, "But will Paradise receive me?"

"Receive you? Certainly! Paradise was made for all those who work like you! Courage, Cabrini, forward! Work onward until death!"

As his attendants were bearing him through the gardens to his apartment, he turned and called back to her, "Let us work, and God bless you Cabrini. Let us work!"

On an August night in Codogno, during a refreshing spiritual retreat, a daughter handed Francesca a cablegram. She prepared herself with prayer before she began, apprehensively, to open it. Normal and routine news came in letters by carriage, ship, and train. A cablegram could only mean urgency, perhaps disaster. The message was from the daughters of the

Granada house, telling briefly of their expulsion from Nicaragua by revolutionaries, and their flight to San Juan del Norte. To the daughter who had given her the cablegram and stood by anxiously, she said laconically, "Our sisters of Nicaragua have been exiled." She silently prayed, and then instructed, "Wire back that they should make their way somehow to Panama. . . . Perhaps they would be kindly received in Panama."

Francesca had been feeling quite happy over the Nicaragua Foundation. The Granada house had been filled with children of the best families and was progressing. In the three years of its existence, the Daughters there had survived three revolutions and were led to believe that their position was secure. After each fratricidal conflict, owing to the unburied bodies of victims, dread diseases and epidemics followed. Fortunately all her daughters remained free from infection, and through their care not one of their pupils contracted illness.

Within days after the arrival of the cable, Francesca received a lengthy letter explaining the expulsion in detail.

When her daughters of the Granada house thought they were at last safe, there appeared immediate danger because of a new dispute in the Government which arose through the entrance of outsiders who excited the liberals, always easily attracted to rebellion. It would happen just at that time that a rich and worldly young girl, touched by the grace of God, was converted and sought the convent. The local superior could not admit her directly, as she first had to obtain permission from the superior general. The girl had recourse to the missionaries' friend, Donna Elena Arellano, who kept the would-be nun in her home. Meanwhile the young lady's suitor, a revolutionary, and her family and friends, by no means sympathetic to religion, attributed the girl's turning her back upon their way of life not to the workings of grace, but to the persuasion of the missionaries. They violently resented what they considered the interference of the missionaries, and shortly

118

afterwards the sisters heard that they were to be expelled. To ascertain the truth of the rumor, the mother superior called on President Zelaya. He received her and her companion with every mark of esteem. He was loud in praise of the missionaries and promised his protection, which left them with a sense of security. The following week he sent a case of prize books for the pupils, which was accompanied by a letter again promising the sisters every protection.

While the sisters were quietly attending their classes and finishing the sewing of some uniforms for the girls, the new prefect of the city, Señor Pedro Pablo Bodan, and the governor, Señor Rivos, impolitely demanded to see the reverend mother. When she presented herself, they coldly and rudely informed her that the missionaries were to leave the country at once, telling her that a steamer was lying in port awaiting their evacuation.

The mother superior pleaded that two sisters were very ill in bed, but they would not revoke the order; and encircling the house with soldiers so that outsiders could have no access and so that the sisters should not have a chance of appealing to President Zelaya, they commanded outsiders who were within the walls of the convent not to leave until the Sisters had first left.

As soon as the pupils heard the news, they arose in a body against these men, crying and shouting. The parents of the pupils rushed to the convent, but their efforts were in vain. The soldiers had orders to kill any who resisted the expulsion of the sisters. Screams and shouts filled the air. It was a scene of desolation. The prefect remained unmoved. In the midst of the disorder, the sisters serenely prepared the few articles of clothing they needed for the voyage, trying to calm the children and their parents. They were determined to show how calmly they accepted this trial, and they promised to return someday. Two hours later, the prefect called forward the

119

carriages which were to convey the sisters to the steamer. The sisters were surrounded by soldiers who accompanied them to the port.

It was like a funeral cortege, for as the news had spread, a great crowd had collected. The people followed the sisters, crying and begging them to stay. For the sisters to leave their country, they thought, was a sign of God's wrath toward them. They pleaded mercy for their sins. At the port, the soldiers formed a cordon around the sisters to prevent the crowd from following, begging for blessings. The sisters passed one by one, as they had to be counted before embarking. A few minutes later two priests arrived on board. They were the parish priest and the chaplain of the convent. They too were banished. The day before, six other priests had been exiled to the port of Corinto on the Pacific.

Donna Elena Arellano, who had expended so much effort and money on the Granada house and who loved the sisters, felt that she could not let them go without accompanying them. This was forbidden under pain of exile, but she decided to accept the penalty. She remained with them all the time they stayed at San Juan del Norte, until they received the order from Mother Cabrini to continue to Panama and a new mission.

Every vessel that left Granada brought some resident of Nicaragua, who came to bring help and consolation to the sisters. Even the Indians of Rama sent the Sisters a substantial sum of money to tide them in their distress.

When Francesca had heard the details of the expulsion, she lost no time conveying the story to all the sisters in her order.

"Daughters warmly and safely about me, you wonder why our sisters were exiled so savagely from Nicaragua? Do not wonder, for as yet these countries are but little advanced in civilization, and full of disturbances and revolutions. There are a few men there who have studied a bit in Paris, London, Germany, and the United States, and each thinks he knows better than the other. They hold themselves in high repute, not

120

wishing to see at the head of government one whom they think inferior to themselves. Then, they seek to make friends and induce them to follow the same ideas. Thus they work on collectively until they succeed by bloodshed in removing the ruling President and placing in the Presidential chair one of their radical group. Very often, one of these satellites, well grounded in these ideas by the first proud usurper, takes the opportunity of overthrowing the one he had previously helped bring to power; in the same manner does a third tyrant behave, and so they carry on in this way. Sometimes one of them, still more ignorant, and not possessing the wisdom necessary for a ruler, wishes to accomplish something even more spectacular, and endeavors to become famous by persecuting religious men and women, blaming them for the evils they themselves have brought about. This is what ultimately happened to our Daughters in Granada."

"My Daughters, you are in suspense and anxious to know what happened in consequence. God knows how to soothe our wounds, and from news I have recently received, we have reason to praise the Most Sacred Heart Who so honors our Institute with banishment, though it is young, poor and the least in our Holy Church. · -- ·

"The expulsion of our Sisters from Nicaragua not only made an impression on the good, but also on the bad. While the Sisters were walking to the steamer between files of soldiers, a big revolutionary, one Don José Pasos, was watching from horseback. A pupil clinging to a Sister, tearfully said, 'Do not weep because you are forced away from us . . . we will be brave. . . .' Though pale, the sister was tranquil and dry eyed. She kissed the child and showed her the crucifix: 'With our Jesus we came, and with Him we leave.'

"At that moment Don José Pasos was touched by Divine Grace. With sudden shame, he galloped off, and locked himself in his home. He had been one of the worst enemies of the Church, attacking Her by his writings and speeches. Having

121

witnessed our expulsion, he has now become one of God's greatest defenders, and went so far as to refuse public office, rather than sacrifice his return to Faith.

"His answer was that a true man could have nothing to do with a Government so brutal, impious and cowardly, whose heroism consisted in oppressing the weak, stamping on religion, and outraging Sisters, whose sole crime was to instruct innocent youth by means of self-sacrifice. This refusal gave room to much criticism and mockery, and made him many enemies, but nothing could make him fall back. He knew well what he would have to put up with, but he said the example of the Sisters helped him. They being innocent, had suffered so heroically, hence why should he not suffer, who merited punishment for his past misdeeds against the Truth?

"Therefore our expulsion has had one great good result for the inhabitants of Nicaragua. Please God we shall return there some day, but not at present, as the actual government cannot guarantee the privileges and liberty which we require for the success of our work."

One incident occurred during the expulsion that, when she heard of it, brought the sunshine of laughter to her heart:

A young, spirited sister, the last to be ejected from the convent, clutching her bag and about to climb into the carriage manned by the soldiers, recalled that in hastily packing for exile she had overlooked her new slippers. She stubbornly held up the line of exodus until she had gone back to her room in the convent and fetched her cherished slippers.

Thenceforward, Mother Cabrini enjoyed referring to the story of the expulsion as "the legend of the famous slippers," and whenever she issued a list of orders that called for diligent memory, she would recommend with a straight face, "Be so kind as to remember every single thing, Daughter, and leave behind not even your dear slippers."

Years of painful experience with political pressures, and the fortitude born of faith and the love of Christ were to stand her in good stead in the face of another disappointment that was to come hard on the heels of the Nicaraguan trouble.

On September 13, 1894, she and fifteen young daughters embarked from Genoa for New York. Her voyages were interludes of rest and poetic sensations. On that trip she wrote in a letter, "Now as I contemplate the sky and sea I seem to view the portals of Heaven which do not close at the end of day, and there the light which emanates from the Divine Face never fails. In that abode exists neither ignorance nor blindness, for everything is seen in God. Neither are there sorrows or sighs, and the body spiritualized lives in harmony with the soul. Friends, reach there at every instant and render the repose serene and sweet.

"Oh, sublime City, send down your beams of light to these regions of darkness, this shadow of death where we still live.

"Come, Oh Supernatural Light, to reveal to us the beauties of that Blessed Country, and detach us from the miseries of this earth; make our eyes so pure that, through the shining crystal of Faith, they may behold the eternal good which awaits us after a short time of sacrifice and self-conquering. He who fights will be victorious, and to the victor the prize is Heaven."

During her absence from New York, civil and religious groups who failed to appreciate the value of Francesca's work, exerted their various pressures upon Archbishop Corrigan. Some of these groups simply did not comprehend the good the missionaries were doing, and in all innocence saw them as expendable. Others, not so innocent, fully realized that the Missionary Sisters promised real and tangible improvements in the immigrants' position. The practical purpose of opposition was logical, for by keeping immigrants voiceless, debased, socially disenfranchised, and quarantined, they insured the continuance of a cheap and malleable labor force. Rapacious exploitation of immigrant labor had contributed to the accumulation of more than a few huge fortunes.

The day after Francesca arrived in New York, she hastened

to pay homage to Archbishop Corrigan. That same afternoon, in return, she received a surprise visit from him.

Smiling fixedly, he nervously told her that the Columbus Hospital did not have a really valid reason to exist; that it was creating jealousy and irritation in certain influential quarters out of all proportion to its small worth. Next, her schools and orphanages were not required in America and could be disbanded, and her wards and pupils could be better taken care of by other and regular institutions. Finally, he said, she and her missionaries were not actually necessary and would do best to pack up and go back to Italy. He elaborated upon the theme of American antipathy towards such minorities as the Negroes, Jews, and her own Italians, and of the hopelessness of dealing with it. According to him human nature could not be changed, and the most discreet and wise thing she could do would be to accept unpleasant reality instead of wearing herself out flying into the face of ponderous social evils that could only be transformed by generations of time. He finished by saying that he sincerely wished she would abide by his decision and not continue to sacrifice herself in vain.

She received the wounds he dealt silently. Archbishop Corrigan was an old friend. It was he who had so enthusiastically assisted her in the purchase of West Park, he who had rented the old building on White Street, so that her classes might meet in a regular schoolhouse and not in the overcrowded little church of San Gioacchino. He had wept with joy at her successes, consoled her at times when others discouraged her, pledged himself unconditionally to help and support her.

Yet even his opposition could only make her stronger. She studied his friendly, florid face. Under her gaze, his fixed smile wavered. And she pitied him.

His reasons for urging her to give up her mission and return to Italy were the very reasons she had to stay and fight the evils he described as an American. He was terribly wrong, and made her all the more determined. She shook her head.

124

"Excellence, in all humility I must remind you that I gave you my reply the first time I had set foot in America: 'The pope sent me here, and here I stay.' "

After he departed, she went among the young daughters whom she had brought from Italy. It was their recreation period, and they were gay.

"My Daughters," she said with an enigmatic smile, "Can you surmise why the good archbishop came?"

"Of course, Mother," responded a daughter, "to bring to our house his benedictions."

"Benedictions?" she chuckled ironically, "Bless your thought, dear daughter, but, the lovely 'benediction' it pleased him to bring, was the ruinous request that we destroy our house with our own hands and run like unwanted aliens back to Italy."

The daughters were stunned.

"Do not worry, my children," she said with invincible calm, "our Spouse sent us here, and here we stay!"

She was not without the help of a high prelate. At that time the vicar-general of the Archdiocese was Monsignor John M. Farley. Though in the first years in New York he was slow to understand her, they later became staunch friends. She called him, "vicar with the good iron heart," for he was a cleric of frank, resolute, and unshakable character. He did many favors for her immigrants. Not long after her disagreement with Archbishop Corrigan, the Church elevated Monsignor Farley to archbishop. The morning following his episcopal consecration he came to her at Columbus Hospital, made a large donation to the hospital, and said happily, "Heretofore, Mother Cabrini, I have not done all for you that I could have. The Lord wants my heart open for your regard. From now on I shall be to you as a father, and you must come to me in your every need."

She told her daughters, "He is a great man of the Lord, and not Archbishop Corrigan, but Archbishop Farley of the good iron heart will be made cardinal." Some years later her prediction came true.

As she strove to prove to Archbishop Corrigan that her mission belonged in America, Providence provided her with a dramatic opportunity to show the worth of her hospital. An Italian battleship arrived in port with the terrifying news that typhoid had broken out among its crew. Other hospitals, fearing epidemic, refused admission to the stricken sailors. Her Columbus Hospital took them in.

This gallantry quickly resulted in favorable attention from the newspapers. The Italian consul offered Columbus Hospital a contract under which Francesca would care for all Italian seamen requiring hospitalization. The public responded with warm regard for Francesca's nuns. The groups that had sought to destroy Francesca could not interfere with the growth of the hospital, nor prevent well-wishers from making spontaneous donations. Furthermore, the honestly doubtful now saw the particular advantages of an Italian hospital. With typical boldness and vision, Francesca perceived that she could give the hospital a better chance for survival in the long run by expanding it radically than by trying to maintain it at its limited size. With a 6,000-dollar loan from the secretary of her medical board, Dr. Charles Lewis, and a large mortgage from the discerning member of the Emigrant Savings Bank, she bought the old vacant Post Graduate and Clinical Hospital on East Twentieth Street.

The structure had to be repaired and renovated. Though it was a cold February, she and a group of daughters moved into its unheated rooms. During the day they worked manually side by side with the construction men, to save time and money. At night, rain and snow often came through the broken windows of the rooms where they slept.

One night, after a day of strenuous labor, Francesca was surprisingly unable to fall asleep. The thought of Monsignor Serrati came to her, and would not let her rest. Of that night

126

she wrote in a letter to Codogno, "That day I had felt a piercing thrust within to pray especially for him. I could not sleep. Instead of making the accustomed acts of love to which we are obliged, a singular sentiment animated me to leave my bed, with crucifix in hand, go to church and pray and pray the night long."

In the morning she received word of Monsignor Serrati's sudden death. She spent the day before the altar, moist eyed and praying with extraordinary intensity. Then she sat at her writing desk and composed a very long letter to her daughters in Codogno, reminding them of his meaning to the Missionary Sisters of the Sacred Heart, eulogizing his rare virtues, his simplicity, and his loving heart. Oh, dear and sacred memories to be relived only in spirit, of Vidardo when she was a schoolteacher, of the House of Providence, and of the old Franciscan monastry that became the cradle of her institute in Codogno.

But she had little time to give to memories. By her own industry, and by example, she established a notable spirit of concord and cooperation between the factions in the Italian colony. They gave her solid support with the preparation of the hospital, and in March, 1895, the new Columbus Hospital, with more than 100 beds, modern equipment, and an excellent and dedicated medical staff was formally approved by the State of New York.

7 ✠ ✠ ✠

TO FRANCESCA this world was one of her Spouse's wondrous creations, a planet inhabited by His children and
lesser creatures that was but small and contained compared to
her love of Him. Her avowed dream was to cover this earth
with Houses in His name.

Having solidly founded her hospital, she began the long trip
for the new South American ventures she had mentioned
to Pope Leo. She made the journey by way of New Orleans. In
the fascinating languid city that had been the scene of the in-
famous lynching she found to her pleasure that her St. Philip's
Street house was a flowering moral oasis.

Only one thing marred her visit to New Orleans, and that
was the inevitable sense of sorrow over the loss of an old friend.
The good Archbishop Janssens, whose help had meant so
much to the successful founding of her house there, whose
friendly, informal visits had been a source of so much pleasure
to her and her daughters, had died. In the manner of meeting
his death, he had revealed the depth and certainty of his Christian character. He had been traveling by ship to Rome when he
was struck down by a stroke in his cabin. He struggled to his
knees, clasped his hands, and whispered, "My Lord, I thank
thee, for I am ready to die."

Francesca, in her own secure faith, rejoiced at hearing of
the pious consummation of his life, yet she could not help
128

missing his friendly presence. It was to the great good fortune of her Missionary Sisters in New Orleans that the man who succeeded Archbishop Janssens was prepared to be every bit as staunch a friend to the nuns. Archbishop Chapelle had shown himself ready to aid the sisters in every way, and sympathized completely with their merciful work with the despised Italian immigrants. Francesca was almost concerned about the smooth success of her New Orleans venture, feeling that the absence of adversity might not demand from her daughters the fortitude she wished them to have. She was a captain who welcomed a storm now and then to test her courage, for anyone could sail a ship in a kind sea.

After staying twenty-four days with her daughters in New Orleans, she left for Panama.

"I keep my promise to write and describe my little adventures and impressions. I travel, work, suffer my weak health, meet with a thousand difficulties, but all these are nothing, for this world is so small. To me, space is an imperceptible object, as I am accustomed to dwell in eternity."

She expressed a thought on prayer: "One whose soul is in disorder, whose mind is wandering with vain, useless thoughts, cannot pray. To pray we must unite the flesh and its feelings to the soul with its imagination, memory, and will. Oh! if the face of this tiny earth were renewed with Faith and Charity! Pray much without tiring, because the salvation of Mankind does not depend on material success, nor on sciences that cloud the intellect. Neither does it depend on arms and human industries, nor on sterile and diplomatic congresses, nor on worldly means. Pray much, for the conversion of sinners and the sanctification of souls does not depend on human eloquence, or the grace of style and rhetoric, but upon our Spouse Jesus alone, Who enlightens the mind, moves the will, sows virtue, and animates us to undertake perfect works."

On reaching Panama she joyfully embraced her daughters who had been brutally expelled from Nicaragua.

"At the Convent I said blessings to the Sacred Heart for giving me back my Daughters whom for four years I had not seen. After a short rest I was anxious to look over the House which good people had obtained from the Government for our school.

"On the south and southwest our House is surrounded by the sea, whose noble waves beat against the walls of the garden, throwing a spray of water, whiter than milk. From here I imagine I can see every part of the earth. It serves as an object for meditation, and this is not disturbed by the desire I have of taking the first vessel that sails to the places where the need is the greatest. But where shall I go? The calls are many, and if I cannot go to all places where we are needed, I will at least strive to do so until I die."

Taking Sister Chiara with her, she resumed her way to South America. During a frightening tempest she scribbled, "The winds roar, heavens darken, the waves arise and threaten to turn the steamer topsy-turvy. All this matters nothing. I have given my trust, I must keep my word of honor, and with faith and confidence. Difficulties! What are they, Daughters? They are the mere playthings of children enlarged by our imagination, not yet accustomed to focus itself on the Omnipotent. Dangers, dangers! And what are dangers? The spectres that surprise the soul, which having given itself to God, or thinking it has done so, still retains the spirit of the world, or at least many sparks of it, which fly up from the ashes and flare at every gust of contrary wind. 'But I am weak!' Who is not weak? But with God's help you can do everything. He never fails the humble and faithful. 'Yes, but I am so fragile!' We are all fragile, yet, when Christ is our strength, what shall we fear?

" 'I have failed in generosity, I have fallen at the first temptation, now I shall not be able to do anything well.' Who has not been tempted? Who has not somewhere fallen? Have you fallen? Then, humble yourself, and, with a lively act of contrition from the depths of your heart, ask pardon, renew your promises to God, then get on your feet and be doing with more courage than ever to repair your defects!"

Intelligently alert and appreciative of God's works of nature, she writes, "The Cordillera presents a lesson to the Missionary, running as it does for thousands of miles, without fear of seas or atmosphere. It teaches us when it rises toward Heaven with its heights and when it humbles itself, hiding in the waves of the sea. It preaches also when it sends out fire, smoke and lava, adding force to the winds that lash within its gorges. In Boyaca, for instance, especially in the Popayan, to which place we have been invited, it thunders fiercely every day, with lightning that seems to reduce one to ashes. In all this one can very easily find food for pious meditation on death."

In Valparaiso she found the Chilean people gay, open, and loving progress almost to excess. An important man of the republic, after hearing of her schools, bellowed, "Mother Cabrini, you must come back within two years when my baby girl will be ready for learning. If you don't, during the war we have with the Argentines we'll take you prisoner, and then make you open a school here. I want my little girl to receive her education from you!"

There were tedious days by railway to Juneal, and then the preparation for the formidable trek on muleback across the Andes to Argentina. At the dinner table the day before the crossing, her fellow travelers spoke of its dangers. They told stories of fatal mists in the pass, of the air so cold it hurt the eyes and brought on nosebleeds.

"A delightful description, indeed! I felt sorry for timorous Sister Chiara, who wide-eyed, heard all this. But when I asked her which way she preferred to travel, over the Andes or through the Straits of Magellan, she answered, 'A thousand times over the Andes rather than by sea again.' So I said to myself, 'All is well.' "

Given long, brown, fur-lined cloaks, she and Sister Chiara looked like monks. The grizzled old muleteer who was to be her guide reminded her of Saint Joseph. She would not let "Saint Joseph" hoist her atop the mule's back, but climbed onto the saddle from a stool, and made Sister Chiara follow her example.

Higher and higher jogged the mule train up the mountainside through the bitterly cold deep snow on the narrow, winding path. As her mule stubbornly insisted on trodding the very edge of the precipice, she tugged at the reins, and with the few Spanish words at her command, implored it to be careful.

"There was a bottomless abyss on one side, dizzying, snow-covered heights on the other, and in front of us a large crevice, long and deep, ready to bury us. The men grumbled about the imprudence of conducting the caravan by this route, and the women shrieked and wept quite hopelessly.

"Sister Chiara lost her speech. Her appearance of the most ultimate dejection, a picture of the world's end, made me laugh. No matter how often I told her to bravely sit up straight, she lay like a wet sack of flour on the mule's back, her head plunged down in refuge on the little animal's neck. Certainly she now repented having chosen the Cordillera instead of the Magellan Straits for our journey. Her only consolation was that when she raised her head I looked quiet and happy as one enjoying a magnificent spectacle. It was truly grand in all its horror."

But Mother Cabrini was to face her own moments of panic. At one spot the trail was cut directly across by a fearful chasm. In order to continue the journey, there was nothing to do but to cross over. The muleteers tested the possibility by urging a few animals to make the leap. Then it was Francesca's turn, for since she had been honored with the best mule in the train, she was obliged to ride first in the cavalcade as well.

Retaining her customary composure, intending to encourage Sister Chiara, Francesca prepared to leap. But, weakened by the thin air, her stride fell short. Only the quick action of the fatherly muleteer-guide saved her. He caught hold of her and

132

pulled her to safety. Francesca dropped exhausted and faint on the snow. By the time she had recovered from the incident, all her companions had crossed the chasm without further difficulties.

She was ready to continue, and soon regained even her capacity to enjoy the scenery. Having toiled to the mountain peak, she surveyed the vista.

"What a majestic sight! I seemed to view the whole world at a glance!"

Then, a day of slipping and sliding down the perilous mountain paths, resting in a hospice where drunken mountaineers and shepherds caroused the night long, and finally the train that raced across the great untouched Pampas to Buenos Aires.

Her eight-months' stay in Buenos Aires was a pleasant and fruitful experience. Though only ten years old, Buenos Aires was a rich, beautiful city with mansions, homes, businesses, a rapidly growing population, and unrivaled public gardens. Father Brogi, whom she had met in Rome two years previously and who was responsible for her coming to Buenos Aires, presented her to the Church authorities and the principal families.

A Father Kierman devoted himself to her cause.

"He helped us until he saw the Academy on a secure footing. Father Kierman is an exquisite soul, and to extraordinary knowledge he adds an admirable simplicity. He seems to have adapted to himself Our Lord's own words, 'Be simple as the dove and wise as the serpent.' "

At first she had a bit of tribulation; an order of aristocratic nuns were disturbed by her earthy, realistic energy, and feared that in some strange way she would damage their particular efforts.

"The devil has neatly studied the nature of things here— giving these dear fastidious Sisters a certain mistaken concept of me, and thus, I prayed Jesus to get the 'Old Beast' off my back."

She covered the various parishes on foot in her search for a house, looking at sixty houses in three weeks, "Sister Chiara and I returning at night with aching heads and indescribable fatigue."

At the exact spot where her shoes fell apart and prevented further walking, she found the house proper to all her needs.

She immediately sent for daughters from Codogno and New York.

Father Brogi had misgivings about her swift, sweeping decisiveness. He wondered that she dared to purchase an extensive property and send for nuns before stabilizing her project with pupils and funds. She answered that if she had waited for secure and comfortable conditions before launching her works, none of her houses would have been established.

Until the new daughters arrived she took care of the sickly Sister Chiara and she herself tended to the household chores. Calling upon her unexpectedly, Archbishop Castellano found her furiously scrubbing the entrance. She looked like any good housewife, with her apron, dust cap, and smudged face. Pretending not to recognize her, he pompously asked to be announced to the mother superior. She laid aside her pail and scrubbing brush, arose, curtsied, and led him into the salon, saying humbly, "Your Eminence, please be so kind as to excuse me while I notify Mother Cabrini." Within minutes she washed, changed her clothing, and accompanied by Sister Chiara, re-entered the salon, exclaiming, "Archbishop Castellano! What an honor! And what a delightful surprise to say the least! Has Your Eminence been waiting long?"

On March 1 her Academy of Saint Rose opened. Soon so many pupils applied for entry that she had to send for more daughters.

It was time to return to her houses in Italy to visit and encourage her daughters there. Taking an Argentinian postulant with her, she left for Italy on August 8, 1896.

134

Passing the equatorial line, they saw the Pinedo de San Pedro rock. At sunset this bird sanctuary seemed a pretty, sailing, city.

"The little angel, my companion, hoped that some day we would establish a Mission there. I asked her if she wanted to convert the sea gulls, who are the only created things that find an asylum there, but she insisted we might find a human being there to convert. Well, of course, she wants to convert the whole world, not missing a single person. And in the fervor of her desire, she appears to have the faith of Abraham, who merited to see his spiritual children multiply like the sands of the sea."

When they were in view of the African coast, she said to her young companion, "Oh, right now, if I had real wings like a bird, I would fly to the land there and open missions. I yearn so to do it. But this cannot be done during my lifetime, and there is too much to be done in the Americas. May God bless and save those good black peoples, our brethren, and their pure white souls."

The world-famed poet and author Gabriel D'Annunzio was on board ship. Learning who she was from other passengers, he introduced himself and invited her to dinner at the captain's table. The brilliant and philosophically tormented author engaged her in a storm of conversation touching upon history, literature, science, God, and man. When he went beyond reason, as she thought, she kept silent for a moment. Then, with kindness and firmness, she affirmed the Christian truths. Slowly, without his noticing it, she induced him to approve what was right according to the standard of truth, justice, and the will of God, and to acknowledge that real happiness was to be found in God alone. Their spirited discussions continued for days. On one occasion, as they were standing at the ship's rail, he candidly confessed that he knew he was a sinful man. But, he said, in order for him to become converted to the better life she suggested and hoped for him, he would have to suffocate

135

and extinguish the whole ardor of his soul and the vehemence of his human and creative passions, and so would have to reduce himself to the condition of a mountain of ice, indifferent to all things, even what was to him the most beautiful and great.

She pointed out to him that the flames of human passions, which always left a void and a sense of dissolution, became changed into celestial flames through grace, and that the supernatural light of heaven, once let into the soul, grew so wonderfully that the human passions became a volcano of divine love, a most real fire that nobody could extinguish.

Telling of her talks with D'Annunzio in a letter to her daughters, she wrote, "Have we not had the brightest examples of the conversions of the human passions for our Christ in this direction—a Magdalen, a Paul, a Constantine, an Augustine? Did they become mountains of ice after their spiritual conversion? Quite the contrary. We should never have had these prodigies of conversion and marvelous holiness if they had not changed the flames of human passion into volcanoes of immense love of God. But the generation of the modern times is too miserable, unfortunate, and stunted of soul. It lives and dies for vanity, spurious pleasures and shoddy goods; it studies anything and everything but religion, and meanwhile, runs with the velocity of a train toward a ruinous precipice. Oh, dear Jesus, what a terrible ruin! Daughters, pray with me for the modern world and say, 'But in Thy mercy turn not Thy face away from them. Arise, great giant of love, arise and redeem these children, O, my Beloved!' "

In grave need of rest, she went to the novitiate of Codogno, where, with 150 daughters, she made her retreat, lasting ten days. In retreat she recruited spiritual strength.

"Remember always," she wrote to her American daughters, "and impress it also on all you have to instruct, that purity of intention in our actions is the life and the value of the same, and is the way to open up the incalculable good which we shall find written in the Book of Life."

It is July, 1898, and she tells of her being with aged Leo XIII.

"He inquired about America, and I told him our Gesu and the crucifix we wear preceded us to success in all our efforts there. 'Child,' he asked, 'where do you fly to now, who calls for you now?' I responded, 'Holy Father, in Paris and London they have asked for Missionaries of the Sacred Heart. There I go to explore in His Name, and back to America.' 'Ah,' sighed the pontiff, 'England, that once was the Isle of Saints, and which through the carnal passions and pride of its king lost the Faith. Go there, child, for England is precious to my heart. But, you are in poor health; how can you undertake so much more labor? I am strong, and I could not do it. It is true that I am very old, but I am still much stronger than you.' The affability with which he deigned to speak to me encouraged me to remark that, as I was his spiritual daughter, I possessed his moral strength which enabled me to go round the world, and I was sure I should not lose that strength by serving dear Jesus Who chose me to be a Missionary of His Sacred Heart.

"Then, putting both hands on my head, he showered blessings upon me, telling me to pray for him, as his heart was overwhelmed with sorrow on account of the revolutions prevalent in many countries. God has spoken through him, so let his blessings be the light that leads us through danger and difficulty!"

It was August, and for the seventh time she left Rome for the West, this time traveling by way of Paris and London. On the twentieth of August she arrived in Paris, and was received in the bountiful care of the best friend of her St. Philip's Street house, Archbishop Chapelle of New Orleans, who was visiting France. With the help of an American lady, Countess Spottiswood Mackin, and a large donation from the French Cardinal

137

Richard, she was able to found an orphanage by October in the Rue Dumont d'Urville. Having satisfied her profound wish for a house in France, she left Paris on October 27th, prepared to indulge a second dream: that of setting foot upon the soil of the great civilized English people.

Surely a part of her enthusiasm for visiting Great Britain was the result of her association with Pope Leo XIII. From the earliest years of his Papacy, Leo had shown the greatest interest in the English people. In his affectionate regard for the country that had led Europe in the development of democratic government, so noble an achievement in Leo's eyes, he had lavished attention on the accomplishments of England's Catholics, striving to encourage the Church in that predominantly Protestant country. In a single stroke, soon after his own election, Pope Leo had aroused the enthusiastic support of the whole English speaking world by making John Henry Newman, a simple English priest who had been born Protestant, a cardinal of the Church.

Francesca's few days stopover in London thrilled her. She was amazed at the friendliness of British clerics, and particularly delighted at the gracious manners of the people at large. Even the humblest working people she encountered in the street showed, she thought, remarkable consideration. She told her daughters in America, "I was astonished by the patience and gentleness of the British people. In other countries they boast much of nobility and courtesy, in London they practice it." She determined to return to England some day and plant the banner of her institute there.

By November, 1898, she was once more in New York. Various churches were applying to the Missionary Sisters of the Sacred Heart for the establishment of parochial schools, offering classroom space. She arranged to set up schools in rapid order in the New York parishes of The Transfiguration, Saint Rita, and Our Lady of Pompei. But in the Bronx she had to

138

rent a large old factory to use as a schoolhouse, and in Newark, New Jersey, she selected two vacant stores for the purpose. After paying the first month's rent the sisters in Newark had only sixty cents with which to face the future.

The dynamics of her philosophy was to start a school and set it in motion regardless of the lack of facilities and funds, for motion, she had discovered, begot motion. She knew that once parents of a parish had a Catholic school for their children, they would not fail it. She knew what she was doing, for she could plainly see the future. Her daring was appealing. Her program offered what the unorganized parishes needed most besides the celebrant and altar stone; the training of the children. Soon after she opened a school, the purses of the rich and poor loosened, banks gave reasonable loans, members of the parish and the clergy rose to the responsibility she placed upon them, and their united efforts produced benches, desks, books, and operating capital. Rarely if ever has a parochial school been allowed to fail by its parish.

The name "Mother Cabrini" began to sound like music to the ears of the clergy and civil authorities, and of all Italians as well. There never was, nor has been since, a woman in all America like Mother Cabrini. Americans, witnessing the accomplishments of the communities rising under her influence— a hospital, orphanages, schools, religious and social centers— slowly began to respect the immigrants, and to cast aside ignorant prejudices.

In 1899 she was summoned for a mission in a new territory every bit as awful as New York had been, if not worse—Chicago. Father Morechini of the Servite Fathers wrote asking her to found a school in his parish of the old Church of the Assumption. In May of that year she went to Chicago with fourteen daughters. There, at least, Father Morechini's cooperation had paved the way in one regard, for he had a splendid building ready. Her problem was to organize students and

139

faculty. During the careful process she came to know Chicago, which she saw as a huge, raw human field, gravely needing Christ.

Diligently, she explored in relentless detail the ugly anatomy of social evils, for experience and her own intuition had taught her how important an understanding of the immigrants' problems was to those who would combat them. Before she founded a house, she studied the significant aspects of a city, interviewing the various human strata, walking miles and learning by seeing the causes and effects of the immigrants' problems. Chicago presented to her acute vision the classic pattern of immigrant life in the New World. It housed some ten Italian colonies, each joined with the colony of another race.

Following the Civil War, Chicago, the "gem of the prairie," with a spontaneous mania for commerce and speculation, developed into a great city, second only to New York. It was the foremost grain mart, lumber market, heavy-manufacturing center, and meat-packing center of the world. As its factories spread, its demands for cheap, hardy labor became more and more voracious. Railroads, bridges, tunnels, canals, ships, ports, and mines were rising on every side, and their building required an ever-increasing flow of strong back and limbs.

After the great fire of 1871, most of Chicago's working class living areas were hastily rebuilt by rent profiteers. Caring little for safety, durability or comfort, these builders created a squalid forest of wooden tenements, which became home for Italians and other immigrant nationalities, as well as Negroes migrating from the South. In the neighborhood of old Hull House, Italians were cheek by jowl with Jews and Greeks. Among the stockyards of the South Side, they were thickly mingled with Croatians, Russians, and Lithuanians, and they shared the Pullman district with Poles and Mexicans.

Francesca visited Italian homes in all these areas. She talked with breadwinners on their jobs, and learned from them the grim, dark truths of their existence. Home was a small flat in a
140

dilapidated multiple dwelling. Invariably there were three buildings, a front, middle, and rear, cramped on a shoestring lot, and narrow alleys separated row on row of deteriorated jerry-built wooden tenements. The plumbing usually consisted of a single water tap in the hallway for a dozen large families, and the common toilet was a hopper-trough in the hallway, in an earthen-paved basement, or under the sidewalk. Occasionally there was an outhouse in the cramped yard. The alleyways were choked with garbage, decomposing animal and vegetable matter, dead cats and dogs, and toilet overflow. The unspeakably offensive odors combined with the stench of the slaughterhouses, stockyards, stables, and the ever-lowering factory smoke.

The vermin were uncontrollable; mothers did not dare leave their infants for a moment because of the savage rats, and families slept with guns under the beds to shoot the rats in the night. Food had to be kept in tin boxes or hung by string and wire from the ceiling.

With the sweltering heat in the congested tenements, typhoid and impetigo were summer's gifts. During winter, rheumatism and tuberculosis blossomed in the bone-damp, freezing rooms, while pneumonia visited at random. Asphyxiation from faulty coal stoves and kerosene heaters in the airless rooms, and tragic flash fires took a heavy toll as well. In the factories where the immigrants worked, the loss of limbs or of life itself was an everyday occurrence.

Children left school to help the family, and went to work side by side with men in the factories, sweatshops, and stockyards. Mothers and daughters did finishing clothing work at home to add pennies. Women and children wandered about the pestiferous city dumps hoping to supplement their meager supply of furniture and fuel. Children were sent to bring back the gleaning of coal along the railroad tracks. The spilled grain about the elevators was salvaged for livestock that was kept in yards or basements or under stoops.

Immoral houses and narcotics pushers were often next door or across the hall from a hardworking, decent Italian family which was doing its utmost to maintain Christian standards and to raise the children without degenerating contacts. Through the flimsy walls could be heard the obscene language of the "sporting women" and their clientele. Or next door to a family might be a group of unmarried laborers, many of whom had ignorantly acquired venereal diseases.

The taking in of lodgers and boarders was widespread. The wife of the workingman, eager for some way to augment the inadequate wage of her husband, always welcomed the extra income gained by providing beds for her husband's fellow workers.

Beds and cots jammed the small, unventilated rooms, with just a curtaining sheet between family and lodgers. The lodger evil, with its lack of privacy, often led to the sad profanation of the home.

The flesh and labors of the immigrant were victimized, and all he could cling to as his own was his faith. That alone could help him to endure, to survive, to struggle with dignity up to his rightful place. No one perceived this with more depth of understanding and compassion than Francesca Cabrini. She knew for certain that wherever there was a priest, a church, wherever a parish was being created, wherever the Missionary Sisters of the Sacred Heart were, there Italian-American life grew vigorously. From all sides came goodness, came people willingly, feeling safer under the protective wings of the parish and with their own shepherd.

Though the mission of hospitals was undeniably the prime expression of mercy, the labor dearest to her, and which she deemed most profound of all, was the education and upbringing of children. They were the flowers of heaven, and the innocent faces of orphans and pupils were to her the mirror of God. Her greatest hope was for the new generation. Children rightly educated, she thought, were so many soldiers, who would do battle against the evils their parents had suffered.

142

On many occasions she would slip into a classroom, take over the teacher's desk, and whatever the subject, carry on the class. She could make of any subject a romantic and beautiful thing. When she left, she would remark with a smile to the admiring teacher, "My Daughter, that is the way to gather God's beloved little fish into your net of learning. Be so kind as not ever to forget, that I was a full-fledged and licensed schoolteacher long before I was admitted into the religious profession."

She wanted each daughter to be a true mother, an exemplar Madonna on earth to the orphans and pupils, and would not suffer the children to experience harsh words, castigation, corporal punishment, or humiliation. She emphasized that only goodness should be showered upon children, for time could never cancel out impressions received by the young. In the little girls of the day she saw the ladies, the wives, and mothers of the morrow. She trained her daughters to guard the girls against unseemly manners, degrading companions, idleness, indecent books, and inane amusements. It gave her joy to watch the children at the sports of baseball, tennis, and croquet. With her funny English, she made the girls laugh by persistently pronouncing hockey as "hawkey." Often when she was not too tired or ill, she would take a position in a game and gaily play.

Choral singing festivals and dramatic moral presentations by the girls gave her pleasure and relaxation. She stressed that girls should be taught the dignity of labor and the practical values of domestic ability and economy. As for the difference between educational quality and quantity, she used to say, "It is better to teach a few rightly than many wrongly, for the properly educated girl is the first link in a chain of interminable good."

In one of her directions she wrote, "My Daughters, in your hands are the new generations. As educators you are obliged to form not only Christians for the glory of Christ and perpetuation of Holy Church, but also solid, patriotic citizens for the prosperity of the Nation and the felicity of the family. Thus, it

143

is yours to mold the decorum of spirit, State, family, and society."

To Father Morechini's delight she filled the school of the Church of the Assumption with 700 children. It was obvious to her that Chicago, with its vast numbers of poor immigrants, needed more of her houses, and before leaving she laid out preliminary plans for an orphanage and a possible hospital.

Not every immigrant was submissive to his exploiters and content to work for wages. An ambitious and imaginative element dared to start small businesses of their own, and in the course of time became affluent. The children of the rich as well as of the poor were in danger of drifting from the faith in the New World. When Francesca got back to New York, she found a new call ready for her. A group of wealthy families came to her and wanted her to open a private school for their daughters. With the wealthy families underwriting all the expense and paying handsome tuition in advance, it was simple for her to fulfill their wish, and in August of that year, 1899, she was able to purchase an estate on 190th Street and Fort Washington Avenue. After making suitable alterations on the property, she opened her first private school in America, the Sacred Heart Villa Academy. Then, immensely tired and ill, Francesca left New York for a long journey during which she planned to visit all of her houses outside of America.

September 2, 1899.

My dear Daughters:

As soon as I had finished waving my handkerchief to the Sisters, I sat on a deck chair, and fell asleep. When I awoke I could not persuade myself that I was alone with Mother Virginia. It was only then I realized that I was far away from the Sisters and felt the sorrow of separation from them. It seemed to me that I still had a word to say to one Sister, to give counsel to another, to suggest something to a third, but already the ocean had isolated me from everyone, while the rainy weather seemed to make me feel sadder. Reflecting upon my vocation as a Missionary, I remembered that I ought not to allow sadness to take hold of me. So I

144

entered into the Heart of Jesus, where I saw all the Sisters, and though I could not speak to them, I asked the Sacred Heart to tell each of them what I had forgotten, or what I had not time to say.

This is the second night I had spent on board the *Touraine,* and still the fatigue which gnawingly clings to me, left me indisposed. I awoke many times, and it took me several minutes to know where I was, for I still imagined I was in New York, and that it was time for me to get up to go on with the work of the Missions which I had begun, and which you, with indefatigable zeal, should continue. I was unsettled by anxiety, for that old man, the devil, has made use of every strategy against me for several months past, even setting the most ridiculous obstacles in my way. But by the grace of God I did not allow it to conquer me.

"When I am on the spot I shall work with might and main, but when Obedience calls me away to work elsewhere, I must leave without worry the previous work, trusting in Jesus that he will give help and energy to the Sisters who have to go on with the work which I have left interrupted. Troubles should never frighten the Spouse of Christ, but render her steadfast. Do not be discouraged by repulses and contradictions, but always go forward with the serenity of the angels, keeping to your path despite every contrary influence. When things are easy, all appears to smile, but difficulties prove where there is fidelity and constancy. Question yourselves well at the two examinations of conscience every day. See if you allow inordinate affections to predominate, and if you behave as you should when exposed to winds, no matter how much they serve to flatter your imagination and desires. Let your lives be a perennial sacrifice of yourselves in behalf of the human race. Oh! the law of love is so beautiful!

"In closing, I must tell you—I'm like a fish—as sick as I am, I feel better on sea than on land."

Disembarking in Le Havre, her first goal was her Paris house, which she found thriving. Having satisfied herself that all was well there, she gave herself a beautiful day, devoted in reverence before the shrine of Bernadette, at Lourdes, and then set out for Madrid.

There were two reasons for her trip to Spain, the land of her dear and cherished Saint Teresa: she had need to gather Spanish postulants to mold into daughters for her South American missions, and she was responding to a call from Queen María Cristina to found an orphanage for the tragic children of officers and soldiers who had lost their lives fighting the Americans during the recent Spanish-American War. Within a few trying months, after tactfully contending with the vain Spanish royalty and temperamental churchmen, she established a college in Madrid and an orphanage in Bilbao. With that, she left for a sojourn in her beloved Italy.

8 ✝ ✝ ✝

IT WAS 1900.

In the year that marked the birth of the world-changing and fateful twentieth century, Francesca Xavier Cabrini reached the age of fifty. Her face, increasingly more purified, retained its pristine youthfulness, but the limited fount of her health was diminishing. Often her weariness was such that she could hardly command her limbs. Not infrequently fever gripped her to a point seeming beyond endurance, and, alone in her room, she would whisper,

"My Spouse, my very own Jesus, I await Thy desire of me with the ardor of a fresh new bride. But, oh, I have done nothing for Thee. Oh, I know I have not done sufficient on earth for Thee."

Again in Italy, instead of taking a well-earned rest, she plunged on to enlarge the scope of her native missions, opening a chapel and a school in Rome, an orphanage in Mariscano, Convents in San Raffaele and Citta della Pieve, and, in Turin, an exclusive academy for upper-class girls and a sanatorium for her ailing daughters.

The problems of becoming a missionary nun, founding an order, and gaining a lasting foothold for her institute, were all behind her. Although those problems had been discouraging at times, they had been inspiring and invigorating. She would now have to face the more nerve-wracking problems of

147

maintaining the elaborate network of institutions she had already founded. With many houses on different continents, the difficulties of sustaining her organization were multiplied. Her solution to these problems was typical of her. Further expansion was the only way to avoid deterioration. As foundress and organizer she could never be satisfied with past and present accomplishments. While she would be sure to deal with the maintenance of existing missions in person, her plans must always run ahead of the number of nuns available, the amount of money at hand, and the approval even of those who supported her aims but who could not keep apace of her. She saw the heroic hardships of establishing new missions as the best antidote to weakness and stagnation. And it is possible she realized her institute would achieve its greatest proportions during her lifetime.

Before leaving Italy she took with her the ever-treasured blessings of Leo XIII. With a group of prelates she was performing before him the rite of genuflection. The ninety-year-old pontiff, impatient to have her by his side, bade her arise, beckoning to her and exclaiming with ringing voice, "Come to me, come to me, Cabrini."

"Holy Father," she said as she approached, "How did you recognize me—how did you know 'twas I among the others?"

"Know you?" he echoed keenly, "Not perceive before me my own true daughter? I know you. You are the one who has the spirit of God to bring to the whole world!"

As she stood before him, she responded humbly, "I want the whole world for the Heart of Jesus."

"The Heart of Jesus!" cried the pontiff exultingly. "Deepest in my heart is this devotion. The Heart of Jesus is the hope of the world! Cabrini, I say to you, you are the instrument of God. He has elected thee to propagate this devotion!"

Then this Pontiff of universal mind and moral grandeur clasped her, warmly asked questions about her American missions, and repeated again and again with vibrance, "God has

148

elected thee. He is with thee wherever thou goest. Cabrini! God has elected thee!"

And priceless were the words of Christ's vicar on earth to her.

On November 30, 1900, she went aboard the *Alphonsus* at Genoa, bound for Buenos Aires. It proved to be a festive day. A large number of daughters and girls from her Genoa house accompanied her in launches to the ship, which lay anchored in the bay. In the salon, the children took over the piano and other orchestral instruments and played her a heartening farewell.

The *Alphonsus* was scheduled to sail at one, and from the fort of Genoa cannon shots signaled noon. The daughters and girls reluctantly descended the gangway to the launches. But at one o'clock Mother Cabrini learned the ship was to be delayed a day for extra cargo loading. She hastened to the ship's rail, and seeing two daughters still lingering upon the shore, she hallooed to them the information. Their response caused her much amusement. "They became so excited that it was quite a wonder they did not try to walk the waters as Our Lord did, to get back to my ship again."

A group of daughters happily returned by small boat to the ship.

"The Captain, moved by the affection of the Sisters for me, said they could remain all night. The Sisters did not need to be asked twice, and so, though they will never have a mission outside Italy, they stayed at least one night of their lives on board a ship."

The first stop the *Alphonsus* made was at Barcelona. Among the passengers who came aboard was a Latin-American priest whom she knew, Father Terradas. He had returned from Panama only a few weeks before. From him she learned dark news of her daughters in Panama, the same daughters who had been brutally expelled from Nicaragua. Father Terradas told her that her Panama daughters were under extreme

149

duress there because of the revolution and civil wars that had been raging for the past three years.

In their scarce communications her daughters had bravely spared her the harrowing facts. At the risk of their lives they gave Christian asylum to the hunted innocent, nursed the wounded of all factions, and even made placating scapulars of the Sacred Heart with the word "Cease" on them to give to the sick and the blood-maddened soldiers. The four horsemen of the Apocalypse galloped unimpeded in the wake of the murderous strife, with bounties of yellow fever, typhoid, smallpox, and the bubonic plague. Notwithstanding the merciful fact that her daughters saved many lives and ministered and consoled without question, the various factions held them suspect, deprived them of ordinary necessities, and kept them at the edge of starvation.

Knowing now the truth of their circumstances, she would not have them sacrifice themselves further, and immediately cabled, "Turn your backs upon Panama even as Lot turned his back upon Sodom and Gomorrah. Shake that evil dust from your heels, and manage to join your Sisters in Argentina, where I will greet you."

At the Malaga stopover, the passengers went ashore, buying the raisins of Malaga to take to Buenos Aires. While the tourists went into sophisticated shops where they had to pay more for the box than the raisins, Francesca fixed her eyes on a donkey which was descending a nearby mountain, loaded with the celebrated grapes. In the evening everyone else returned to the ship with elegant boxes, while she carried a rustic basket and an abundance of raisins acquired for pennies. At table someone offered her a bottle of wine, and she, wishing to reciprocate, sent to her cabin for one of the bottles of wine her daughter Mother Augustine had packed for her.

"They asked me if it was Malaga wine. 'Yes, of course,' I replied, 'My bottle is in Malaga, is it not?' " They enjoyed my joke, drank the wine, and were surprised at its exquisite taste,

150

especially the Bishop of Montevideo. They could scarcely believe that such good wine came from my own dear Lombardy."

In a letter written aboard ship she could not help but speak of her habitual illness, "my faithful old friend that never leaves me" and the bone-aching fatigue that drained her. But on the day of the Immaculate Conception, her poetic contemplation of mankind's Mother renewed her spirit, and she added to her message, "Today I feel better because it is the Madonna's day."

Not long after she arrived in Buenos Aires her Panama daughters succeeded in getting there too. She received them joyfully, as though they had returned from the inferno. Taking them to her, she sighed, "Oh, my Daughters, did you think you would never see your mother again? But how pale and thin you have become. Your mother must restore you in body and spirit. We must pray for the souls of the godless who have afflicted you; how right is our great Holy Father in Rome who tells us modern man is racing toward the precipice and the abyss, for the learning of man today is the school of death and destruction." And she listened with heavy heart to the bitter experiences of her Panama daughters.

In weighing the advent of the Twentieth Century, no interpretation could so cleave the blind and culpable core of our age as her words. "Daughters, how sad it is to see those who, through their own most grievous fault, have allowed the darkness of incredulity to gather around them. We have occasion to feel great sorrow in seeing men who, after abandoning the Catholic religion, after having rebelled against Jesus Christ, reach the precipice of Atheism, Pantheism, and Materialism. 'There is no God,' the first say. 'There is no difference between good and evil,' the second say. 'There is nothing better than to accumulate riches by all possible means, and give way to pleasure,' exclaim the last. By means of their egos and insensate theories they have upset the world, and many have

151

lost their good reason. From such errors have come all the misfortunes that affect the present and menace the future.

"No! The faith of the common people is not to be despised. They may not be able to express why they believe, they may not know how to defend their belief, but they do know the reason of their faith. How many illiterate souls, by reason of the purity of their hearts, have raised themselves to God in sublime contemplation, thus showing that those mysteries that are superior to science and to the mind are not superior to the greatness of the human heart!

"No! the mind does not understand the mysteries of our Holy Faith, but the heart, that has the gift of faith, feels rather than understands that they are the mysteries of love. We are the children of God. He has deigned to enrich us with all that is necessary to obtain our temporal and eternal felicity. Let us pray that we and all creatures may give glory to God in time and eternity, that His most holy law may reign and govern us and all men from one end of the Universe to the other!"

Her seven months in the Argentine were fruitful. The Buenos Aires school was paying for itself and expanding. The Argentines were anxious for more of her houses and brought ample funds to her. She was able to place her daughters who had suffered in Nicaragua and Panama in three new houses, in Flores, Rosario, and Villa Mercedes.

Then, like the titan who, in his battles became strong every time he fell upon the earth, Francesca, ill and downed with vast weariness, sailed for the land of Rome that was her holy renewing earth. She was invalided in Rome for weeks until one day, the ninety-two-year old Leo XIII, ever concerned for her health, sent her a basket of oranges especially picked from his private Vatican grove. The beautiful fruit was symbolical to her, as though coming from the hand of her Spouse to the hand of His vicar and thence to her. Soon after she had eaten some of the oranges she left her bed and went to the

152

pontiff. This proved to be the final time on earth that she was privileged to see her staunchest friend.

Refreshed and eager for more missions, she summoned a whirlwind energy. She visited all her Italian houses and the House in Paris. Swiftly, she established her first English house in Brockley, outside of London. Then she set sail once again for the United States, her most fertile field, to take up again the mission entrusted to her by her beloved pontiff.

The founding of her Houses were not performed by magical means. Her efforts were zealous and methodical alike. Cutting the cloth to fit the time, she applied herself practically to the conditions of the age in which she lived. She did not have to create a missionary field; it was here waiting for her. The need for Italian-speaking nuns, in the unorganized immigrant colonies was critical and ripe. After her first houses in New York had demonstrated the special worth of her institute, dioceses in other states gladly invited her to open houses. It was a period of unparalleled development in American history. The face of the United States was changing from day to day. The automobile industry was newly born, and electricity, oil production, communication, transportation, land speculation, commerce, and construction of every kind, were advancing rapidly. It was the age of the booming materialism and abuse of labor that invoked Pope Leo's immortal encyclical *Rerum Novarum*, the Christian Magna Carta of Labor. But, in justice to the times, it must be acknowledged that, with all the material expansion, hearts then were open. Philanthropy was not institutionalized, and rich men were often spontaneously generous. Many a self-made man, remembering his own tenement childhood and struggles, or abased poverty in Europe, gave Francesca large donations for her missions. Without the gallant help of wealthy men and women, the existence of many of her houses would have been impossible.

Not all immigrants had settled in the Eastern cities. Great

numbers of the more adventurous made their way west. There were large concentrations of Italians in the mining and agricultural industries and cities of Colorado, California, and Washington. The limited parishes and priests pioneering these colonies were grievously overburdened and needed schools and teachers.

In July, 1902, Francesca was on her way to found a school in Denver, which then had the sole diocese in Colorado, a state whose area exceeded that of Italy. Bishop Matz of Denver had requested her aid, writing to her of the good her missionaries could do in the Italian mining colony there.

Soon after she arrived in Denver, Bishop Matz gave her the old church on Palmer Avenue to convert into her school. Once the renovations were under way, she was anxious to visit the mine-working fathers of the school's future pupils. She journeyed by zig-zagging railway up over the brilliantly colored mountainous masses of rock and down through the canyons to the gold mines. She and her daughters entered cage hoists and descended deep into the man-made labyrinths, walking by candlelight through miles of low shafts to reach the miners.

Men, fathers of families, stripped to the waist, sweated and begrimed, the muscles of powerful arms and shoulders straining with pick and bar and shovel against gold-flecked ore, hear the music of a woman's voice. They turn and to their amazement see before them in the shadowy tunnel a fragile, smiling nun. She holds aloft her silver crucifix.

"My good brothers, we come down into the bowels of the earth to you in the name of your Creator, He Who pines for your filial love."

Nuns braved the treacherous depths to come to the men, addressing them in the sweet mother tongue and bringing them the faith of their dear Jesus, the Jesus of their childhood, the very Jesus of their ancestors and progenitors, the saddened Jesus whom, in America, they had forgotten.

154

The hearts of these men expanded so that at first they could not speak. They removed their caps, humbly kissed the crucifix in Francesca's hands, knelt, and signed the cross.

The presence of Francesca Cabrini and her daughters in the treacherous underground caverns where they labored seemed miraculous. Angels, brides of Heaven, had come to them in their daily, long darkness, and that visit they would cherish in prayer and memory to the end of their days.

Lodging was arranged for the nuns so that they could remain a few days to commune with the men. After work the men prepared Italian food and a sip of wine for them. Changed to clean clothes, their rugged faces scrubbed, hair and mustaches brushed, the immigrant miners reverently gathered about their Italian sisters in the dining shanty, to hear of the parochial school she would bring to Denver for their families. And each, in his dialect, spoke of his life. They told of dangerous work, of frequent maiming injuries and the destitution that resulted, of fatal accidents that left uncared-for widows and orphans. They described their years devoid of sacraments and religious guidance, years of corrosive isolation from families, of animal-like subsistence in bunkhouses. They complained of fraudulent labor contracts, petty exactions, and exorbitant charges for board, tobacco, and workclothes in the wage accounting.

How strange and wonderful it was for the men to whisper long-unsaid prayers with her and her daughters in the rude, womanless mining camp, and to know that at last God had sent inspiration through her to their souls.

Before she departed from a camp, the miners would voluntarily make up a purse for her mission, and promise to come to the church in Denver with their families.

Commenting upon man's perilous efforts to wrest the yellow metal from the earth, Francesca wrote in a letter to her daughters,

"Man avidly seeks the wrong gold. When will the children

155

of God learn that the smallest act sanctified by a pure intention, is the richest gold, and deposited where thieves cannot steal?

"It is important for our Daughters to visit the mines and see with their own eyes the awful labors men go through for temporal gain. Under the earth our Daughters remind the men of their families and religious duties, comfort them in their miserable conditions, and always leave them happier, or at least more resigned to their poverty. The fatigues of our Daughters climbing up the steepest mountains and going down through the terrifying mine tunnels are rewarded by the smiles which light the faces of the brave hard-working men on hearing their Italian language resounding gently and gracefully in those black vaults. Do you want to know the fate of most miners? The miner toils away from the sun year after year until old age and incapacity creeps over him, or until a landslide, poisonous gas or an explosion or drowning or an accident of some kind ends the life of the miner, who then does not need a grave, being buried in the one he has lived in most of his life.

"Oh, if the voice of religion at least could reach these poor men, and teach them to make holy and noble such arduous work, and to render it fruitful for Eternity, what a boon it would be for them!

"Thus you see the tremendous responsibility resting on those who take away the gift of faith from the working classes, for in so doing they rob them of every hope of the future life, banishing the love of God from their hearts. Take away the supernatural principles and dictates of our Holy Faith, and what remains but wickedness and the indulgence of every passion? Pray, my good Daughters, that the number of Missionary workers may be increased, and that they may be really zealous and good-hearted, because the efforts of such are capable of arresting the materialism and unbelief which,
156

like a most subtle ether, infiltrates itself everywhere, causing immense and irreparable damage."

November 19 was a lovely day, with the sun's rays sparkling on snow-covered Denver. As the 200 children dressed in white were taking their places in the center of the old church, Francesca Cabrini said admiringly, "The wealth of the future is not in the gold of the hills but in these our precious children, who certainly are living gems of the best quality, though at present they are rather rough and unpolished." The two side aisles were crowded with parents. In the center was a stage adorned with the papal colors, in the middle of which hung a portrait of the pontiff. Gazing with love upon the picture of Pope Leo, Francesca said to the daughters by her side, "Leaning on the rock of the Vatican, I have nothing to fear, but, on the contrary, have in that protection a pledge of celestial favors."

With modest smiles the miners and their wives hid the pride they felt as they watched their children. Speaking in Italian, Bishop Matz opened his address dedicating the Missionary Sisters' new school with the Lord's words, "Suffer little children to come unto me, for of such is the kingdom of Heaven."

When Francesca was satisfied with her Denver school, she returned to the east to expand the missionary field there. Her health continued to trouble her markedly, but if ever under duress she questioned the ways of the Lord, or in her human heart relented before her own rule of obedience, she never betrayed it. If anything, she manifestly regretted that she was not doing enough for her Spouse. Despite her bodily weakness she urged herself to accelerate her missions, and was impatient over every retarded and unfruitful moment. With expert speed she founded an orphanage in Arlington, New Jersey, and added an annex to the overcrowded Columbus

Hospital in New York City. As soon as she was satisfied that these and the other eastern houses could get along without her, she left for a long-planned trip to the midwest to expand her mission in Chicago. When she arrived, she wanted to open an orphanage, but the new Archbishop Quigley, a man with an extraordinary feeling for the immigrants, convinced her that the immediate need of the Italians was a hospital. After weeks of begging, she went to the Archbishop and triumphantly announced, "Excellence, our Italians are right with us. We have gathered from them a thousand dollars. Now we begin the hospital!"

"A thousand dollars!" echoed the Archbishop with kindly laughter, "*One* thousand dollars? Dear Mother Cabrini, do you know how many-many 1,000-dollar bills we must have to buy a big hospital?"

She nodded. "Surely I know, but to start is to win. I have begun houses with less, with no more than the price of a loaf of bread and prayers, for with Him who comforts me, I can do anything."

The property she first thought of buying was an old empty building that belonged to the Alexian Brothers. Though it was large and well-built, Archbishop Quigley, who was familiar with it, felt that it was not suitable for a hospital, for it was located in a commercial section alongside railroad tracks.

During her quest for a hospital building she inspected two properties, one a modest building of likely price in Vernon Park, the other the six story North Shore Hotel in Lincoln Park on the Lake front. Owing to mismanagement, the ultra-fashionable Hotel had failed, and was being offered at a figure far below cost. It was a sun-bright winter's morning when she saw it. Glistening snow covered the attractive natural surroundings, and nearby was the convivial scene of sportslovers iceboating, skating, and racing horse-drawn sleighs on the frozen surface of Lake Michigan. The sight of the imposing,

158

sympathetic stone structure containing 250 rooms, made her catch her breath. She longed to have it. She mused on what an ideal haven of mercy she could make of it for the afflicted, the injured, and the convalescing. It was a sin to see it vacant when it could be accommodating the unfortunate children of God.

She shook her head and said to the daughter at her side, "Why do I waste time dreaming of this estate as a hospital for our poor emigrants when it is obviously too sumptuous for us? Come, we have nothing to try here." Then, she reflected, "Are the vultures of age and illness making me timid? Am I letting my lack of courage counter God's will? Maybe my sweet Jesus wants me to acquire this property for the poor!"

There followed many weeks of dollar by dollar begging, the selling of subscriptions, and dealings with the owners of the hotel, who had come down to the fixed low price of 120,000 dollars.

Completely exhausted, she was for the first time in all her bold financial ventures assailed with concern. The purchase price would be only the initial step. Then there would have to be renovations converting the hotel to hospital requirements, no end of equipment, medical and surgical supplies, salary funds, insurance, and so on. If she made a costly wrong move, the mission in Chicago would be discredited and the immigrants' sufferings prolonged indefinitely. Should she settle for the smaller, reasonable Vernon Park building, or brave the splendid North Shore Hotel? Heretofore, a dream, an instinct, had always suggested her decisions. Now, despite fervent prayer, no dream, no sign indicated the answer. Thus, she presented her dilemma to Archbishop Quigley, fully expecting the prelate to dismiss the huge, ambitious North Shore Hotel dream in favor of a safe move.

Without hesitation, Archbishop Quigley chose the grand edifice and beautiful grounds of the North Shore Hotel, and gave

159

her lively encouragement. That night she said to her daughters, "I marvel constantly at the ever-surprising character of this blessed America. Mark you with prayers and thanksgiving for this New World. Today, an American bishop, not Italian, mind you, has seen fit to feel that a majestic building in an elegant locality was not too good for the needs of the poor Italian people."

Having raised only 10,000 dollars, the thought of meeting the purchase price of 120,000 dollars, frightened her. After pensive moments, she relaxed and confidently smiled. "Shame on me for worrying. Our Lord has spoken through Archbishop Quigley, and to obey is my duty. Wanting this great property for the Italian hospital so much, the Lord Himself has to see to it that all issues well. So be it!"

The hotel owners had committed the entire plot of the hotel's original land with the purchase terms. Francesca was not by nature mistrustful, and for the most part her experiences with businessmen and their promises had been good. But her insight and understanding of human frailty often stood her institute in good stead. She sensed something peculiar in the owners intention, and before signing the contract observed a simple, practical precaution. At dawn, a few days before the transaction, she went to check the dimensions of the property. A policeman who happened to be nearby watched wonderingly as she and two daughters measured the plot, using in place of a regular tape measure a length of clothesline, with knots accurately spaced a foot apart. She quickly discovered that the owners had moved the surveyor's landmarks, with the obvious intention of keeping a considerable section for themselves. Because of her shrewd precaution, the ruse was easily frustrated.

In July, 1903, while Francesca was in the process of taking over the North Shore Hotel in Chicago, her earthly master and patron, Leo XIII, died. The father on earth of Christ's children, he who had directed her mission to America, the Eagle

160

of God who had held her to his breast and assured her of paradise, had preceded her to the reward.

Pope Leo's death had to be a blow to Francesca. They had become almost a part of one another. They were as one in their devotion of the Sacred Heart, and in their incisive comprehension of the ills and injustices of their time. The Divine Will had planned and arranged this paternal and filial association, for they were both absolutely right and required for the times. Pope Leo led the Holy Church through godless flames, and Francesca was a conscious instrument in the pontiff's hand. She eagerly shared his specific goals and endeavors. No one could have better directed Francesca, as foundress and missionary, to the works she might best accomplish in her age than the humane Pope Leo. When Leo assumed the papacy, godlessness and materialism had been gaining ground, even in Catholic countries. His predecessor had been continually beset by the encroachments of anticlerical elements in Italy itself.

By the end of his life, Leo had not only reversed the waves of European godlessness, but, during the last phases of his pontificate, was responsible for the revival of Catholic strength in Protestant countries as well. He did more than denounce the evils of materialism, he found positive answers to the moral problems raised by the new age. In his long battle to translate his profound principles into action, Francesca was one of his finest warriors. She, in turn, had learned to rely completely on his unqualified support, and his personal interest in her mission had been a constant source of inspiration for her.

Though she felt the loss of his physical life dolorously, her spirit was not darkened. According to her faith, his death was the beginning of his blissful, true life, for which she was happy, and she was certain that from above, she had in the soul of the grand pontiff an even more valid intercessor for her mission.

With the election of Cardinal Melchior Joseph Sarto to the Holy Chair as Pope Pius X, she commended her houses to

161

salute his accession with prayer and joy and to take to their hearts his immediate message, "To Renew All Things In Christ."

Obstacles more fretful than serious detained her in Chicago and delayed her plans for a trip west. As soon as the wealthy residents of Lincoln Park learned that the fashionable North Shore Hotel was to become a hospital, they tried to influence the municipal authorities to prohibit it. With the help of Archbishop Quigley, who stood resolutely on the side of the Missionary Sisters and the poor, Francesca was able to shame the selfish opposition into silence. The task of raising funds for renovating the hotel into her hospital was formidable. Many of her own beloved Italians had succeeded in Chicago, and they could have helped her—but they did not. If this was a disappointment to her, she made no complaint. Long experience had taught Francesca that the love of God and the exercise of charity were not the privileged possession of her own faith or her own people. As so often before, when financial conditions seemed despairing, donations for the Chicago hospital came from non-Italian Catholics, from Jews and Protestants. Actual and threatening difficulties were more than balanced the day the world-renowned Catholic doctor, J. B. Murphy, proffered his services as president and head-of-staff for her hospital.

Once the Chicago Hospital project was well underway, Francesca was eager to move on to the as yet untouched area of the West Coast. She hastily delegated responsibility for the reconstruction of the hotel building to other sisters, and set out for Seattle.

On the seven-day train trip across the continent, she was tormented with a high fever. The daughter with her wrote,

"As we traversed the Arizona desert, the hot sun refracting from the fiery sands made the interior of our car a fur-

162

nace. Knowing how much Mother was suffering, I could not stay still, and finally exclaimed, 'What a brutal sun!'

"Despite her pain, Mother answered me, 'How now, you lament what God sends? God Who with His wisdom has created the sun, God is your Spouse, and you criticize His work? The sun is one of the most superb things of His creation. It truly gives a living vision of the purity and potency of God, with its splendor and warmth. Never permit yourself a similar expression again. We have always to be content with whatever is sent to us by Jesus. He is our Spouse and we are not to annoy him with complaints about what He does.' "

The northwest, teeming with exhilarating growth, was still experiencing open lawlessness, upon which she humorously commented,

"What a place! Here, tempestuous men, wearing pistols like soldiers, shoot each other without ceremony. In these wild and virgin territories there is no dearth of troublemakers, cheats, and violence. It is not uncommon for vengeful railroaders to blow trains up in the air with dynamite. And as for bandits, from what I hear, it seems all the brigands of the United States are having a happy, profitable reunion in the Northwest."

Young Seattle, the Queen City, crowned twenty hills overlooking Puget Sound. The snow-capped peaks of the Rocky Mountains rose on one side, the Olympic Mountains on the other. The city's verdant hills were bathed by the sea and perfumed with lemon and orange blossoms. The dark green background of forests, and the piney air made Seattle, to Francesca, "the garden of America."

She was happy there; the climate was invigorating, and the Italian families clamored to have her. How good it was to sit at the table of one's own people!

"With a loving heart," she said, "honest bread, a plate of spaghetti, wine, and a mouthful of fruit, is an exquisite feast. In the vision of the Lord, the humblest abode, illuminated with the faces of children, is a palace!"

163

She chose the summit of Beacon Hill, that smiled down upon the city and the bay, to erect a building to house a small church, a parochial school, and an orphanage.

When construction began, she took a pick and dug a hole where a supporting pier of the chapel was to rise. Then she wrote on a sheet of paper,

"Seattle Wash. 18–2–1903, 1133 South Twelfth Avenue, Beacon Hill. *Nel pilastro angolare della Cappella provvisoria —Mount Carmel Mission—delle Missionarie del S. Cuore di Gesu, La Madre F.S. Cabrini ha deposte le seguenti medaglie: 1. Piox X; 2. Leone XIII; 3. Gesu e Maria; 4. Crocifisso e Madonna del Buon Consiglio; 5. Beata Virgine del Buon Consiglio e S. Antonio; 6. Sacra Famiglia, tre Cuori; 7. Il Redentore e Leone XIII; 8. Madonna di Pompei e Leone XIII; 9. Un Crocifisso; 10. Abitini del S. Cuore e della Madonna del Carmine. A tutta questa nobilissima e santissima Famiglia e alle Anime Sante del Purgatorio e affidata la prosperita di questa missione, per; la salute di un numero innumerabile di anime degli Italiani di Washington e dell' Alaska. N.B. le medaglie sono depsote nel pilastro angolare della Cappella N.E. Indi firmo in ginocchio e fece cadere le medaglie nella fossetta da lei preparata e che di nuovo riempi di terra."*

Thus having recorded the place, time, and person who deposited the listed religious medals there for the prosperity of the mission and for Italian souls from Washington to Alaska, she placed the note and medals in the hole, and on hands and knees refilled it with earth.

When the simple chapel was ready for worshippers she did not have the price of a church bell. She and her daughters went in twos, climbing the different hills, hallooing, "Come to the Holy Mass, dear ones! Come to your church!"

Within minutes, parents and children would emerge from the cottages scattered in the valleys and on the slopes, and come running and waving to the Sisters, "We come, good Sisters, we come!" And from the hills in every direction they

164

followed the nuns, like long lines of chicks behind a brood hen, to church. In a letter to her daughters she wrote, "Deprived of parish, priest and Altar, our Italians here have been many years away from God. Still, I found the Faith deeply rooted in them. Therefore, by means of kindness and courtesy it is not difficult to bring them back to God.

"It is very moving to see men and women of advanced years weep with emotion upon beholding their own first Italian church in the New Land, hearing the Word of God in their mother tongue. They are reminded of the old country, so long abandoned, and the ever-dear memories of their childhood— the steeples, the Squares, the solemn processions in their native land to which they will never return. I expect much from this mission."

During Lent the worshippers came so early for the Holy Mass that many of them made the Stations of the Cross three times over and more before the service actually began. In sun, wind, and rain, at the sweet calls of the nuns they came.

At evening, their candles and lanterns made a jubilee of sparkling lights among the hills as they came to vespers.

The fathers of families could return to the orchards, fields, forests, fishing boats, quarries, and their various labors, content that their children were guided in God's way, and that their little homes were blessed.

Mother Cabrini had often been asked how she felt about America.

"America? The Vicar of the Lord sent me here. Codogno is my heart and Rome is my intellect, but my wish is to die in this vast field of Christian hope, and for my worn-out remains to rest in the peaceful cemetery of the Convent in West Park, New York."

It was in Seattle that her feeling for America came to flower. One day, she quietly went to the city hall and announced that she wanted to become an American citizen. It was not that she loved the land of the past the less, it was that she loved

165

America and its future the more. In Italian-accented English she supplied the routine information about herself and her life. When requested to pose for the identification photo, she blushed and nearly fled from the building.

Leaving the city hall, proudly holding her first citizenship papers, she confided to her accompanying daughter, "I presented myself to the authorities for the purpose of becoming an American citizen, but not to be photographed like an actress! Oh, I did not want to be photographed. I pray no one sees that dreadful picture!"

"I am nobody, nothing. As for my likeness, I wish it to be imprinted only upon the Sacred Heart of my Spouse."

Constantly aware of her role as spiritual mother to her daughters, she maintained maternal touch with a steady stream of letters. These were circulated throughout her houses, so that each daughter might benefit and delight in them. Many letters bore the deep and lasting wisdom of the epistles. For the education of children, "those young hearts which, soft as wax, are ever ready to receive impressions," she stresses the joining of intellectual with religious instruction, "so that they may realize those high truths which alone can awaken in them the love of virtues and the control of passions."

As she aged and became more infirm, her sense of the profound and the ludicrous sharpened, her exhortations grew softer, and though she told of peoples, places, and events with a girl's enthusiasm, her writings achieved a mellow, earthy quality. Many things seemed to her downright comical. In Seattle she learned about Eskimo life from an old Alaskan Jesuit. She passed on the information to her daughters so that, if she opened an Alaskan mission, they would not be overly surprised by the habits of the igloo dwellers.

"Their manner of taking food is strange to say the least. If you are invited by some great personage, such as the head of a tribe, you must not imagine you are going to eat cooked

166

food. In front of the head of the family you see two plates, one with the raw fish and meat and the other empty.

"Now his work begins, for the good host chews all the food which is to be given to the guests. This ceremony over, all the guests proceed to eat of this 'well-prepared dish.' And, that is not the worst of things practiced there!"

As an American citizen she became more interested than ever in the nation she had made her own. Enroute to New Orleans from Seattle, by way of Colorado and Texas, she gloried in the natural beauty of her new-chosen country.

"For hours the train ran between walls of inaccessible heights which touched the sky, whilst below the winding river flows, alternately impetuous and calm, reflecting in its pure water of variegated colors the extraordinary rocks, a scene which would be the delight of our mineralogy and geology classes! These mountainously sculptured gems are the works of the Immortal Artist, Whose existence men dare to deny and to forget while the wondrous works of His hands speak so eloquently."

She defines the endless Texas plain, its fertility and suitability for every kind of cultivation, as "virgin lands, full of life and promise."

At a station stop she visited an Indian Reservation called Coeur d'Alene, where the Jesuit Fathers had a mission. She relates how the Indian smokes his pipe while the Indian woman, with her baby strapped to her back, works.

"We should be grateful to Christianity, which has raised the dignity of woman. Before Mary, what was woman? With Mary, a new era arose for woman. She is no longer a chattel, but equal to man; no longer a servant, but mistress within her domestic walls; no longer the object of disdain and contempt, but elevated to Mother and Educator, on whose knee generations are built up."

She shakes her head in discouragement over still-prevailing "ridiculous superstitions" among the red men.

"When an Indian dies, all of the tribe has to weep by the corpse whether they want to or not, chanting their grief the whole night in a monotonous strain like this, 'You were so very good, oh, oh, oh. You had a lovely wigwam, ah, ah, ah.' When morning dawns, the chief, in pagan regalia, arrives, and the face-painted Indians beg him to tell them if the deceased has gone to heaven or hell. He commands them to bring a bowl of bread and water. They hold the unconventional belief that if the dead is destined for heaven, it needs nothing. Of course, the deceased does not return to take bread and water; consequently the tribe concludes it has gone to heaven, and makes merry over the corpse, dancing, singing, shooting guns, partaking of strong drink and a great banquet. Poor souls! These are they whom Christ saw, in all the horror of His Imminent Passion, the uselessness of His agony for so many souls. The trials of the first Church are just the same after twenty centuries, and it is not to be wondered at, for Christ has always been the sign of contradiction. And so it must be with the Church, in this vale of misery and tears."

One night on the train during that trip, the daughter sitting opposite her said, "Mother, I had a dream concerning you, and the devil."

She leaned forward to listen; just at that moment a rifle shot crashed through the train window exactly at the spot where her head had been.

The frightened conductor said to her, "That bullet would have killed you if you had not moved your head when you did. It is a miracle. Sister, you certainly have someone looking after you."

She serenely replied, "Calm yourself, sir, that bullet could never have found me, for the Sacred Heart protects me."

The daughter described her dream:

"Mother, in the fantasy of slumber the devil appeared and said, "I know too wisely and well your habit. It is painfully familiar to me. You are one of Cabrini's Missionaries. Thus, I

168

want you to inform that woman that I am not going to waste my time with her anymore, for on account of all the astute provisions she takes against me, the tribulations of my thousand disguises and maneuverings have profited me cursed nothing." Then he shook his fists and wrathfully wailed, "Ah, if only I could, I would make mincemeat of that old nun!"

"A likely dream, my dear Daughter," she chuckled, "Mister Satan's anguished sufferings to snare souls to his domain are almost touching enough to make a Saint weep. Ah, poor devil!"

9 ✠ ✠ ✠

WHEN she arrived at New Orleans, she found that the St. Philip's Street house, which served as church, convent, school and orphanage, charming and spacious as it was, could no longer contain the constantly increasing number of orphans, and a house solely for the orphans was a pressing need. At that time the Italian colonies of New Orleans resounded with acclaim for a wealthy shipowner, Captain Salvatore Pizzati, known as "The old Sicilian wolf of the seas," who had amazed the Italians by donating 40,000 dollars to the Lazzarist Fathers. Upon learning of the old captain's sentiment toward religious philanthropy, Francesca said to the superior, "God wants me to go to Captain Pizzati on behalf of your orphans." And she went to the Captain's door immediately.

The captain answered the bell, and she introduced herself.

"Mother Cabrini? What Christian has not heard of you! Come in, come in, Mother Cabrini. But my, how tiny you are to do such mighty works!"

Francesca smiled, then came firmly to the point. "How is it, good Captain, that when my daughters come to your door for the sacred and blessed charity of orphans, you tighten your purse and limit your Christianity to pennies?"

"It seems the Lord sent you to me. What shall I do first?"

"Captain, would you be so kind as to visit the St. Philip's

170

Street house and see with your own eyes sights that would soften even a heart made of stone?"

Captain Pizzati came to the orphanage that night. In the dormitory, by the glow of the votives before the Statue of the Sacred Heart, he saw the clean little beds crowded from wall to wall and heard the sweet sounds of the slumber of hundreds of infants and little girls. He put his hand to his heart and whispered, "Mother Cabrini, their breathing is the angelic music of Heaven!" She nodded and paused by a crib in which two baby girls were placidly sleeping, though jammed together. In a silvery whisper she said, "Captain, you are Christian and Sicilian, and so are they. Their earthly fathers and mothers are dead. They have Jesus now as Father and the Missionary Sisters of the Sacred Heart as their loving mothers. But they are wanting a larger roof and beds.

"The saint of fishermen and the Keeper of The Keys, guided you safely over the many perilous seas and has retired you with the health of an oak and much wealth. Will you not in turn be as Saint Peter to these orphans in the stormy seas of this life, and prove that your baptized name, 'Salvatore,' has been God-given and truly stands for 'Deliverer?' "

Tears burst from the old captain. He kissed the sleeping infants, then stood up and said huskily, "Blessed Mother Cabrini, why did not you yourself come to me sooner and properly open my old eyes to this overcrowded paradise of cherubims? By now these little angels would not be sleeping like two loaves uncomfortably in one bag. I would gladly have seen to their needs long ago. Without delay, find a nice piece of land, get an architect to draw beautiful plans, and I, fortunate old Pizzati, will pay all expenses for the erection of a grand orphanage."

After he left, Francesca and the mother superior knelt and thanked with prayer their Spouse's Sacred Heart. But Francesca, prompted by the acute insight that had warned her of the hotel owners' intended dishonesty in Chicago, was not easy

171

about the captain's promise. "The moods of mortals are similar to the weather," she said to the superior. "We must be alert to the psychology of this world with the same realistic methods that the successful American businessman applies to his industry. Mark you, if I allow the large-hearted Sicilian captain's tears to dry, his compassion will conveniently disappear, and so will our new orphanage. From experience I know the fancies of our affluent *paesanos*. In the morning I must be posted at his door to strike his heart again while his eyes are still warmly wet. First I will refire his generous soul by assuring him of some high decoration from Pius X for his munificence—perhaps he will be made a Cavalier of Saint Gregory Eminent. Then I shall firmly direct his hand to sign with pen and ink 'Salvatore Pizzati' to an ironclad contract before a lawyer, holding him irrevocably to his promise, for the good of his soul."

Francesca did as she had said. Pizzati had not forgotten his emotion over the plight of the orphans the next day, and he was overwhelmingly pleased by the offer of high decoration. He cheerfully signed the contract she had arranged. How fortunate Francesca's uneasiness about the old captain's promise had been! Just as she had anticipated, ambitious Italian liberals, seeking grants from the philanthropic old captain for their own gain, badgered him to rescind the large sum he committed to her orphanage. Pizzati weakened and tried to annul his written agreement with her, but she would not hear of it. One morning a pompous political functionary representing her opposition came to the convent and suavely attempted to coerce her into renouncing the Pizzati contract.

To the disappointment of his colleagues, he returned defeated. "You complain that I failed?" he said. "How would you have fared in the face of such fury? Little Mother Cabrini, who seems mild as a dove, stormed at me with the mien of a lion, saying, 'You cannot hinder the work God has put in my hands, for the interests of the orphans and the poor are sa-
172

cred!' Her God and the law are with her. I tell you, if we try to prevent her new orphanage, she will win, and we will pay dearly. You just do not fool with this woman Cabrini!"

"To insure ample plenary indulgences for Captain Pizzati's soul when he goes to Heaven," as Francesca put it, she went the limit with the captain's bank-account. She bought a great tract of land on Esplanade Avenue, valuable land that stretched to the St. John Bayou. There she built a most splendid stone orphanage.

In June, 1905, at the French Hall, in the presence of applauding civil and ecclesiastical authorities, Archbishop Chapelle pinned the Order of Cavalier of Saint Gregory Eminent upon the chest of swarthy, grizzled, old Captain Salvatore Pizzati. Francesca had kept her word. The decoration had been expressly and significantly sent by Pius X. And what a happy man was the old philanthropist, grinning with embarrassed pride at accepting so signal an honor!

The early 1900's were turbulent days. All kinds of blatant dishonesty flourished alongside the impulsive charity of such men as Captain Pizzati. During her victorious battle of New Orleans she received a telegram from Chicago. "Mother Cabrini. Serious trouble with the work on the hospital. Come at once. Archbishop Quigley."

At the Chicago railroad station the Archbishop greeted her with bad news.

"Mother, I am sorry to have to tell you, but the renovations of the North Shore Hotel have gone wrong. We are already 40,000 dollars in debt, the end is not in sight, and today foreclosure is threatened. I feel you will rescue it somehow. Thank God you are here. If you had come a day later, you would probably have found your distressed daughters sleeping in the park like derelicts."

It is an unfortunate fact that more than a few contractors look upon work done for the Church as an easy opportunity

173

for fast and swollen profits, bleeding the good, sweet religious to the extreme with all manner of dummied items and false statements. This is especially true in construction alterations. In hard competitive construction, when contractors feel that the workmen are not extending themselves sufficiently, it is not uncommon to hear the foremen shout, "Hurry it up! What do you think you're working on, a Catholic Church?"

One glance at the mess the contractors had made of the North Shore Hotel renovations for the new hospital in her absence was enough. She put her hand to her forehead and exclaimed, "Greedy, heartless contractors have combined here for me the ruins of Jerusalem!"

An anger she had never known arose within her. "Oh, these contractors! The devil of bad faith is in them! This moment I could devour them alive!"

In all her years she had never before permitted herself to lose her temper. The religious must not find excuses to behave like those whom they wish to save. Shocked at her own outburst, she inclined her head and begged God's forgiveness for having given way to rage.

Promptly she obtained consulting engineers, and compared the renovation blueprints and specifications with the deliberate disorder she found. She checked and listed the false and the inept work, unnecessarily demolished floors and walls, duplicated labor and materials. Then she summoned the contractors to her lawyer's office, and confronted them with undeniable evidences of damages and fraud. Seeing no other way out, they brazenly questioned her authority. The plumbing contractor, in an offensive tone, demanded, "Lady, just who are you?"

She answered by placing before them her credentials, upon which Leo XIII had written and signed, "alla benmerita Madre Cabrini, Superiora Generale delle Missionarie del S. Cuore."

In a vibrating voice she said, "Sirs, you violated a sacred trust, and robbed hard-gotten money while the sick poor wait and suffer for their hospital. Remove your signs, men and
174

equipment from my job. You took cowardly advantage of my inexperienced nuns while I was not here, a most shameful deed before the eyes of God and society. I discharge you, and your looting claims will be dealt with in a court of law. Mother Cabrini is now the contractor who will finish the job."

Many a businessman has wished he had the staunch qualities of her generalship. When a move representing much time and effort failed, she dropped it and turned forcefully in another direction. Now she did not sit and weep in "the ruins of Jerusalem," but went among the Italian working class and recruited bricklayers, carpenters, plumbers, tilesetters. They vowed they would stand by her and convert the hotel into her new Columbus Hospital.

"Look, Mother, no trowel is surer and faster than mine!"

"God bless you, Master Pietro."

"Madre Cabrini, my plumbing layout is the new method that saves time and money!"

"Mother, come to the sixth floor, and just you feast your eyes on our plastering!"

Under her smiling direction they assiduously proved the manliness and gallantry of the God-loving proletariat, working with a herculean drive as though the building were to be their home, and she their true mother.

"Mother," they exclaimed with reverence and pride, "see what your children do for you!"

She was with the hardy men the day long, bringing them food and wine at lunch, and in turn sharing their robust sandwiches. They doffed their caps and signed the happy cross at the sight of her. When the whistle signaled the end of the working day, Francesca, with her habit, hands, and face smudged with plaster, paint, sawdust, and brick dust, blessed them each by name, and said to them, "Good night, my brothers and sons. Go to thy homes and dear ones with joy!"

The date fixed for the opening of Chicago's Columbus Hospital was February 26, 1905. It was to be "the Day of the

175

Lord," she said, "because it was all His work." Craftsmen and decorators, doctors, internes and nurses, priests and sisters swarmed about the edifice night and day. The work seemed to increase instead of decrease.

Though a hospital in 1905 was at best somewhat primitive according to today's standards, it still had to be a complete self-serving community. Before she could think of receiving a single patient, she had to arrange and provide physical requirements: proper heating and ventilation, laundry, kitchen, pantry and dining room facilities, storage space for medical supplies, a reception salon, examining rooms and nurses' stations, a stable for the horse-drawn ambulances, chapel, and living quarters for the help.

Men and women from all branches of medical science supervised the installation of equipment for their offices and operating rooms, the X-ray room, and the laboratories.

Amid the hectic activity Francesca was tranquil. She saw that diverse labors were coordinated rapidly and done accurately, and made sure that when she opened the doors of the hospital, the public would have no reason to find fault.

By February 26, 1905, "the Day of the Lord," the hospital was finished. A great celebration was planned, and even a surpassingly clear sky, with a sun that made the blue waters of Lake Michigan sparkle, seemed to participate in the feast.

The opening of a hospital, though a milestone event for the medical profession, does not ordinarily awaken excitement in the public. Great, then, was the happiness of the worthy Archbishop Quigley when he arrived to speak at the ceremonies and found 4,000 people crowded into the chapel and reception rooms waiting to hear him. Several thousand people of all races and creeds stood out in the street, as there was no space for them inside at the ceremony. Never had there been such enthusiasm over the opening of a hospital in the United States as there was on this occasion.

The morning ceremony was purely religious and consisted

176

of the blessing of the house by the archbishop, followed by a long procession of people. There was a Solemn High Mass, with a sermon by the archbishop. A pleasant surprise awaited the congregation at the close of His Grace's sermon, when the archbishop read a telegram from Pius X, who sent his blessing. Francesca later wrote to the sisters at her mother house:

"You, my Daughters in Rome, who are so privileged at seeing His Holiness so frequently and receiving his blessing, experience holy emotions in your souls. You can imagine, then, with what satisfaction and gratitude this telegram was embraced by the doctors and guests. It came as a heavenly message. It was as precious as the distance is great which lies between these shores of America and the Vicar of Christ.

"I look upon the blessing of His Holiness as a pledge of heavenly favors, for I have always noticed that success attends every work which has been sealed by it. The hand of the Holy Father is never raised in vain. Now the Chicago Columbus Hospital has begun its beneficent work for American humanity, and great numbers of sick seek its shelter."

By the time the Chicago hospital was opened, Francesca's institute had grown into a vast network. She enjoyed the exhilarating work of founding new missions, visiting new places, and establishing her sisters among new friends. But at times the problems of sustaining the work that she had already done were more serious than those involved in expansion. Certainly they were problems of a different kind, far more annoying and far less stimulating.

While she was engaged in salvaging the Chicago hospital from the chaos wrought by dishonest contractors, word reached her from Rome of one such problem. A small group of headstrong young daughters at the mother house had banded together to protest her ways of managing the institute. Their own ideas were more liberal, more "modern," as they called it, and more constructive, they believed. They were also utterly impractical. These young reformers scoffed at total obedience as an' obsolete conception, unsuitable for the new century. The foundress was ill and aging. How much longer could she live? Should the future of the institute depend entirely upon one person? Did Mother Cabrini alone have the attention of the Lord?

Why did directives to the mother house in Rome come by remote mail from Mother Cabrini? Why was not the mother general at Rome where she belonged instead of forever traveling? Was there proof that the Lord demanded their blind and slavish obedience to a chance superior? Should there not be a responsible body of sisters who chose the superior for a house? Why could not they have a voice in decisions? They were thinking only of an illustrious and dynamic future for the institute. Suppose Mother Cabrini suddenly died, would the result not be chaos? Many regulations born of Mother Cabrini's early life and the old-fashioned days would have to change and broaden with the needs and tone of the new exciting century. Was not the venerable foundress confusing maternalism with the self-appointed powers of matriarchalism? The time was ripe for the institute to be run as a modern religious organization and not as a parochial family in the hands of an almighty mother.

The few misguided daughters of Rome had the sympathy of certain liberal-minded priests, who presented the case of their grievances to the sacred congregation governing rules and prelates, together with their emotional but vague plans to alter the institute. An overwhelming majority of the daughters, who remained faithful, upheld the cause of their absent mother with vigor. The august body did not ponder long before dismissing the rebels with paternal advice to return to their good senses and Obedience.

In giving his judgment, Monsignor Giustini, secretary of the sacred congregation, remarked, "By the fruit is known the tree. Mother Cabrini's works blossom from the hand of God.

She is a woman who by herself bears the weight of many houses. Your Mother Cabrini, dear Daughters, is a superior woman. I not only revere her, but humble myself at her feet."

What was her sentiment in regard to this incident? The revolution of these few young daughters was a violation of the allegiance she hoped for from them. Yet, who was she to expect perfect fidelity, when the Son of God Himself had been and still was doubted and denied? She must not give way to the sting of rebuke. She wrote to Rome:

"Dear Mother Superior, I recommend that you treat this light-headedness with soothing manners and much pity, as does a proper mother of family who takes a thousand cares for her sick daughters even when they turn against her. The petty revolution I attribute to their nimbleness of mind, rather than to voluntary malice. All I wish to preserve for the Institute is simplicity and family spirit. If all the Daughters in their Mothers' Houses were perfect, there would be no need for the exercises of virtues. What then? Of course it would be paradise; but, has any mortal seen paradise in this world? I expect my Paradise in the next world, not this. Truthfully, I am too worn with my present toils to be disturbed by this tempest in a tea cup. I could almost laugh at the gyrations of these rebels to reach castles in the air. Seriously though, without the training of discipline and the inculcation of an iron fortitude for them, I could not in all conscience leave our Daughters to the grave responsibilities and perils of missionary work.

"Woe to us if we followed unrealistic and utopian notions! It would be necessary for us to close our Houses and live in ivory towers far removed from urgent daily combat against the misery of the world. I regret to say that I cannot accommodate and surrender to sick heads, but it is my care to cure them, and I do wish you would be so kind as to read aloud to the petulant the following remedy:

"On the Standard of the Missionaries of the Sacred Heart

179

is written, *'Imitation of Christ,'* which suggests negation of self and detachment from deluding worldly passions for intimate union with God. The heart must be in the custody of Obedience, Chastity, and Poverty.

"No one is called and ground beneath this Standard by force, and it is for this reason that all are given a long time to think before offering their sacrifice. The nemesis of the soul is conquered by love and not by open or obscure force, as the good Jesus desires no one in the family of His Divine Heart by force. Oh, Daughters, does this precious little family of the Sacred Heart please you? If so, go forward with courage, take an axe to the roots of your defects, and you are quickly a saint. You are not pleased with our family of the Sacred Heart? Then you waste your time as a Missionary because you harm yourself and your Sisters and never will become a saint.

"Do not waste further time, Daughters always so dear to me, in vain fantasy. Keep your feet on earth, for fairy castles in the air you can never adorn. There is no easy way, no substitute for goodness and the imitation of your Spouse. I pardon you with my entire love no matter what you have said or done, but I do wish that your contrition and sacrifices come gladly from your willing hearts. In penitence make a Holy Communion after my intention, and then let us think no more of the incident as though it had never occurred. The good Jesus blesses you and encloses you very well in His Sacred Heart."

This loving message immediately brought the few rebels in the order back upon Francesca's practical path. Thereafter, they gave their utmost fidelity to her.

Much later, on her next visit to Rome, she was walking with a daughter on the Via delle Umilita, when they saw a priest coming toward them. The daughter whispered, "Mother, this priest approaching is one of those who abetted the young rebellious Sisters. Ooh, that is he!"

"Oho," Francesca exclaimed triumphantly, "so this fellow

is one of our 'fine friends'!" As she came face to face with the priest, he blushed guiltily when he recognized her. She gave him a long, luminous look in return and smiled with an expression of infinite charity.

Another and far more painful trial occurred while Francesca was busy with her work on the Chicago hospital, when New Orleans fell prey to an epidemic of yellow fever. It was impossible for her to feel at peace when any of her daughters were suffering or in danger, and she suffered particularly if she could not be with them to help. But, occupied as she was with urgent work in Chicago, she could not rush to New Orleans. The most she could do was to communicate with her daughters and pray for them, their orphans, and the inhabitants of the stricken city. Once she had thought the New Orleans mission got on too smoothly to exercise her daughters' souls. In the scourge of yellow fever, they showed how staunch, despite their relatively easy life, they had remained. The sisters quickly arranged to have the orphans and those nuns who were not physically strong moved to the open country on the Gulf of Mexico, away from the death-infested city. The congested, unsanitary tenements of the immigrants and Negroes were the best target of the terrible plague. The city was completely unprepared and its medical department helpless. Fatalities grew to incredible proportions. Death bells rang constantly, and corpses were piled unceremoniously in morgues and undertaking parlors. Getting the bodies out of sight and underground was a major problem.

In most cases medicines, and prayers suddenly sought and recalled, were of no avail, and superstition became the confederate of Death. To the poor Italians and Negroes, the incomprehensible rituals of medicine and the presence of somber black-robed priests seemed harbingers of the unwanted visitor. It was imagined and rumored that priests and doctors, for some punitive mysterious reason, were spreading the fatal germ.

The sisters consecrated themselves to the struggle against death. At first many of the stricken, ignorant and hysterical, imagined that the sisters were conniving spies for the doctors and priests they so dreaded. But miraculously, patients tended by the sisters recovered. Thousands began to clamor for their help. The sisters converted their two houses into infirmaries, and devoted themselves with indefatigable zeal to the sick, medicating, cleansing, soothing, feeding, counselling, and consoling, as though they were themselves members of the stricken families.

The germ did not neglect a single home. In many homes parents and children alike, within days, lay scattered in various cells of their miserable hovels like reluctant effigies, cold and rigid in the profound silence of death, exterminated, claimed only by the mass burial ground. With courage that men will never know, disdaining mortal contagion, nausea, and rest, Francesca's daughters cared for the ill and dying day and night, wherever they were. The rooms of the St. Philip's Street house, and also the convent rooms, the chapel, and the courtyard were filled with prostrate women and children whose faces were pale as wax. Great numbers of the little ones were destined to become orphans raised by the sisters.

Archbishop Chapelle, the humane man of Christ whose loving care had so helped Francesca's mission in New Orleans, hurried to the aid of the sisters in this crisis. While helping them in their merciful work, he fell victim to the fever, and after suffering briefly, he died. Not long after the chapel bell of the St. Philip's Street house intoned his passing, the yellow fever epidemic disappeared.

Francesca's prayers had been with her heroic New Orleans daughters, and by the grace of Heaven not one of them fell ill during the decimating plague.

During those macabre days the stricken had cried and begged for the Missionary Sisters of the Sacred Heart. No one
182

had then said nuns were unnatural beings, impractical idealists, mystics, and dreamers. And, while death had gorged itself in New Orleans, many who had hated and hurt the lowly immigrants had been mercifully saved by the daughters of Francesca Cabrini.

From Chicago she went to Denver, where she found the school she had opened the year before flourishing. The cheerful predictions Bishop Matz had made had been realized, and now the zealous prelate wanted her to establish an orphanage. Owing to the frequent disasters that befell the miners, Italian orphans were very numerous.

She analyzed the map of Denver, and plotted the likeliest direction of its expansion. By carriage and on foot she traversed the outlying countryside, and chose an inexpensive property at an isolated location miles from the city. The site was magnificent. It lay at the foot of the Rocky Mountains, upon a pleasant hill that sloped gently to the banks of the Rocky Mountain Lake. The house was in the midst of an orchard rich with fruit-laden trees.

Bishop Matz and others of Francesca's friends thought she had lost her mind. The location she pointed out was an impossible wilderness, cut off from transportation and communication.

"The growth of Denver must branch out within the proximity of the location I have decided upon. Your fears are needless. I am certain the area of the new orphanage will be the scene of important development soon." Not long after, her prediction came true, and most profitably.

During her Denver stay she taught the catechism to the miners and prepared them for Holy Communion, which many of the elderly had not received for fifty years. With a priest and several daughters she visited the poor miners and their families, in their small huts, and prepared them for the beautiful sacraments.

At recreation one evening, before evening prayers, a daugh-

183

ter handed her a newspaper showing the citizens of Denver presenting to President Roosevelt, who was visiting the state to hunt bears in the mountains, a laudatory plaque of solid gold inscribed with gems. She shook her head and then remarked to her daughters: "Mortals glorifying the mortal. They should know that God alone has put into the mind of man the divine spark of intelligence. The poet, the statesman, the artist, the scientist, all owe to God the genius that makes them outstanding, and the Church, amongst the titles she gives to the Holy Ghost, calls Him the Spirit of Wisdom and Intellect. It is meet, therefore, that we should draw water from the source, and so, after having worked on our part and studied assiduously, we must have recourse to Our Lord and expect from Him memory, intelligence and success. Cardinal Ximenes used to place himself at the foot of the crucifix when there were critical questions of State in hand. Asked by his Ministers why he did so, he answered, 'To pray is to rule.' Pray, then, Daughters, but not at length, for with all the work we have to do, you have little time and must pray briefly but with fervor. The world today is going back to paganism. In spite of its gigantic progress in science and commerce, it has forgotten prayer, and hardly recognizes it any more. And that has come about because, with pagan materialistic sentiments, man makes a god of himself and creatures, and loses the idea of the relations that exist between himself and God.

"Our good God, Who, as the child recites in the Catechism, has created heaven and earth, is almost banished from the world—there is no place for Him. Man has made an idol of himself, which he worships, and so does not pray to, or adore, the true and only God. No wonder, then, that after superhuman efforts for Aaron's golden calf, nature, weak and impotent to fight any longer, or to attain what it seeks, abandons itself to despair, suicide, and crime. Prayer would have obviated all this. Prayer is like incense rising to Heaven, and draws exhila-

184

rating graces from Heaven. It strengthens the strayed soul, giving it back peace and calm."

The young daughters who heard her words were deeply moved.

When she was satisfied with her plans for the orphanage in Colorado, she left to found a mission in California, "which," she said, "opens another page of the book of the beauties of the Universe . . . a pale image of the Most High."

Seated in a coach of the Santa Fe Railway, which was taking her to Los Angeles, her glance swept across the stretching plains. Around Denver, they were dotted with the cottages of the Italian agriculturists. Further on, there were vast tracts of uninhabited land and untouched soil. But her thoughts were upon retirement. Many times recently she thought herself almost at the termination of her mission in this life, and then new work cried to be done, work that she could not neglect without neglecting the holy interests of the glory of God and the salvation of souls. She had never considered herself sanctified, or very different from other religious mortals. Now, she could no longer deny her human longing for rest. More and more, her frail, worn, delicate body and limbs pleaded to her to call a halt to her monumental labors. Her mind clamored for detachment. Most urgent of all was her love of the perfect Spouse. Her love begged a restful preparation for that ultimate meeting. It longed for the sweet meditation, the hours and days in which the bride could relish sounding her love so precious, so that with the consummation of the nuptial, she could enter His heart gracefully, and with entire belonging.

"When, and where, and how will she stop?" asked the passion of more than fifty years.

As if in answer, her thoughts suddenly veered and flew to her immigrants, who in such awesome numbers landed every year on the Atlantic shores, overcrowding still further the already populous cities of the east. In the west there was yet room for many millions, and its fertile soil would offer living more congenial to the Italian immigrants, as well as a field in which to apply their agrarian knowledge.

This swollen, gorging stream of peoples should have had its course humanely and intelligently directed. She knew that the Immigration Department was approaching the problem more with words than with action. The solution, however, presented almost insurmountable obstacles, not only because of the almost 4,000 miles which separated the Atlantic from the Pacific, but more especially because it was difficult to find good-hearted people who would occupy themselves with the work and would not speculate in the sacred interests of the poor.

Poor immigrants were systematically cheated by those who pretended to be their protectors. They were gulled into signing their "X" on legal papers that kept them in bondage for years to parasites. If, upon seeing how they were cheated, they tried to escape, their persecutors employed lawyers, process servers, and sheriffs to bleed and crush them. Francesca, considering these practices, wrote:

"This deception is all the more hideous, because these so-called protectors know well how to color their private interests under the cloak of charity and patriotism! I saw our dear Italian fellows working on the construction of railways in the most intricate mountain canyons, miles away from habitation. They are separated for years from their families, and deprived of the holy joys the peasant in the old country has on Sundays at least. In Italy the peasant is able to put his hoe aside, go to divine service and hear the priest, who reminds him of the nobility of his origin and of his destiny, and of the value of work consecrated to God. He has one day in the week to devote to his family and to honest amusements, and is thus able to resume his work with his mind invigorated.

"I do not mean to deny that there are advantages in these

186

immense fertile lands. They certainly could offer the immigrant work and a decent life. I can assure you now that in my journey through our Missions in my new country, America, the evidence of the Christian good that is being done by our Houses for the immigrants is of the greatest comfort to me. That which, being women, we are not allowed to do on a large scale, such as helping to solve important social problems, which eventually decides the stability or doom of the nation, is being done in our little sphere in every State and city where our Houses have been opened. In them the orphans, the sick, the unwanted, and the poor are sheltered. The good done simply by our coming into contact with a great number of people is incalculable.

"The relation between the Sisters and the people is inspiring for all. The poor people call them Mothers and Sisters, and they feel these words are not without meaning, for they know that truly maternal hearts correspond with such titles. They feel that the hearts of the Sisters palpitate in unison with theirs, and that, having put aside all thoughts of themselves, the Sisters make their troubles, their interests, their pains, their dreams, their joys, their tragedies, their own. All this, however, is not our merit, but the fruit of the love of Christ and of the prodigious fertility of our Holy Religion, the true friend of the people, the light which guides them in the darkness, the house of refuge, tower of strength and port of safety."

Francesca observed keenly each sight and detail of her trip. She made note to tell her daughters later about the Garden of the Gods, where Manitou, the deity of the Indians, dwells among brightly colored rocks scattered in thousands and sculptured by nature—now imposing, now grotesque, sometimes austere, sometimes frivolous. She saw high upon a rock the nest of an eagle who for years had lived there as queen of the mountains, but when a hunter killed its young eaglet the noble bird left, never to return.

She stopped in the coal area of Trinidad where her daughters

187

went regularly, to go down into the mines to speak to the men. The visits of the sisters were rays of the sun in the bowels of the earth.

When the train left the city of Trinidad, it slowly ascended the mountain district. She beheld austere mountains whose summits were whitened with shining snow, hills green with pine and reddened by the colors of the rock and soil, sharp peaks which seemed to touch the sky and on which the eagle alone rested, plateaus where the hardy goat back from his mountain excursions came to browse upon the grass, and where the slow ox and proud buffalo pastured together, quite unconscious that in the neighboring glen the howl of the white bear echoed. Here and there silver streams descended among the rocks and soon became torrents which, in rapids and waterfalls, followed their beds of many-colored rocks. The name Colorado was most appropriate for that enchanting country, to those most beautiful natural parks, where the hand of man could never add greater beauty than that with which nature had enriched it. Here Francesca exclaimed spontaneously, "How wonderful is my Spouse in His works!"

She stopped in Albuquerque, and again her love embraced the Indians.

"The Indians show an erect forehead and aquiline nose, with a proud intelligence shining over their countenance, whilst the penetrating eye reveals the hardiness proper to their race, not to mention their nobility and kindness. Attracted by the silvery Cross, they asked to be allowed to kiss it. Whilst satisfying this innocent desire of theirs, I thought, 'How many among these uncivilized peoples do not yet know God, and are sunk in the darkest idolatry, superstition and ignorance, without anyone to do them a little good.' Oh, how the heart of the Missionary suffers when, kindled with zeal for the glory of God and the salvation of souls, she feels her very forces paralyzed by her powerlessness to enter into every place where the interests of God call her! They seemed to fix their eyes upon me and

188

seemed to say in their mute languages, 'Why do you not come and bring the light of your Faith amongst us? Oh, generous and Christian souls! Why do you not listen to the call of your distant brothers? You do not lack courage, energy, intelligence or heart. Why leave hidden and buried so many beautiful gifts with which the Lord has endowed you, and not employ them rather for the benefit of those who do not know the true God? Why do you not reflect that these talents of yours, employed in the service of the Lord, will produce immense merit on earth and glory in Heaven?' Thus spoke the poor Indians of Albuquerque to my heart, and a keen feeling of regret makes my heart bleed at not being able now, through lack of assistants, to remain amongst them and to apply myself to their spiritual and intellectual culture."

From the train she contemplated the Arizona desert, that far-flung territory intersected by chains of mountains, profound abysses, and extinct volcanoes, and penetrated with various colored peaks and mountains of gigantic forms, so diverse that they seemed at one moment like castles with turrets and towers of defense, at another like colossal monuments adorned with an infinite number of columns and marvellous sculptures. The Petrified Forest was to her a wood of huge, casually strewn jewels, and she thought that to describe the magnificent panorama of the Grand Canyon was a task beyond the ability of even the most gifted of writers.

"It is a labyrinth of dreamlike architectural forms. There is no reason to envy the pyramids of Egypt or the majestic mausoleums of the Pharaohs, decorated as they are with the most curious ornaments, when nature can produce these marvels, resembling sometimes lace or veil, and giving at other times a vision of festoons hanging from the rocks painted in an endless variety of colors.

"Diaphanous tints of great delicacy are also to be seen. The dignified mountains which dominate this abyss mutate their color according to the hour of the day, so that the rubies you

189

see now change themselves later on into emeralds, become as dazzling as diamonds under the powerful rays of the sun, and in the evening time, glow like sapphires. In the presence of such an imposing spectacle, man feels very small. In the eye of the Faithful, this is an image, though a faint one, of God."

She loved California immediately. It was even more beautiful, she said, than Italy. She was rhapsodic over its blue-bell sky, sunny climate, and lush vegetation. As soon as she arrived in Los Angeles, then a city with only 150,000 inhabitants, she began the search for suitable grounds for a school and orphanage. There was not a hill or valley which she did not visit, and always with an increasing admiration of God's goodness, which was so clearly seen in that privileged part of America. To her every valley was a natural sanatorium.

"It was precisely on one of these hills," she wrote, "that I found a place adapted to our work, and I can say it was prepared for us by the Sacred Heart, for the palm trees in front of the house hide it so nicely that it seems like a real Convent. We are but a short distance from the town, and at the foot of the hill where our House is situated, the Italian families live, so that the Sisters find themselves in a few minutes right on the field of work and are quickly able to reach the School that good Bishop Conaty is erecting for us."

Another letter, written not long afterward, describes the progress of the mission:

"I have had a short restful vacation in gorgeous Catalina Island and in the breathlessly sweeping Sierras. Already our Sisters have begun their work, not only in the behalf of the Italians but also the poor lovable Mexicans, who are numerous here and in dire need of help. Priests are so few here that the heretics have long since sowed their cockle in this beautiful country. I have never seen a place in which there was a greater number of sects, and of the most ridiculous kind. The divine sun and perfumed flowers seems to draw them like flies. Returning home one evening I had to pass through one of the

190

principal streets, when my attention was attracted to a group of women and men prostrate on the ground at the corner of the street, crying and beating their breasts, whilst one of them preached in a loud voice that they should be sorry for their sins. A musing gentleman told me to wait a minute if I wished to see a funny sight. Then, quite suddenly, they all stood up and clapped their hands and danced with joy. This practice of theirs has given them to think that the sins they had wept over were pardoned, and so they are called the 'Holy Jumpers.' There are also the 'Nazarenes,' who profess to live without eating or drinking—if so, an economical way of life. Christian Science holds sway everywhere. In the center of town these people have a big tent, where there are written in large letters the words of Holy Scripture referring to the miracle performed by Saint Peter at the door of the Temple, and there they 'perform' their 'miracles.'

"There the lame walk (?) and the blind see (?), in the presence of those foolish enough to allow themselves to be deceived. But a poor lame man who, in good faith, went in the hope of being cured, was badly treated on one occasion. The spirit invoked was unwilling to obey and perform the demanded miracle. The Minister shouted, 'Lord, listen to us because we are holy and innocent, and come immediately after you!' But it was of no use. The poor man remained as lame as ever, and the minister was so displeased and enraged, that had the man not hobbled out of the tent in a hurry, it would have gone ill with him!"

Having finished for the present her work in Los Angeles, she returned to Chicago, where she found Columbus Hospital thriving. In her twelve-months' absence, 1,000 patients had been treated, and 350 operations performed with splendid results.

"When I arrived, Dr. Murphy, president of the hospital, asked me what I thought of my children—alluding to the many doctors who work there night and day. I answered that I was delighted. It was not a question of children, but of physicians and surgeons, some of whom are already famous in the medical world; yet, you should see how humbly they submit to regulations I dictated, after having studied carefully the local conditions.

"If discipline is necessary in a school, it is essential in an institution of this kind, where the dangers of abuses are great. If I am now able to leave Chicago with a tranquil mind, it is because I know my instructions are carefully observed. Regulations are helpful not only to the Religious but to everyone, for human nature is prone to tire, relax, and change according to events. To persevere in our good resolutions, in spite of difficulties and aversions, strengthens the character and assures happy success to individuals and institutions."

Mother Cabrini's loving guidance of her children was firm indeed!

10 ✠ ✠ ✠

IT WAS twenty-five years since she founded the cradle of her institute at Codogno, and she had in her hands 1,000 brides of Christ distributed in fifty houses. There were 5,000 orphans and thousands of pupils who fondly called her Mother, 100,000 patients who had been treated in her hospitals, and again many thousands of orphaned girls and pupils who had grown to Christian womanhood under her standard of the Sacred Heart.

She was on the threshold of the evening of her life. Against the setting sun, light and shadows alternated joy and pain— but in these, her declining years, more pain than joy.

Dreams of retirement continued to attract her, and she regarded the work of the immediate future as the finishing touches to her life's mission.

Her main concern was the perfect training of her daughters. She wanted them to carry on the mission of the Sacred Heart, for with her slowly fading health, at any time she could be called to that death which would be the beginning of her true life. Since the turn of the century she had thought she could not live long, and this conviction had been an important reason for her earnest insistence on expanding her institute during the years since then. She was in fact very ill. The training of her daughters to carry on her work was, therefore, her particular concern.

To every house she brought strength and wisdom. To a

daughter who wanted undue attention, she said, "I do not like querulous victims—those souls who weigh and consider their sufferings and sacrifices. With one ounce of the love of God one bears burdens silently and joyfully. The way to Heaven is so narrow, so rocky, so thorny, that no one can travel up it, except by flying. No one can fly, except with wings, and the wings do not attach to the body, but to the spirit. There are three degrees of perfection. Of those of the first degree who say, 'I would,' hell is full; of those of the second degree who say, 'I will,' but with velleity, purgatory is overflowing; and of those of the third degree who resolutely say, "I will at any cost!" Heaven is filled."

Often she would tell her daughters the parable of contentment, the story of the farmer who claimed that he always had all that he desired. When he was asked how he could claim that everything was to his liking, the old farmer replied, "When the good Lord makes it rain, I want rain; when He gives me pleasant weather, I want pleasant weather; when He makes it warm, I am content with that. And so, you see, all things go to my liking."

When someone wanted to present Francesca with a relic of a Saint, she refused the gift, saying, "From my earliest childhood I have promised my Spouse that I would never preserve or cherish a memento of any person, no matter who he or she may be. I am sorry, but I cannot accept it."

To a daughter who was given to untimely and embarrassing remarks, she gave this admonition, "I am a woman, and know women. Keep your tongue under control. We women do not guard it nearly enough; we are inclined to levity. We would have good judgment, if we wanted, but for pride; our disposition is definitely one of levity. Consider the Madonna: She had to undergo great suffering; her soul was plunged into a sea of bitterness. And yet, what sweetness, what profound peace possessed her soul! Neither the poverty of Bethlehem, not the anxieties of the flight to Egypt, nor the agony of Calvary

194

availed to disturb her. You have seen the traces of ineffable sorrow in her mien, but you have also seen there the calm of unruffled peace, produced by her perfect conformity with the will of God. I would wish, that in admiring Most Blessed Mary, all my daughters would become so many little immaculates."

In urging imitation of Mary for her daughters, she was sharing with them one of her own most cherished devotions. Ever since her childhood, she had tried to model herself according to Saint Ambrose's description of Mary: "Her movement was not indolent, her walk was not too quick, her voice not affected or sharp; the composure of her person showed the beauty and harmony of her interior. It was a wonderful spectacle to see with what promptness and diligence she performed her domestic duties, to which she applied herself with great solicitude, but always with tranquility and great peace. Her forehead was serene, and a modesty more celestial than terrestrial pervaded her every movement. Her words were few and ever dignified, prudent, and joyful. In Mary, all and everything was well regulated."

Whenever trouble clouded a daughter's face, Francesca would say, "Child of mine, you should be grateful for the cross darkening your countenance, and I envy you, for of crosses I have none. When you are beset and suffer, console yourself by yourself and carry it with a manner no one can discern. And here am I, without any cross!"

The daughter, thus dulcetly reproved, quickly felt comforted, realizing that a cross for the real missionary was a dear treasure, and not to be called a cross.

When a daughter was being rather boisterous, Francesca would advise her that her Spouse did not care for bustle and noise, but preferred to dwell in a quiet, recollected soul.

Once, when she made a modest daughter the head of a school with many hundreds of pupils, the daughter exclaimed in consternation, "Mother, what a grave responsibility! So many innocent young souls for me to guide!" To which she answered, "Do you think that the profit of those souls depends upon you? You do not think Jesus works in them? Misery to us if the production of the good fruit depended upon our poor ability. We have but to do our best and work with much simplicity and without preoccupation. For the rest, we must be confident that, for us, Jesus thinks of everything."

Spiritual books saturated with sentimentalism, obscurantism, fantasy, affectation, and their affinities, she would not tolerate. She wanted words and thoughts to be plain and clearly understandable. She always kept spiritual conferences with her daughters brief, lively, and practical.

If, when she visited a house, she saw long faces, and noted an air of dejection or bad humor, she would not ask what was wrong. Instead, she would put afoot some new work that required movement and more active life that obliged the daughters to get out of themselves. In a few days they would become serene. Once during recreation period, she saw on a daughter's face a look of utter melancholy. Simulating exactly the daughter's sad, pensive expression, she sighed tragically, raised her eyes to heaven, dropped her chin upon her breast, and sang in a woe-begone voice two strophes from the despairing, "Desolate, heaped with vexation am I." To the amazed daughter she said tenderly, "Child, you have troubles? With fifty houses to think about, I have none. Let us abandon ourselves to God, oh dear daughter mine, let us be conducted and guided by Him, let us do His Will, and then our faces will not be pulled, but always placid and radiant."

She gave her attention to all her daughters equally, for all were equal as His children to her. She never commanded, but rather used always the phrase, "I beg you the charity of doing for me," this or that.

Presiding over affairs so complex that they would have taxed even the greatest of executives, she had no office, and owned no portfolio. She cared nothing for possessions of any sort, and on many occasions she exchanged with her daughters her Nuptial band, so dear a reminder to every religious.

196

From the day she left her home in Sant'Angelo for her Spouse, He was her sole desire and attachment. All other longings, for family, home, and material things, she had carefully put aside. She never revisited her birthplace of Sant'-Angelo. One of her daughters demonstrated in many little ways a marked attachment to her parents. In a breaking voice, Francesca said to that daughter, "In the entire giving of myself to our Spouse, I have left behind family and friends without ever being curious about them. I have not permitted myself to follow certain deep-seated inclinations in order to illustrate detachment to my daughters, but I see with you I have not been successful by my example."

At Mass she would become immersed in love. After a service and cantata in a chapel, a daughter asked if she had enjoyed the choral. She answered in all ingenuousness, "No, Daughter. Was I to leave off hearing the dearest voice of my Jesus to listen to your singing?"

During a feast of the Sacred Heart, she remained a long time in the chapel, immobile, transfixed in adoration. Then she retired to her room. A daughter went to her with important business. She sweetly interrupted the daughter and said with ecstasy, "Today belongs to my Jesus, and I am interested in nothing else but Him. Come to me tomorrow with the problems of the institute. Daughter, take Him to you today, forget everything, for this day 'tis He Who does all."

She had written with fine, clear letters in her note-book, "You do know, Oh, my Jesus, that my heart has always been Yours. With Your grace, Most Loving Jesus, I shall follow in Your footsteps to the very end of the course, and that, forever and forever. Help me, Oh, Spouse, for I want to do so fervently, swiftly!"

Thoughts of retirement were blissful dreams, but for the present, there was work to be done. Francesca visited her houses in Argentina and Brazil.

The superior of the Sao Paolo, Brazil, house had with long

197

and strenuous efforts collected a goodly sum of money. She did not bank it, for she proudly wanted to hand it to Mother Cabrini upon her arrival in Sao Paolo. When she and Mother Cabrini went to deposit it, the banker shook his hand and informed them that that particular issue of currency had been called in months before by public proclamation and could no longer be honored. The accompanying daughters wept with dismay, and the superior was so wounded by the cost of her oversight that she took to bed with fever.

Next morning, Francesca visited the distraught superior and found her trembling in bed. She said soothingly, "Daughter mine, is one of His spouses so easily vanquished? For shame. Your loving mother has said not a complaining word to you about the nullified money, and you have let the fever assail you?"

"Mother, Mother, our mission had such need of that money," cried the superior, "and because of my stupidity it is worthless and gone!"

"Sweet Daughter, God gave it, and God saw fit to take it back. You are not at fault. Please do me the favor of forgetting all about it. Now, rest, dream, pray, and tomorrow you leave your bed, and without fever."

Cardinal Arcoverde, from Rio de Janeiro, wrote to her, "Mother Cabrini, I have a million souls to save; help me!"

The train from Sao Paolo to Rio de Janeiro passed through pestilential marshlands, and during the journey, Francesca was bitten by a malaria-bearing mosquito. By the time she reached Rio de Janeiro, she was suffering lassitude and nausea. Then began the paroxysms of intermittent chills and fever. At the Convent of the Good Pastor, where she and the daughter with her were staying, they thought at first she had contracted typhoid or yellow fever, but a blood test revealed the parasites of malaria. For ten days she suffered the head-splitting, bone-shivering fever, and then began to respond favorably to the quinine she was given. Though she accepted this cross with

198

characteristic good humor, she fretted to pursue her mission. To her companion she said gaily, "Daughter, the doctor tells me I must have absolute rest, but the only absolute rest I hope for will come with my death. See, that is how it goes; when I had a great deal to do I had no time for the luxury of sickness, but as soon as I slacken my pace, I fall. The best medicine for me is to tackle a lot more work and to move faster—for when I move at high speed sicknesses can not catch up."

As soon as she was able to leave her bed, she began the arduous search for a house for her school. Despite her illness, she rose at dawn each morning to scour the metropolis. Often she was so weak from the aftereffects of the malaria attack that every exertion left her breathless. Her eyes blurred, and she could barely stand.

As so often, there were influential factions hostile to her work. That did not bother her. By now she had known opposition often enough in her long years of founding Houses to regard it calmly, and went on with her duties. It took her little time to make her preparations, and soon she was ready to open her school.

At just that time, a violent epidemic of smallpox came upon the city. Among the first victims was one of her daughters. Francesca immediately isolated her in a cottage, which she called the villa, on the convent grounds. Soon another daughter, Sister Gesuina, was stricken with the ominous symptoms of chill, headache, backache, and vomiting. More concerned with the work of the mission than with her life, Sister Gesuina concealed her condition, fighting to continue her duties. But all too quickly, the signs were unmistakable. Francesca, the first to notice, put her arms about Sister Gesuina and said, "Daughter, Daughter, why did you hide this awful fact from your Mother? Come, child, to your sickbed in the villa."

She tried desperately to find a little place, "a hole in the cool, safe mountains" for her stricken daughters, but to no avail. In the city, the disease raged, claiming hundreds of lives.

199

Those who owned houses in the mountains locked themselves in and away from contact. More daughters were stricken. Who but she was to take care of them? The ordeal was almost beyond comprehension. There were few doctors in the city, and they, like their colleagues all over the world, at that time, knew of nothing that would cure small pox. Even today, there is no specific remedy for the disease. The empirical therapy then consisted for the most part of applications of heat and cold, and milk baths that invited bacterial complications, only added to the hazards of the disease. Francesca did more than pray. Having isolated the infected daughters in the villa and personally undertaken their cure, she gave them ample fresh air and fresh drinking water, calomel, and saline purges. She sprayed phenol against the putrescent odors. She nourished them with boiled skim milk, brushed glycerine on their skin, sterilized everything they used, as well as her own clothes coming and going.

Her beloved daughters presented a most terrible sight. Their flesh was a confluent mass of pustules, their skin purplish, their faces swollen, their eyes deeply sunken. Day after day, she was with them.

All her patients except Sister Gesuina passed the crisis and responded to her ceaseless, intelligent, tenacious care. The health authorities, fearful that the school children would be infected, demanded that Sister Gesuina be removed to the public pesthouse, and for the sake of the school's future she had to acquiesce. Her heart was torn at the thought of parting with her mortally ill daughter. Her sole comfort was the sainted disposition of that daughter who, when informed that she would be carted to the house of death, though delirious with fever and pain, quickly said, "Surely, I will let myself be taken, for I do not wish this mission of the school to be endangered in the least just because of me."

From a safe distance a curious crowd watched the horse-drawn ambulance wagon of the lazzaretto arrive. Sister Gesuina was not aware of the doctor while he checked her fleeing pulse, but she heard Mother Cabrini whisper, "Dear Gesuina, 'tis time for thee to leave." And at the sound of that gentle voice, which was to her the voice of obedience, the dying daughter sat up. Assured that she had her Crucifix in her hands, and the Scapular of the Madonna about her neck, she whispered cheerfully, "Let us go," and then collapsed into coma.

Francesca's birthday was a few days later. On that day, she received word of Sister Gesuina's death. "As my gift today," she said softly, "The Spouse, has called our daughter, His bride, sweet Gesuina, to Him."

The faction opposed to Francesca's mission hoped that the tragedy of the smallpox epidemic would drive the religious school away. While she was passing through the crowded Central Square, a young lady of fashion, who belonged to the hostile group stopped her and ironically offered her condolences for Sister Gesuina's death. Francesca's eyes flamed, and she exclaimed, "Your malevolence does not escape me. But, you who labor to ruin the work of the Sacred Heart will eventually have to accept most bitter wages!" Then in a lower voice, she added kindly, "My disdain is directed not against your person, fine young lady, but against the evil in you." She smiled and turned away. As she was leaving the Square, the daughter with her exclaimed, "Oh Mother, what a royal dressing down you gave her, in front of all those people!" She chuckled. "Daughter, I have malaria and sundry other debilities, and am aging. In fact I am utterly worn out at present. Nevertheless, before those creatures who think themselves better than God, I feel stronger than a lion." That courageous public reprimand put an end to the unreasonable opposition, and, in fact, transformed the hostile into respectful and thankful friends of the school.

Francesca was determined that never again should an epidemic threaten her daughters and pupils. She found a healthy refuge in a spacious estate outside of the city in the picturesque

201

mountains of Tijuca. The grounds were resplendent with palm trees, flowers, and cascading streams and made a perfect setting for her school and convent. Before she left Rio, she held a festive scholastic service, which was attended by her former enemies as well as those who had supported her from the first.

Her work in Rio done, she returned to the United States. She spent the next two years visiting all her American houses, tending to necessary reorganization. In 1910, when she found herself again in Chicago, she undertook another major expansion. The Chicago Columbus Hospital had become so well known for its medical services that it drew patients from all over the United States. Archbishop Quigley, his heart ever close to the welfare of the immigrants, suggested that she open another hospital, this one to be strictly for charity patients. Although she was sixty years old, she charged into the task with the semblance of eternal youth. The new project seemed to rejuvenate her. Like a young girl she hastened about the city looking for a building.

Her poor should have a nice building with quiet surroundings. In one of Chicago's elegant residential sections, her eyes lighted upon a fine large property that she thought would be ideal for her free hospital. On impulse she rang the bell and asked if the property could possibly be for sale. The impulse seems to have been inspired by Providence, for the owner was a widow of means who had long dreamed of performing an act of true charity. Soon the estate belonged to the Missionary Sisters. Immediately, the wealthy residents of the neighborhood protested. They did not want a free hospital in their midst, and put pressure on doctors and politicians to help them in their opposition.

When politics and bribery did not deter Francesca, her opponents turned to more desperate measures. One night while the building was being renovated, the temperature dropped to twenty degrees below zero. During the night, Francesca received word that something was wrong. She hurried to her new building, and found there a scene of deliberate sabotage. The water pipes had been cut in many places, flooding the building and freezing into heavy layers of ice. She had the water main turned off at once. The next morning, she, her daughters, and their immigrant friends hacked away at the ice-covered floors with picks and axes. Soon they had repaired all the damage. Thereafter, she had a few rooms made habitable and moved in to protect the work.

A few weeks before the opening of the hospital, she awakened one morning before dawn to find dense black smoke filling the building. Arsonists had broken into the basement in the dead of the night, poured oil on all the floors and set it afire, disregarding the lives of the sisters. She and her daughters bravely fought the flames until the firemen arrived. The following night she made sure the doors were bolted, and stayed awake herself all night to act as sentinel. As she had anticipated, the hired arsonists returned and tried to force the basement door. As soon as she heard them, Francesca rushed out into the street and called the police. She succeeded in frightening the criminals away, but they were not caught.

Francesca was certain that her antagonists would not dare to set fire to the hospital if it housed bedridden patients, so she did not wait for the formal opening. She quickly moved in sixteen patients, and within three days the hospital was filled to capacity.

The enthusiasm of the immigrants for their new hospital was boundless, and Pope Pius X sent a telegram of benediction on the occasion of its opening.

The wealthy interests who had opposed the hospital were by no means silenced, but the work was so urgent, and Francesca's competence so well appreciated that she found support from the most diverse sources. Even anticlerical organizations joined her fight. All the humane elements in the community united and subscribed to her charity hospital, each according to his ability and means. Societies paid for the bulk of the

203

equipment and the furnishing of the operating rooms; individuals supplied the needs of sickrooms. Long tables were set up in the reception hall to receive gifts. The rich and the many poor came gladly, among them many non-Italians and non-Catholics. Supplies came in torrents day after day.

Having put the new hospital on its feet, Francesca realized that it was far from large enough. Not worrying about whether or not it could be built within her lifetime, she prepared the design of a vast edifice.

In 1910, the affairs of all her American establishments were in order, and a visit to her European houses was long overdue. In March, she sailed for Italy.

It was the Holy Week when she sailed. What a joy it was for her to rest her malarial-wracked body and limbs. The sun and sea had always been her best medicine; yet even aboard the ship she continued to feel ill. More than ever she longed to retire to the pastoral hills of West Park. She yearned for time to meditate above the ever-moving Hudson, to relax her spirit. She wanted to wander the fields and gather flowers, to select herbs and compound salutary teas and medicines for the ill, to prepare for the sweet death that could not now be distant.

From the Rome general house she announced her determination to relinquish her position, and asked the institute to convoke an assembly for the purpose of electing a superior general to replace her. She fully expected her daughters to understand that after thirty years of incessant work, she had neared the end of her physical resources. The most practical course the institute could now take, she thought, was to replace her with a younger woman. She, steeped in hard-won wisdom, would counsel from her peaceful, contemplative retirement.

Mother Cabrini's proposed retirement was a shock to her daughters. It was impossible to imagine that anyone on earth could take the place of their mother-foundress while she was alive. Pope Leo XIII had proclaimed, "Cabrini, thou art the

204

elect of God! We must work 'till death, and paradise awaits!" How could they think of displacing their Mother who had been elected by God!

Without letting her know, every one of her fifty houses exchanged impassioned letters. No, they would not disobey their mother. Yes, they would vote for a superior general to serve for life—and that mother would be Francesca Xavier Cabrini.

It was not that they deceived her. They simply obtained the signature of every daughter, and sent the unanimous result to the Assistant-General in Rome. Under the direction of Cardinal Pietro Respighi and other eminents, the Assistant-General obtained confirmation from Pope Pius X for Mother Cabrini to be designated superior general for life.

The daughters arranged to present their loving decision to her as a birthday surprise. On the morning of July 16, she noticed in the chapel an unusual profusion of candles and flowers before the altar of the Madonna, but did not connect its splendor with herself. After Mass a great number of smiling daughters surrounded her, offering heartfelt good wishes for her birthday. When she commented ruefully on her age, all the daughters spontaneously proffered their own lives, saying they wished their remaining years should be added to hers.

"Dearest Daughters," she responded, "Tell me. Just what could I possibly do with a lot of dead nuns?" Mischievous laughter greeted this remark. Francesca was puzzled. "What is behind all this excitement?" she asked. "I have never seen you as festive as you are today."

They answered in chorus, "Mother, this day is very special!"

Not in the least enlightened by this answer, she shrugged.

"Every day is the Lord's, and therefore special. Thank you, my good Daughters, but I have work to do."

Later in the day Cardinal Vives y Tuto, prefect of the Sacred Congregation of the Religious, summoned her and a large group of daughters. Now, she thought, her wish to retire would be honored.

Her daughters crowded about her, struggling to keep their faces straight, and the cardinal did his solemn best to look serious. "Mother Francesca Xavier Cabrini," he began in a severe voice, "You petitioned to retire?"

"Yes, Your Eminence."

"Mother Cabrini, will you obey me?"

"Eminence," she answered most humbly, "I have always been obedient, I am obedient, and I shall always be obedient."

"Very well then," said the cardinal, beginning to smile, "Since you have run your institute so badly until now, your Daughters, the Sacred Congregation, and His Holiness Pius X have decided to give you the opportunity of doing better in the future. Therefore, you are to remain superior general of the Missionary Sisters of the Sacred Heart for the rest of your blessed life!" And the Cardinal broke out into hearty laughter.

"Most Reverend Mother Cabrini," said the cardinal, as he signed the document, "this is the happiest moment of my religious life."

The joy of her daughters was indescribable. They presented her with an album containing the signed names of every one of her daughters, and a long letter which spoke of their love for her. The words of Saint Tobias perfectly described their feelings: "Honor thy mother in every season of thy days; and it becomes thee to record how much and often she has suffered for thee."

After reading the letter to her, her daughters sang a joyous hymn, and one by one knelt and kissed her wedding ring. She looked upon them tenderly.

With gentle humor, she said, "Had the procedure been held in the proper democratic manner, surely I would not have been accorded complete approval."

The daughters gaily and emphatically protested.

"Well," Francesca asked with twinkling eyes, "what about all those who wanted to be superior general? Are their hopes shattered?"

Her daughters laughed heartily.

The moment of whimsy passed, and Francesca, deeply moved, addressed her daughters soberly.

"Your Mother I have always been," she said. "And had you permitted my retirement and elected another superior, I would have remained in my heart your very own mother. Since you want me to serve as your mother *in perpetuo,* I obey your wish. You must know that in the future I shall remain as rigorous against your defects as in the past. I shall continue to correct you with frankness, not allowing one fault to get by. Who of you can say that I ever kept quiet when it was necessary to reprove you?"

With one voice they responded, "No one!" And valuing her priceless maternal candor, they thanked her with overflowing hearts.

The long-cherished dream of devoting her final days to preparation for the union with her Spouse dissolved, she pulled together her waning strength to urge on her mission. In August she hastened to Paris to seek another shelter for the orphans there, as the rented building that housed them had been sold. She trudged the streets for two months, but her search was in vain. Finally, when she could remain in Paris no longer, she left that problem to her Jesus, and went on to England. Months later, the Italian ambassadoress Donna Tittoni, found an elegant villa at Noisy Le Grand for the French orphans.

In England her mission was crowned with success. After a few months of diligent search, she was able to transfer her daughters from their modest house in Brockley to a large residence in the London suburb of Honor Oak. Her English daughters sadly perceived her progressive debility. Some two or three times a day in the course of her work, she had to climb the stairway to the elevated trains. Each time she became white and breathless and had to stop every few steps. When her daughters tried to help her, she would wave them aside and assure them with a smile that her weakness was a temporary indisposition.

Just when the affairs of the London house seemed to be in order, a legal involvement regarding the property arose. She could have left the problem to the lawyer for the institute and her English daughters, but she was reluctant to leave the England Pope Leo had loved so, whose people had so delighted her with their courtesy, for she felt that she would never see it again. So she stayed on until the business of the London house was settled.

When she was free to leave England, she returned to Italy for a sorely needed rest. In Codogno she performed her spiritual exercises with the observance and fervor of one who prepares for death. Following her retreat, she spent days perusing and systematically categorizing the papers of the archives.

Those yellowing documents told stories of invincible dreams that became brick and stone houses of many chambers and chapels. These many buildings, offering homes to abandoned infants, shelter to the sick, wholesome surroundings to school children, were important. More important were the dedicated human beings who worked within their walls. Throughout the too-small world, young sisters were developing into other Cabrinis. They instructed children, mothered orphaned babies, cared for the sick and injured. Through their example, sinners returned to Christ. The papers reminded her of His works accomplished by His Will through her frail hands. She was faithfully putting her House in order before she departed.

"Daughters," she asked one day, "is Antonia Tondini still alive? If by God's grace she is, bring her to me. I would like very much to see her once more."

When she was told that Antonia Tondini had been brought to the convent and was in the reception room, she was delighted. She greeted the shriveled old woman with an affectionate embrace.

208

"Antonia, God bless you. I have thought of you with affection so often, and longed to see you."

The senile Tondini was confused. "Francesca . . . Mother Cabrini . . . pardon me. For the love of God, pardon this old woman. I do not understand your goodness. You were but a girl, and I a stiff-necked woman. Somehow, we did not get along. I did not mean evil . . . life is strange. And now, why do you stoop to the sight of me, why did you ask for me?"

"Antonia Tondini, blessings on you. Much has happened since last we were together. What you refer to, I have forgotten long ago. How has it been with you? Are you well, are you at peace?"

Before Tondini left, Francesca knelt before her.

"Antonia Tondini, please forgive me for any displeasure that, involuntarily, I may have caused you."

The trembling old woman wept like a child, and Francesca arose and kissed her hands. Later, a daughter who had witnessed the moving scene said, "And she made you suffer unendurably; is it not true, Mother?" To which Francesca answered with simplicity, "Antonia Tondini was given by God not to know any better. She truly thought, when she treated me the way she did, that it was for my good."

In the cloistered quiet of Codogno she reviewed her past in the little city. She relived the soul-trying years in Antonia Tondini's frenetic House of Providence—truly her greatest trial, and yet the dearest. In a sense, she had never really left the House of Providence. How often throughout the busy years had she thought of the building after it was vacated! How often in her heart she saw the deserted floors and doors and windows and walls and roof that sheltered, even though poorly, her first orphans! Always the drab structure whispered of tenuous hopes, dreams, tears, and silent and spoken prayers. Yes, the House of Providence had been the crucible that tempered

209

the strength of her charity. To her, the injustices, doubts, threats, and injuries were the testing and trying storms that had formed her.

Then, there were the sweet orphans who were later to become her first daughters. She remembered as though it were again taking place the hour and moment that she gave her holy vows.

Ah, Codogno, birthplace of her institute. It pained her unutterably to leave Codogno now. As the carriage bore her to the railroad station, she turned to look at the scenes of her youth—the convent, the chapel, and her first house—with the presentiment that she would see them again only when looking down upon them from Paradise.

She returned to Rome. Soon after came chronic anemia joined with a severe malarial attack. She suffered acute chills, fever, and faintness. For months she was too ill to leave her rooms, though she repeatedly tried to resume the work of the institute. Finally, her fever and nausea become so severe that she could not raise her head from her pillow. Her daughters were desolate, for she had been reduced to a shadow.

During the latter part of March, as the early flowers were blooming in Rome, she called the directoress of the Rome house.

"Daughter, Columbus Hospital in New York is desperately overcrowded. We must have a new building. Pack my traveling bag; I am leaving for America."

"But, Mother," protested the devoted daughter, "ill as you are, how can you think of making the voyage?"

The daughter was deeply concerned for her, but Mother Cabrini said smilingly, "Fear not for me. Work and God's wondrous sea will be my medicine."

Knowing that she would never return to Europe, she wanted to visit all her daughters in Italy, France, Spain, and England; but she felt that her little time would be better spent at work.

210

Instead of personal visits, she sent a circular, praying her daughters to understand that the hours pressed against her fond wish to see them. She told of the task before her, the building of a new Columbus Hospital in New York.

"We need a vast sum," she wrote, "and I have nothing. I have only the benediction of the August Pontiff, but his written recommendation is as a treasure in my hand."

She also wrote to her daughters with tenderness of Christ's love for them. Of death, she says, "Beatified is this death that our Spouse has earned for us with His Sanctified Passion and Crucifixion. I leave you in His Heart, wherein I pray that you implore graces for your Mother, who so much loves and thinks of you."

A group of daughters accompanied her to Naples, where she was to embark for America. As was her custom, she made arrangements for them to have dinner aboard. To mitigate their sadness at her departure, she ate a bit of fish and made light of her illness, pretending that she felt completely well. She would talk of nothing serious, and marshalled forth her natural humor. When it was nearly time for the ship's guests to leave, she said sadly, "My Daughters, 'tis late." Each step they took as they slowly descended the gangplank, was a blow to her heart, for she knew it was the last time she would see them. Her look followed them with the most profound affection.

11 ✠ ✠ ✠

IT WAS the spring of 1912 when she arrived back in New York. The old Post Graduate Hospital that she had made into her Columbus Hospital had served valiantly for eighteen years, its merciful arms ever open to the afflicted and the poor. But now it was painfully overcrowded, and its facilities sadly limited. With bold vision Francesca decided upon an edifice that would cost 1 million dollars. To many her proposal was fantastic. For a year she knocked on doors and turned here and there, trying to raise 200,000 dollars to initiate the great new hospital. Her failure to get the money did not discourage her. She could visualize the future, and knew that the new hospital she wanted would not remain an illusion. With as much confidence as if she had the million dollars in her hands, she called a young architect, and with him designed a majestic modern building of ten storys.

She devoted herself so energetically to the project that she denied herself even a sojourn in pastoral West Park, and urged on her lessening strength relentlessly. One morning she came to the threshold of her room, her face pale and her beautiful green-blue eyes glowing. The daughters near her room were horrified to see her swaying weakly. "Daughters mine," she gasped, "I am dying, I am dying." Raising her hands imploringly, she cried, "Come, oh Angel of death, come!" She collapsed into unconsciousness.

212

Her daughters' care of her was prodigious. They labored desperately to sustain life within the tiny worn being. A benefactress had donated to the institute a modest health refuge for ill nuns, a lodge atop the Mount of the Holy Cross in Colorado. When she was well enough to travel her daughters sent her there to convalesce. She protested that it would be valuable time taken from her work, but her daughters insisted that she rest, and she obeyed them. With one daughter to look after her needs, she settled down in a log cabin amid the gleaming snows on the mountaintop. She was delighted with her peaceful surroundings.

She loved to watch the soaring eagles, and when a distant hunter shot one to earth, she sorrowed for the proud winged creature of God who fell victim to the gun of man. In the pure, dry mountain air she gradually gained strength. The solitude and peace allowed her time for blissful meditation.

After weeks of rest and prayer, she said to her companion, "Daughter, eternity is for rest and bliss, not this brief life. I have stayed too long upon this delightful mountain. The children of Los Angeles require another school. Let us be moving and doing."

In Los Angeles, as everywhere, needs far outweighed means. She quickly acquired four lots, but could raise very little money to build a school. A general contractor was out of the question, but there was always an answer to a problem. She sent for sturdy construction-wise Sister Salesia, the bricklayer's daughter who, since their rudimentary addition to the Codogno house twenty-seven years before, had gathered much practical building ability. Learning that an amusement area called Luna Park was to be leveled for business purposes, she lost no time in bargaining for the wooden buildings that were to be demolished. She hired expert Italian carpenters and hardy laborers by the day, and rented big horses and wagons to cart material.

The workmen, daughters, orphans, schoolchildren, and good friends of the parish formed a gay army. With hammers, pinch

213

bars, and crowbars, they attacked the doomed frame structures of Luna Park.

It was a strange sight to see nuns and children climbing ladders, beleaguering the roof of the dancehall, carefully ripping apart the gambling stands and the gaudy postered shacks of the amusement park.

Francesca personally supervised the work. She was everywhere at the new building site, with a wide-brimmed Mexican sombrero on her head and a bamboo cane in her hand. She reigned supreme from morning to dark in wind and hot sun and rain, directing her cheerful gangs of orphans in the systematic sorting and stacking: the window sashes here, doors and jambs there, moldings here, clapboards there, wainscotting there. There were special buckets for hinges and screws, locks, and other hardware. And the orphans made the work a great game. They competed in yanking nails and hammering them straight for reuse, and had fun whacking the powdery lime mortar from bricks to be laid in foundation, chimney, and stoops.

Each day at noon she drove a horse and cart between the demolishing work at Luna Park and the new building site, bringing lunch and wine to the men, and hot coffee, sandwiches, and sweets to her daughters and the children. The work was strenuous; faces became tanned in the good California sunshine, and often her first-aid kit was needed for injuries. The communal labors were lightened with laughter and song, and blessed with prayer.

After thirty-one days the collecting of building materials was completed. Since she had more than she required for the building she had designed, she had the surplus, even to the last nail, loaded on a freight car and shipped to the Denver orphanage to serve toward expansion there.

Now, she had to leave Sister Salesia with the responsibility of the construction, and hurry to meet an urgent problem in Seattle. The Seattle orphanage happened to be right in the

214

path of a planned city highway, and she had to provide the orphans with another shelter. She resorted to her practice of painstaking exploration on foot, to the dismay of her daughters, who begged her to spare both herself and them from the gruelling pace she set.

But despite her sixty-three years and her precarious health, she would say, "You young ones are fatigued? Very well, I will search by myself."

After days of fruitless searching, even she was reduced to a relentless exhaustion. She placed a map of Seattle before her daughters, put her finger upon a location, and said, "Go to this section, look it over thoroughly and report to me your findings."

"But, Mother," responded a daughter, "permit me to say that I doubt if there is anything suitable there. I know that section well, and there is nothing, just nothing there."

"Just the same, Daughter, go there, and then tell me what you have found."

That night the daughters returned to the convent greatly excited and exclaimed, "Oh, Mother, we went exactly where you told us to go, and found a little paradise on earth!"

She listened to their enthusiastic description, and then said, "I knew it would be a beautiful place. I saw it all, in my dream last night."

The following day she saw in reality the property that had appeared in her dream—a villa atop a hill, which commanded a breathtaking view. The proprietor told her that the estate belonged to his wife, and that she would not part with her Eden for all the gold in the world. Her daughters were downcast, but Francesca, when she left, calmly remarked, "That paradise will be for our orphans . . . somehow or other."

They descended the hill to the village below, and began the journey back to the convent. Francesca and her daughters were exhausted. Evening was falling, and at that hour the trolleys were few. She hesitated to hire a taxi because of the cost, but was concerned about the fatigue of the daughters with her.

While Francesca debated with herself, she saw a chauffeur-driven limousine approaching. It carried only one passenger, an elegantly dressed lady. That decided her.

She raised her cane and signaled. The lady had her car stopped and graciously offered to drive them back to the convent. On the way, Francesca talked with the lady, and in the course of the conversation the lady learned that she was talking to Mother Cabrini, whose work she had long admired. Francesca talked of the paradise she had seen and wanted for her orphans. At the convent door she said to the lady, "I am grateful for your goodness, and pray that the Lord will always recompense tenfold whatever charity you perform."

The lady's eyes grew moist. "Mother Cabrini, the property you saw today, the 'paradise' you speak of—I own it. I had never thought of parting with it. But, if I may be allowed to enter your Holy House for a moment and receive from your hands, a glass of water in the name of Our Lord, your little orphans shall have their 'paradise' with all my heart."

Visiting the orphans in their new home and seeing the villa and grounds, Archbishop O'Dea could not cease repeating, "Beautiful, marvelously beautiful! But tell me, Mother Cabrini, how did you do it, how did you acquire this magnificent property?"

With a smile she answered, "Excellence, I paid for it with three treasures: my love, a dream, and a glass of water in His name."

Having acquired the beautiful estate, Francesca made it known throughout Seattle that she needed 100,000 dollars with which to build a proper orphanage on it. Scarcely a week later, two American gentlemen came to her with 160,000 dollars in cash. The gift was intended to cover the cost of a splendid chapel as well as the orphanage. The only condition they required was that they be allowed to remain anonymous. She complied with their request, and not until many years later was it known that the grateful donors were Patrick Heensy and William Pigott.

216

Her great Seattle project safely under way, she returned to New York and a problem at West Park. The civil authorities had complained that the distance between New York City and West Park made it difficult for relatives and friends to visit the orphans. To solve the problem Francesca decided to open another orphanage closer to the city, and began to look for suitable property along the bank of the Hudson not far from the city. At Dobbs Ferry, which enjoyed the quiet atmosphere of the country and yet was convenient to New York, she found an old house for sale. She inquired about it for the purpose of finding out how expensive property in that area was. As she had expected, the price was exorbitant.

"Mother," said a daughter, "it is useless to look for a house here. This is a neighborhood of millionaires, and they would hardly be interested in our cause."

In answer, Francesca went to the most sumptuous estate in the area, which lay on the river side of the street. She regarded the large fine building and cultivated grounds with possessive and approving eyes.

"What are you up to, Mother?" asked the daughter timorously. "This is a private school for wealthy boys. Furthermore, it is Protestant!"

"Protestant?" Francesca replied. "Well, well, very good. In that case the wealthy Protestant boys will have to pack and leave for the sake of our poor little orphans!"

In answer to her ring, the son of the president-owner appeared. The young man, who also taught at the school, was somewhat disconcerted to find himself facing an elderly Catholic nun. Confidently, Francesca asked whether the property of the school were for sale. At first the young teacher was disposed to be uncommunicative, but Francesca's rare personality impressed him. He could not help being drawn to her, and invited her and her daughters in to inspect the building.

The school had excellent accommodations—classrooms, dormitories, kitchen, dining room, chapel, gymnasium, swimming pool—all in perfect condition.

The young man informed her that she might tempt his father to sell the property if she offered him 100,000 dollars.

She gracefully responded that she would make her own calculations as to its worth. As he escorted her to the door, she gazed at the property thoughtfully and gave her daughters a look that said, "This is just the place I want for our orphans."

She went to wealthy men for the funds. She presented her cause directly, using the plain words of Paul. As usual, her solicitations were effective, and she got the school.

She planned a festive opening for the Dobbs Ferry Sacred Heart Villa. The date was to be March 31, the twenty-fifth anniversary of the day the Missionary Sisters of the Sacred Heart had first set foot upon American land. She wanted a jubilee celebration, to give thanks to her Spouse for the blessings that had prospered her work.

Beautiful as the house and grounds were when she took possession, Francesca could think of improvements that must be made before the gala opening. Happily, she and her daughters undertook the work themselves, with Francesca assigning the chores.

"Daughter, the glorying of the chapel, once Protestant, and now to be only of the holy faith—is yours. And you, Daughter, are horticulturist and custodian of gardens. Daughter, yours are the hands to make the cook pots sing." One by one, she distributed the tasks among them until at last, she paused and reflected, "To each and all have I ordered, and here I have left myself without a duty. But, come to think of it, there is one more office to be performed: that of brightening with paint the face of our house; Jesus has made me omit that command, because He wants me to do it!"

With a painter's cap on her head and the skirt of her robe pinned up, she applied herself with joy. The can slipped from her grasp, splattering her from head to foot. Laughing, she righted it and continued to daub away. Her daughters held the ladder steady when she climbed its rungs, and whenever they

218

begged to relieve her, she protested, "Be so kind as to tend to your own work. This is my special chore, my pleasure!" For fifteen days she dipped and brushed until she had completed her job.

When all was ready, she invited Cardinal Bonzano, Apostolic Delegate to the United States in Washington, to celebrate the jubilee Mass, and preside at the opening of the Dobbs Ferry orphanage.

Although the good cardinal assumed that the Dobbs Ferry orphanage would be an inconspicuous provincial affair, he graciously agreed. When the day came and he arrived, the mansion, with its extensive grounds, lavish gardens, and beautiful, capacious chapel, surprised him. As guests began to arrive for the ceremonies, his surprise turned to astonishment at the magnitude of the celebration he was to preside over. Carriage after carriage arrived to discharge dignitaries of the highest rank of both Church and state. The orphans filed into the chapel in a seemingly endless stream. With their faces sparkling, hair beribboned, and spotless dresses neatly starched, they were as pretty as the flowers of the gardens.

Seeing them, the cardinal turned to the modest little nun at his side and exclaimed, "Mother Cabrini, your heart is supreme for these orphans. You have given them a cardinal's villa to live in!"

After the Holy Mass, Cardinal Bonzano addressed the large and enthusiastic audience that had assembled in honor of the occasion. He spoke of Francesca's sacrifice, and heroism.

"Thirty-five years ago," he said, "this family of the Sacred Heart did not exist. Today, it numbers sixty-five illustrious houses and 1,500 Daughters."

His words, he said, could not demonstrate the fruit of her labors. Her schools, orphanages, and hospitals testified most eloquently for her.

"It is not the Church alone that is indebted to our Mother Cabrini. This nation of America owes her profound gratitude, for within her fold she raises children who will become sane, inspired citizens, who one day will help to form the soul of this new land."

Francesca, seated quietly alongside the impressive churchman, contemplated the beautiful orphans with joy. Her thoughts turned to her first orphan in America, the ragged little girl from Mulberry Street, whom she had dressed with cloth from her own habit. How her Spouse had multiplied the worth of a few yards of His bride's robe!

It was during the happy commotion of this jubilee that, by stratagem, the rare and final photograph of Francesca Cabrini was taken. In it, she sits with folded hands watching His children, calmly smiling. The serenity of her smile seems to say, "Glory not to me for I am nothing. Glory belongs to God, Whose works are here before us."

The next morning found her again at work with her daughters. Father O'Keefe of the nearby Hastings parish had begun the excavation for the foundation of his new church. The building site was on a great layer of rock that had to be blasted and removed. She obtained from him at no cost a huge quantity of rock, gathered stonemasons and volunteers, and erected a wall on the river side of the grounds. As she described the work,

"I could not bear to see the quality rock from the excavation of the Hastings church go to waste. With hammer, trowel, and mortar, friends who are experienced at these things freely raised the long high wall. When it was completed, I playfully remarked to these good men that it would be fun to have a little castle atop the wall overlooking the grand Hudson. Within a week, the men fashioned a castello as if by magic.

"I directed the work, spending every day in the open air and sunshine, with my cheap little cane in hand, and a big, gay straw hat on my head, looking for the world like a genuine

220

peasant. Thus did I make of summer's soft season a nice companion."

Then fell the shadow of the terrible cloud that was to darken her closing days. Sarajevo. The twenty-eighth of June, 1914.

The news from the capital of Bosnia, now Yugoslavia, that Archduke Francis Ferdinand had been assassinated, heralded the world-embracing madness of war.

From that day, she was inwardly to sorrow and weep, her breast a tomb of tears for the numberless wounds inflicted upon the heart of her Spouse. She told her daughters that the black announcement of war was the beginning desolation of desolations. Each house in the European inferno would now have to trust for their safety to the heart of the Spouse. The corrupt, the licentious, the irreligious, had outraged divine love, and were to reap for mankind a harvest of wormwood. She begged her daughters to renew their spirits in Christ during this doleful trial.

Each day the newspapers vividly described the massive flow of destruction. She read of stark armies smiting His human creations, and knew that hourly, daily, weekly, monthly, the holocaust was an ever-spreading torrent, compounding its horrors, killing and mutilating men, women, and children, turning to rot that which He made fleshly in His image. And a grave veil lowered over her smile to stay. Rest and sleep were scarcely for her any longer. Instead she gave ceaseless prayers for peace amongst His children.

Why could she not be by the side of her menaced daughters in France and England? But that was impossible. She wrote to them, exhorting them to remain brave and tranquil.

"Dearest Daughters, let the mantle of your charity cover all without question. Gather all the dependents of the dead and wounded and homeless. Now is the hour to stretch out your hands to all victims of disaster, the poor, the rich, the believing, and the unbelieving. From your bastion of Christ's love Providence will not be lacking, but will abide with you in abundance. Take to yourselves the abandoned babies, for they are His emissaries of the future on earth, the Christian fathers and mothers of a better tomorrow."

The day after Pope Pius X promulgated his immortal encyclical of peace, she wrote a telegram of appreciation. But in the heat of wartime feeling, the words "peace" and "love," seemed treasonable, and censorship prevented her message from reaching the pontiff.

Melchior Joseph Sarto—Pius X—as priest, as bishop, as pope, was always an apostle. He loved the people, and his heart bled for them in mortal anguish as he saw the First World War crushing their cities, their homes, their work, their lives. So deeply did he grieve over it, that he withdrew within himself and died.

Upon the death of Pope Pius X, the conclave of cardinals, elevated Cardinal Giaccomo Della Chiesa of Bologna to the papacy. This new pope, Benedict XV, devoted all his energies to alleviating the atrocious consequences of the murderous war. Bravely he denounced the First World War as a blind, "useless struggle," and he pleaded for immediate peace and the unity of all nations under the reign of Christ. Francesca Cabrini shared with heart and soul the new pontiff's aspirations, but in the hysteria of the wholesale slaughter, there were all too few to heed the call to peace.

Her sorrow over the war did not distract Francesca from the work at hand. Indeed, she was too distressed to find relief in anything short of intense activity. In August of 1915, she began a big new mission in Seattle. On the way to the western city, she confided to one of her daughters, "Actually, I had no desire to take this trip, nor had I in mind any more missions. But for some months past the Lord has been trying to make me understand that while so many are destroying, I should

222

build, and He has made me to feel that I have a labor to perform in Seattle."

Trembling with intermittent chills and fever, she gazed from the train window at the passing landscape, and continued as if in soliloquy, "If my Lord wants this mission accomplished He will return to me the strength which has almost totally abandoned me. He is doing so, and that is why we are on our way. Truly, I do not feel quite able, but think how much worse I would be if He at this moment were not sustaining me."

The trip required many days of sitting upright in the coach. When the train ran through the intense heat of the desert, she suffered agonizing pain. She said not a word about it, but at night, when she thought her daughters were sleeping and would not hear, soft, intense groans escaped her lips.

In Seattle, she planned to open a foundling home. Archbishop O'Dea and the public seemed to favor the idea, but life had long since proven to her the instability of human beings. She did not depend upon them, but sought rather, the favor of Heaven, choosing the sainted mother of Mary as patroness for the babies who would never know their earthly mothers. She bought a statue of Saint Anna, and confided to her the care of the foundlings' future. Just at that time her daughters of Rio de Janeiro sent her a beautiful statue of the Child Jesus. When the statue arrived, she quickly summoned all her daughters, and as they stood about the statue, she exclaimed, "How adorable He is. He only needs to speak!" Comforted now by her two celestial patrons, she proceeded to work.

The property she selected for the orphanage was a fine big building that had been the Perry Hotel. The enterprise had gone bankrupt, but its situation was not publicized. It was a fine structure, located in the center of the city on Madison Street and Boren Avenue. With difficulty, Francesca found out that the principal trustee of the Perry Hotel estate was a "Mr.

223

Clarke" who was in New York. She was afraid that open inquiries would alert competitive business interests to her plans, so she prudently refrained from investigating further. Thus, she had to contact Mr. Clarke without knowing his first name. She telegraphed her New York daughters, "Find a certain Mr. Clarke, who is in possession of the Seattle Hotel Perry, and ask it as a donation to charity."

There were at least 200 Clarkes in the New York City directory. The daughters kept telephoning Clarkes until they finally found the right one. Two daughters went to him and timidly relayed to him Francesca's request. He was not only a shrewd man of the world who lived by and for dollars, but also a Protestant. Astonished as he was to be approached for such a tremendous donation to a Catholic charity, he was not too shocked to refuse with vehemence. The two gentle daughters nodded silently and left.

Francesca's next telegram instructed the daughters to return and make Mr. Clarke some sort of an offer. With the simplicity, truthfulnesss, and obedience that they learned from her, they again went to Mr. Clarke. As they mentioned money this time, he listened. Their humility impressed him, and he could not help admiring their obedience to their insistent mother in Seattle. Gradually, he became willing to negotiate. After a series of visits from the angelic missionaries and some ninety telegrams exchanged with Mother Cabrini in Seattle, he assumed complete responsibility over the heads of the other trustees and offered her the Perry Hotel for the extremely low figure of 150,000 dollars.

"Mother, do not let the Perry Hotel get away from you," said Archbishop O'Dea. "Even at 200,000 dollars it would have been most reasonable. Before this Mr. Clarke changes his mind, give him a binder of 100,000 dollars."

Fatigued beyond expression, she went the rounds of the rich and poor, begging and borrowing. The most she could glean was 10,000 dollars, which Mr. Clarke accepted. The
224

subordinate trustees, upon learning that he had committed the hotel to Francesca's institute for an incredibly low price on the strength of a slender binder, were irate. To add to the turmoil, bankers and profiteers, who were themselves interested in the property, closed all mortgage doors to her and anxiously awaited the few months that would surely bring the forfeiture of her deposit. She became the talk of the Seattle money world. The efforts of the aspiring speculators even succeeded in discouraging friends who had promised her aid. They said among themselves, "Mother Cabrini is elderly and ill. Her temerity is too great. She wants our donations to buy a colossus. Where experts have failed, how can she expect to succeed? Our money will do better in war bonds and munitions stocks."

Even Archbishop O'Dea became cautious, and provided her only with a lukewarm and ambiguous letter of recommendation. With it, she limped from bank to bank. The opposition was merciless; no bank would consider giving her the mortgage money. From November, 1915, to the early spring of 1916 she solicited every wealthy individual, every bank, every possible source of funds in Seattle. They responded only as stone walls.

Archbishop O'Dea was a well-meaning cleric, as became his office, yet he was not blessed with the stature of sainthood. He contributed to her cause nothing but the fanfare of authority and that he kept at a discreet, but revealing, minimum.

Who, then, would help her? Soon her option would expire. Should she capitulate? It was the Lenten season. During the Forty Hours devotion, she had her daughters, three by three, and her little orphans, ten by ten, adore the Sacred Heart. As they did so, she offered herself at the feet of her Spouse, ready to drink from His will the sweet or bitter chalice of events.

The days of prayer strengthened her, and as the time for the fulfillment of the contract grew nearer and nearer, she was calm. One day, she took an indelible pencil and went to the statue of Saint Anna, who had in her hands a book from which she was reading to the child Mary. On the open pages of the book she wrote the sum she needed, and whispered, "Saint Anna, mother of the Madonna, I place before your eyes that which I need, so that you may think upon it and procure it for me."

The evening before the deciding day, her daughters watched her with quiet despair. That evening she knelt in prayer before Saint Anna, not even leaving her post to eat. The bell of the convent door rang, startling the daughters. The young daughter who answered came to her and whispered, "Permit me, Mother, there is a gentleman at the door—" The daughter broke off, looked to her in confusion.

"What is it, Daughter?" she said. "Why do you hesitate?"

"The gentleman seeks you at this hour of night, and he is surely . . . Hebrew!"

The card the daughter handed her informed her that the man was Mr. Hilberg, president of the Scandinavian Bank. She smiled and pressed the card to her heart. "Daughter," she said, "quickly and most respectfully, admit Mr. Hilberg. Last night, while I slept briefly, I had a dream of great good."

Tall, slender, clean-shaven Mr. Hilberg, a man of impeccable courtesy, bowed and said in a gentle voice, "Mother Cabrini, when you came to my bank for help, I was out of town. I returned only a few days ago. I have unquestioning faith in your purchase of the Perry Hotel, and in your purpose. Please allow me to place myself at your disposal for whatever monies you require. What amount of mortgage do you wish?"

She led him into the chapel and to the statue of Saint Anna.

"Mr. Hilberg, she who directed you here to me, knows."

He read the great sum written upon the book in Saint Anna's hands and made a note of it. Then he smiled at Francesca and nodded assuringly.

"Good Mr. Hilberg," she said, "will you accept a glass of wine and a bread biscuit from the Missionary Sisters of the Sacred Heart?"

226

With born gallantry, he replied, "Yes, please. I would consider it a very high honor."

She turned to a daughter, "Daughter, be so kind as to bring to us in the reception room, two bread biscuits and two glasses of wine."

The daughter did not ask him, nor did Francesca or Mr. Hilberg let on why he had come. His compassionate eyes told more than enough.

The following day, April 21, 1916, the contract was signed. On April 30, she was in possession of the great Perry Hotel, and Francesca and her Daughters prayed heartily for grateful blessings always to follow their friend in deed, the knowing man of Old Testament faith, Mr. Hilberg.

Francesca's unprecedented difficulties in raising the purchase price of the hotel gave her much grave thought. It was still wartime, and at best there was little sympathy for foundlings. Money was going into war efforts and war relief. Though there was no dearth of foundlings and orphans, how could she nourish and maintain a huge charitable institution now?

During a recreation period she overheard two young daughters discussing her. Said one, "Our dear Mother is so concerned about the new house that she hardly sleeps." She said to them, "You are wrong. I really do not have worries, because I have consigned each house to the Sacred Heart. He has to think about them; I leave the guidance to Him." Then she added, "Saint Anna, being destined as the patroness of the new house, the worries devolve upon her, and it is she who has to work. She herself will do all for the new house. Already she has begun: Last night, in a dream, she told me what to do. In my mind she wrote, 'The time is not propitious for your original intention here. Turn about your plan so that it walks on its own legs.' Thus Saint Anna instructed me to relinquish my desire of a foundling home, and indicated instead a hospital that will do works of mercy and yet sustain itself."

On the twenty-fifth of May, the archbishop visited the new House. Admiring the structure, he asked, "Mother Cabrini, why have you workmen here making changes? What are you going to do with this grand building?"

"A hospital, Your Excellency, a work that will support itself."

The archbishop nodded, but remained significantly silent. There was at that time a Catholic hospital in Seattle. Clannish elements in the Church thought that another one, to be directed by nuns, was unnecessary and undesirable. These factions joined with the disgruntled individuals who had tried to prevent her purchase of the Perry Hotel. The doctors who were to form her medical staff were influenced by the opposition and withdrew their services. But that was not all. On the festive day of the Sacred Heart, she received an official letter from the archbishop, coldly prohibiting the opening of her Seattle Columbus Hospital. Coming from the shepherd of Seattle, this was the most pointed of thorns. Wracked and strained by a mortal debility and unreasonable conflict, she exclaimed, "How appropriate that this message should come today, on the day of the Sacret Heart!" And she said no more.

That evening at spiritual exercises she strove to conceal the pain that oppressed her. But in the days that followed, her sorrow became deeper, and ineradicable.

It was not only her problem with the hospital that pained her so. Her new country was arming to enter the arena of death. Crazed by the spirit of war, the self-appointed guardians of Americanism began a poisonous campaign against Catholic institutions which they branded "foreign." Inquisitorial commissions investigated her institute. Civil authorities and renegade Catholics sought to close her schools and orphanages. Letter after letter came to her, bearing threatening news. She exhausted her days and nights sending counsel and encouragement to her houses, urging them to seek the strength of the Sacred Heart and stand their ground, come what may.

As for her problem with the Columbus Hospital in Seattle, she decided to initiate a program that would not conflict with the work of the other Catholic hospital. Facilities for physiotherapy and electrotherapy treatments for various crippling afflictions were sorely needed. Archbishop O'Dea, she was certain, would not prevent her from opening a hospital offering such treatment. Somehow, she believed, a great Seattle Columbus Hospital would ease its way into being.

One day, a young matron from a family above reproach, presented herself. "Mother Cabrini, I come to you with all veneration, as you are the beloved of heaven. I am expecting my first child, and I pray that you will be its protectress. Please, Mother, allow my child the grace to greet the light within your house."

Weeks before the date the doctor told her she would have her baby, the young lady was surprised to find a Missionary Sister at her door with the message, "Mother Cabrini requests that you summon your doctor and come quickly to our Columbus Hospital, where your maternity bed awaits you."

The young lady complied. A few hours later her child, a girl, was born. Since it was premature and its life tenuous, Mother Cabrini herself baptized the infant, naming her Columbina, "the little dove." Her birth was the small ray of sunshine that began to thaw the hostility against the Seattle Columbus Hospital. The happy young mother's doctor, family, and friends stimulated forces to the aid and approval of the hospital. At length, the opposition melted away and the work initiated, according to Francesca, by Saint Anna prospered.

12 ✠ ✠ ✠

FRANCESCA KNEW now that each day of her life was in doubt, that the end which would be her glorious beginning, was almost within reach. She longed, before she died, to visit a few of her other houses.

In the fall, while her daughters in Seattle were gathered about her, she told them she was leaving for Los Angeles. Noticing that they had to struggle to keep from weeping, she comforted them, saying,

"I will return tomorrow."

"Oh, Mother," a young daughter exclaimed tearfully, "forgive me, but how can you say you will return 'tomorrow' when the trip to Los Angeles alone takes three days?"

She answered, "Dearest daughter, did you not know that everything we expect, everything we want, everything that is to come is 'tomorrow'? Therefore, I return tomorrow."

At that moment, the dinner bell rang. She extended her hands, and said,

"Behold little daughters, we are together in a final breaking of the Christian bread, for when I return to you, it will be ... tomorrow." After dinner, she spent the evening alone in the chapel, before the Sacred Heart.

To her daughters in Los Angeles, she looked pale. She was visibly suffering. The trials she had borne in Seattle had left

230

her spirit hungering for quiet and prayer. Upon her arrival, she stood in the garden, gazed at the daughters about her with deep maternal tenderness, and sighed.

"Ah, flowers of my soul, doves of my cote, how surpassingly good it is to be with you in beautiful California!"

When they saw her, the orphans burst into the garden, running to her and crying, "Mamma! Mamma Cabrini is here!"

On Christmas Eve, her daughters sang the High Mass, while she herself assisted. After Mass, the Sisters intoned the *Te Deum,* and she lifted her voice so melodiously, that as they sang they were enraptured. She led the long file of brides to the crib to kiss the Infant Jesus.

The last day of the year she gathered her daughters in sacred retreat. At midnight, while they prayed for peace in the newly born year, the sounds of celebration could be heard from the streets. There were firecrackers and gunshots, horns and whistles and singing.

A young daughter whispered excitedly, "Oh, Mother, listen to the uproar."

"Very well then, little Daughter," Francesca answered. "Let us have our own celebration, and greet our Spouse for the year 1917. Let us raise our voices to the Sacred Heart in an improvised hymn."

Winter gave way to spring, while Francesca rested, and enjoyed the sunny California climate. She would sit for hours in the garden, deep in spiritual meditation. When the orphan girls came to the garden, she would put sweet after sweet into their small hands. The many and various birds flew to her feet, and received from her biscuits and seeds and crumbs of cake and bread. Her daughters, youngest, young, and aging, came to their mother, and for them she had inexpressible affection.

"Daughters," she said one day, "why do I rest here as though I were already in paradise? The new Chicago hospital has problems. Pack my bag, I will go to Chicago."

They pleaded with her to stay and prolong her rest, but in vain.

"Now, Daughters," she said. "Who knows, maybe my famous Chicago doctors will transform me with their magical arts into a young woman again. Would you not want that?"

And she made them smile through their tears. Though they simulated cheer, each one, unaware that her sisters did likewise, came to her room and suggested that she would content herself more readily with Mother's absence if only she had a token, which she could keep safe for Mother until her return. And each received the answer, "But, Daughter, what shall I give you as souvenir, when I am a nothing and possess nothing?" Yet, not to deprive them of their innocent and loving wish, she discreetly left with the Superior a blessed memento for each.

The day she was to leave, she tottered out onto the balcony. There in the garden below, were her daughters and orphans singing for her. The birds left the trees and fluttered to her. As usual, she gave them a little bread. Then she said to them,

"Dear little ones, tomorrow, not I, thy mother on earth, but, thy Father above, must care for thee."

And her daughters and orphans knew they were included.

Her arrival at the Chicago Columbus Hospital on April 18, 1917, was at once the occasion of joy and sadness for the daughters who met her. Praise God that she had returned to them, but oh! how devastated, how emaciated, how sorrowfully changed. They furtively wept as they saw her assisted from the automobile, bent and leaning with trembling hands upon her cane. She was barely able to walk.

She did her best to mask her weakness, and immediately wanted to travel about Chicago and attend to the affairs that brought her there. Her daughters begged her to allow them to put her to bed. In a weak voice, she insisted that active work would help her. But finally, when she' was on the verge of collapsing, she consented to let the doctors examine her.

The doctors quickly recognized the relentless malarial progression. She dutifully submitted to weeks of rigorous treatment. Gradually her chills and fevers diminished, but the treatment left her without strength. To allay the just fears of her daughters, she exclaimed laughingly, "Shorten your long faces and stop worrying. The pathological test shows that my blood is as pure as a baby's!"

Each morning her daughters had her taken for an automobile ride out of the city to the wide open countryside and farmlands. In the forests and amongst the fields she would slowly and painfully gather leafy branches and wild flowers with which she delighted to glorify the altar of the chapel.

In spirit she was again and always the Francesca who listened as her father, Agostino, revealed to her spacious heart the pastoral wonders of the creator; the Francesca who walked the woods and fields with her devout mother and sister. Her life returned to the goodness of beginning.

During her excursions over the plains, a nostalgia for the farm life of her childhood came over her. She impulsively decided to acquire a farm for the institute, to help supply the hospital with fresh produce. She extended her rural ramblings until she found an appealing farm in Parkridge.

In her long years of bearing the light of her Spouse from land to land, she had spent hours and days and weeks in carriages, ships, and trains, months and years in the concreted streets of turbulent, crowded cities. Now, well-nigh powerless as the end of her life neared, she reached to the past, her earliest days in Sant'Angelo's rustic Eden. With the excitement of a child, she stocked her farm with horses and cows and goats and pigs and chickens, and she revelled in the simplicity of nature that was so harmonious to her being.

During July she engaged in the spiritual exercises, being the first before the altar at five in the morning, and not missing a single devotion. On the closing day she directed laudations to the Sacred Heart with such passion that her daughters, seeing her apparent strength, believed that she was recovering and would bless their company for years to come.

Even she wondered at the seeming revival of health. Was not the Groom ready for her? Did He want more accomplishments from her? Would she have to abide the weight of life until the dreadful war was over and His peace descended upon torn humanity?

But this animation was only a temporary grace to her daughters' hopes. In November her weakness returned, and heralded the consummation of that love for which she had so long lived, labored, and suffered. She began to slip away. On the morning of the twenty-first, the birthday of Pope Benedict XV, as she went toward the altar to receive Holy Communion, her breathing came with extreme difficulty, and she reeled. Leaving the altar rail, she staggered and was about to fall when daughters surrounded her and brought her to bed.

" 'Tis only a slight indisposition, my children," she said, "the debility resulting from a restless night. Do not scold me for my activity. Was I to remain in bed and thus lose my Communion on the pope's birthday? Never! Even if I were really ill, I would have wanted you to force me out of bed and to Holy Communion. Do not concern yourselves with me. Take care of yourselves so that I may worry the less about you."

More and more now she wanted to be with her daughters. One of the older daughters, Mother Antonietta Della Casa, the superior of the hospital, suspecting the gravity of her condition, gently begged her to spare herself and forego the community recreations.

"Oh, no," she protested, "it is now only at their recreation that I can be together with my daughters. If I am not one with them after their valiant day's work they might feel that I do not love them. I will try to keep them happy with my presence during their recreation even if I were dying right then and there."

During recreation, with efforts that she carefully concealed, she would surprise her daughters with small delights. Like a mother who knows the particular taste and preference of each of her children, she would have an apple for one, a pear for another, a bon-bon, a caramel, cakes, and cookies. As their eyes spoke their filial love and veneration, maternal satisfaction glowed within her.

On December 8, Feast of the Immaculate Conception, she suggested that each daughter write in her own way from her heart an adoration to the Blessed Virgin Mary. That evening, at dinner, they read aloud what they had written; some had expressed themselves in English, some in Italian, some with verse, some with prose, some in the form of an epistle, some in prayer.

She listened and nodded with pleasure. Then she said, smiling in appreciation, "I want you to know that your mother feels that each one of her children has made our Madonna happy." Her soft, smooth face wrinkled with delicate humor, and she added, "Furthermore, when the institute runs short of profound preachers and romantic poets, we will come to you for sermons."

Apprised that a model hospital was under construction in the city, she wanted to inspect the project and see if there were any new features that she could adapt for her hospitals. The daughters exhorted her not to venture out into the severe cold and wind.

"Why do you obstruct my wishes?" she asked. "I am obligated to do all the good that my Lord desires from me."

That evening when she returned from her journey, a vast feebleness came over her. She was chilled, and had acquired a cough that proved unrelenting.

A few weeks before Christmas, she sent for the stewardess and said, "Do me the pleasure of providing each daughter with a new habit for Christmas Day. And, please, would you be so kind as to get for me too, a fine, fresh habit? This Christmas everything has to be special. We must prepare to exult in an exceptional manner this coming feast of feasts!"

Though completely depleted physically, she busied herself with letters and season's greetings for her houses, and the many prelates, doctors, and benefactors who were her friends. To . the daughter who was to print the order's Christmas cards, she said, "I wish on the cards the words of the psalm, 'Oh, send out Thy light and Thy truth; let them lead me; let them bring me unto Thy holy hill, and to Thy tabernacles.' "

The daughter looked at her in consternation.

"Does it not seem to you, Mother, that the verse is not consonant with the festive occasion of the Nativity, but is a sentiment more fitting to the thought of one departed, a soul in Paradise?"

"Yes, yes, that I know," she answered smilingly, "This Christmas that verse goes well. Leave it the way it is."

Learning that, because of war restrictions on sugar, the parish did not intend to give the school children the traditional Christmas sweets, she ordered candy at all costs for the children, deeming, "Without the sweets so delicious and dear to the little ones, Christmas is not Christmas. War or no war, the innocents will receive their Christmas-party sweets from the Missionary Sisters of the Sacred Heart!"

On Friday, December 21, she awakened early, feeling acutely the terrible last-stage ravages of malaria. But she rose above her agony, went calmly to Mass, and remained worshipping in the chapel throughout the adoration without betraying her extreme weakness. Later, she watched her daughters with pleasure as they filled hundreds of gay packages with candies for the children of the parish.

She was helpless. How strange it was for her not to be able

to work. Oh, at last, at last, she was unable to labor. The incredible toils were over. She was no longer needed, and the work of the Missionary Sisters of the Sacred Heart could go forward without her.

Now, her daughter-brides could bear on the light of the Spouse as she had. They were little saints on earth. They would be as other mothers bringing other brides, and they, in turn, would bring still others, and so it would be throughout all the generations to come. Her life's purpose was fulfilled. Now she awaited His call to the wedding feast with unclouded peace.

When her daughters returned from the children's party, she wanted to hear every detail of their enjoyment. Were the little ones surprised? Did they think Mother Cabrini would forget them! What faces did they make? Who said what? Despite untold suffering, she remained with her daughters, taking to her heart each moment of their loving nearness. She had them, too, eat of the Christmas candies, and they were cheerful and gay as she wanted them to be. Before they went into the chapel for evening prayers, she lingeringly bestowed upon them her final benedictions.

The next morning, Saturday, December 22, 1917, was to bring the moment she had envisioned with fullest reality all her life. It was to bring the moment of her glory, the day reserved for the bride and the Groom, and she, Francesca, the bride.

She had not the strength to quit her bed, to go to the altar and breakfast with Christ. The superior of the hospital, Mother Antonietta Della Casa, came to her to bid her good morning, and receive her blessing. She responded to all Mother Antonietta's questions about the day's work. A young daughter came to her and asked if she would like a bowl of nourishing broth.

"Very well, Daughter, bring it to me if you so kindly wish."

Then she said, "Children, all I desire, is that my room be

put in order. Sweep the dust from the floor—especially before my rocker, where I will sit, and receive. I am a bit weary, and later will arise anew."

Mother Antonietta reported to her at 11:40. As Francesca advised her about her work, Mother Antonietta listened obediently. Heaven had deigned for Mother Antonietta to hear her melodious last words on earth.

Alone again, she arose, and locked the door. It was the time to contemplate privately.

As a tiny girl of seven in Sant'Angelo, before the altar, she had first been visited by Him.

The moment of the anointing of the Sacred Chrism, I felt that which can never be described. From that moment I was no longer of the earth. My heart began to grow through space ever with purest joy. I cannot tell why, but I knew the Holy Ghost had come to me.

Daily, hourly, since then, she had breathed her love to Him. Now through with the world, she offered herself, and she felt His hand lifting from her the burden of life.

A sweet piercing found her breast, and blood red as roses trickled from her lips. The arduous years disappeared, and her life seemed brief as a moment.

He was arriving, and she was awake to the day and to the hour. He was coming to take to Him her flame.

Behold the Bridegroom cometh; go you forth to meet Christ the Lord.

She wished to gaze upon her daughters in farewell, and could not tarry. She turned the key, unlocked the door, and rang the bell. Then she sat in her rocker, and waited serenely. The time for words was past. He was at hand.

Mother Antonietta and daughters rushed to her side.

"Mother, dearest! Oh! No! Sainted Mother!" they cried.

Mother Anonietta took her into her arms.

Beatitude immersed her. Her veiling eyes said:

You are my daughters, as olive plants round about my table.

238

Rejoice. After you shall as virgins be brought to the King. Rejoice, my Daughters, for you are the chaste generation with glory!

Her daughters receded as she obeyed the Light.

With thy comliness and thy beauty set out, proceed prosperously, and reign. Come, thou spouse of Christ, receive the crown which the Lord hath prepared for thee from everlasting.

In that moment began the eternal and true life of Saint Francesca Xavier Cabrini.

EPILOGUE

WHEN FRANCESCA had founded the West Park orphanage and Convent in 1890, she had stood upon the slope overlooking the Hudson and said, "I wish to be buried here." In accordance with her wish, after a solemn Requiem Mass celebrated by Archbishop Mundelein in Chicago, her body was transported to New York. Bishop Hayes celebrated a second Requiem Mass in Saint Patrick's Cathedral. Then her body, accompanied by thirty-three Daughters, representing the thirty-three years of the Lord on earth, completed the journey to West Park.

On January 2, 1918, hundreds of orphans, dressed in white and carrying lilies and candles, followed her casket from the Convent Chapel to its sepulchre.

In 1928, the investigations concerning the sanctity of the Foundress of the Missionary Sisters of the Sacred Heart began. The traditionally critical Apostolic Process probed her every act and work, and confirmed cures of hopeless afflictions as the undoubted result of prayers to Mother Francesca Xavier Cabrini. In regard to two of the miracles the highest medical authorities testified for the Congregation of Rites. One was the case of Sister Delfina Grazioli, cured at Columbus Hospital, Seattle, of adhesions of the pylorus and duodenum, which according to the unanimous diagnosis of the doctors was incurable. The other was the case of the infant Peter Smith, cured of blindness caused by the mistake of a nurse who had acciden-

241

tally applied a fifty per cent solution of nitrate of silver to the child's eyes.

The Beatification of Mother Francesca Xavier Cabrini took place in the Vatican Basilica on November 13, 1938.

On July 7, 1946, St. Peter's wore a holiday appearance. Its venerable and imposing pillars were decked with magnificent ancient damask hangings. Countless electric lights and candles were grouped around the pontifical altar.

The bronze statue of St. Peter standing in the nave had been clothed in a richly embroidered cloak of finest silk. On the floor lay a thick green carpet. Paintings depicting Mother Cabrini in the act of performing miracles hung from the balconies on either side. Monks of every order, each in distinctive garb provided a splendid array. There were chamberlains of cape and sword in early Elizabethan costumes, mace-bearers and penitentiaries, Swiss Guards in the multicolored uniforms designed by Michelangelo, Noble Guards in black topboots, white buckskin breeches, red tunics, and shining helmets, and Palatine Guards. Whitehaired Cardinals in scarlet mingled with bearded patriarchs from the East, mitred Bishops with choirboys, apostolic couriers with master porters of the Red Rod.

The activities in the Vatican began just after seven in the morning, when the Cardinals, patriarchs, Archbishops, and other dignitaries who were to participate in the canonization began to arrive at the Sistine Chapel. While these were forming for the procession to St. Peter's, the Pope arrived in the sacristy of the Chapel accompanied by his privy chamberlains. There he donned the vestments he was later to wear in St. Peter's Basilica. Then, wearing the tiara or triple crown, he entered the Sistine Chapel. He removed his tiara and knelt in prayer. He then intoned the *Ave Maris Stella,* which the choir continued while the Pope remained kneeling.

At the end of the first verse the Pope, wearing the mitre, took

242

his seat on the portable throne known as the *Sedia Gestatoria* and was carried in it to his place in the procession. At the door of the Basilica the Pope was received by the Chapter of St. Peter's. Trumpeteers of the Palatine Guards had taken their stations in the dome of St. Peter's, with the result that their music floated down on the congregation like that of a "Choir of Angels." At the Pope's appearance, they flooded St. Peter's Basilica with melody.

In front of the papal altar, the Pope descended from the *Sedia Gestatoria* and knelt in prayer. Then he rose and took his place on the throne. The Cardinal Procurator of the canonization approached the Pope, accompanied by a consistorial advocate. The advocate knelt and, speaking for all Cardinals present, earnestly begged the Pope in Latin to inscribe Mother Cabrini in the Catalogue of Saints.

Pope Pius replied, through the secretary of briefs, exhorting the faithful to assist him in imploring divine assistance, by the intercession of the Blessed Virgin, of the Apostles Peter and Paul, and of all the heavenly court, before making a decision in a matter of such grave importance. Everyone knelt, and two cantors intoned the litanies of the saints, to which all made the responses.

After the litanies, the consistorial advocate again approached the throne and "more earnestly" repeated his previous request to the Pope. The secretary of the brief replied in his name that all should implore the help of the Holy Ghost, source of all light and wisdom.

The Pope then knelt at the faldstool and prayed during the singing of the "Miserere." On rising, the Pope intoned the "Veni Creator Spiritus," falling to his knees again during the first verse, and standing during the rest of the hymn. On regaining the throne the Pope was once more approached by the consistorial advocate, who "most earnestly" repeated the previous formula of petition.

The secretary of the briefs replied that the Pope, convinced that the canonization was pleasing to God, had resolved to proclaim Mother Cabrini a saint.

At these words everyone rose. The Pope, wearing the mitre, seated himself on the throne in his capacity of teacher and head of the universal Church, and made the following solemn declaration in Latin:

"In honor of the Holy and Indivisible Trinity, for the exaltation of the Catholic Church and the increase of the Christian religion with the authority of our Lord Jesus Christ, of the Holy Apostles Peter and Paul, and by our own authority, after mature deliberation, ever imploring divine assistance, and by the advice of our venerable brethren the Cardinals of the Holy Roman Catholic Church and of the Patriarchs, Archbishops, and Bishops, present in the Eternal City, we inscribe in the Catalogue of Saints the blessed Francesca Xavier Cabrini, ordaining that her memory be celebrated every year in the universal Church on the day of December 22, in the name of the Father, Son, and Holy Ghost."

As soon as the Pope had uttered these words the consistorial advocate knelt before him and, after thanking him, begged him to order publication of the apostolic letters proclaiming Mother Cabrini's canonization. The Pope replied, "We have decreed."

The Cardinal Procurator thereupon ascended the steps of the throne and kissed the Pope's hand and knee. The consistorial advocate, turning to the prothonotaries apostolic, requested them to draw the act of canonization.

The Pope then rose and intoned the Te Deum, which was continued by the choir and faithful. After a prayer sung by the Pope to invoke the new saint, a Cardinal deacon recited the Confiteor, adding the name of Saint Francesca Xavier Cabrini after those of Peter and Paul.

Meanwhile an apostolic subdeacon approached the throne, bearing the papal cross. The Pope, after removing his mitre, chanted the absolution and gave the apostolic blessing.

244

The canonization proper was followed by a Pontifical High Mass that lasted until 11:45 A.M. During the Mass the Pope received the gifts that by tradition are presented to him after canonization. They included two pigeons, two doves, two canaries, two green finches, two loaves of bread, a cask of wine, a cask of water, and six tall candles.

The Pope was approached by Frederick Cardinal Tedeschini, Archpriest of the Basilica, who offered him the purse containing twenty-five coins, of Pope Julius II "for a well-sung mass."

Then His Holiness Pius XII delivered his homily.

"While human beings are transitory and all grow old little by little and fall in ruin, the glories, the initiatives and the works which flow from Christian holiness, on the other hand, not only are preserved with the passage of time but prosper and flourish, sustained by a marvellous force.

"Similar to the grain, to the mustard seed, which is the smallest of all seeds, but which when it is planted develops and becomes one of the largest of plants, so they grow every day and in the end invade the whole world.

"That fact, which frequently is verified through the dispositions of Divine Providence in the annals of the Church, today above all is comforting at a moment in which men need as never before the splendor and fruit of saintliness.

"We therefore think of this with great comfort while, under the influence of the divine grace, we honor with the halo of saints the blessed virgin Francesca Xavier Cabrina. She was a humble child who distinguished herself not by tribute or wealth or power, but by virtue. From her most tender years she preserved the whiteness of innocence, maintaining it carefully with the thorns of penitence; and with the advancement of the years, prompted by instinct and supernal ardor, she dedicated her entire life to divine service and the greater glory of God.

"Although her constitution was very frail, her spirit was endowed with such singular strength that, knowing the will of

God in her regard, she permitted nothing to impede her from accomplishing what seemed beyond the strength of a woman. Thus, with the help of grace, the humble institute of nuns which she founded in a short time spread through Italy, to America, and to many cities of the world. She gathered endangered youth in safe houses, and taught them right and holy principles. She consoled the spirit of the imprisoned, giving them the comfort of life eternal and urging them to resume the right path and to remake an honest life.

". . . Men need as never before the splendor and fruit of saintliness. Nations and peoples will learn from her—who ardently loved her Fatherland Old and New and spread the treasures of her charity and labors even to other lands—that they are called to constitute a single family, which must not be divided in ambiguous and destructive rivalry, nor dissolve itself in eternal hostilities, but join the brotherly love born from the commandment of Christ and His divine example.

"May this new saint, may Saint Francesca Xavier Cabrini implore from the Prince of Peace and from the Father of us all that with hates spent, the spirits placated, public, private, and international relations will be regulated not by unbridled desire for selfish advantage, but in justice and equity, restoring to mankind the true peace from which the common good flows. Amen."

The profoundly deep, low-throated bells of St. Peter's quivered in the sunlight. The four hundred churches of Rome joined and joyously sang forth their peals and chimes, as a pure white dove winged away from the Pope's side, unerringly found an opening in the lofty dome, and flew skyward.

About the Author

Born in 1911 in West Hoboken, New Jersey, Pietro Di Donato was the first son of devout Italian immigrant parents. The death of his father, a bricklayer, was immortalized in the author's first novel, *Christ in Concrete,* which burst upon the literary scene in 1939. At that time, the author supported his seven brothers and sisters by following his father's trade and wrote when he could find the time. Today, Pietro Di Donato lives on Long Island with his wife and sons. His new novel, *Three Circles of Light,* received critical and public acclaim. *Immigrant Saint* is his first book of nonfiction, and to the life story of Mother Cabrini he brings an intimate knowledge of the Italian soul and a rich spiritual heritage. He is currently doing original research for a book on the life of St. Maria Goretti.